W9-ATR-557

Ending It:
DISPUTE RESOLUTION IN AMERICA

Descriptions, Examples, Cases, and Questions

SUSAN M. LEESON

Professor, Political Science
Associate Professor, Law
Willamette University

BRYAN M. JOHNSTON

Director, Center for Dispute Resolution
Associate Professor, Law
Willamette University

ANDERSON PUBLISHING CO.
Cincinnati, Ohio

© 1988 by Anderson Publishing Co.

Library of Congress Cataloging-in-Publication Data

Leeson, Susan M.
  Ending it: dispute resolution in America / Susan M. Leeson, Bryan M. Johnston
      p.   cm.
  Includes bibliographies and index.
  ISBN 0-87084-404-0
  1. Dispute resolution (Law)—United States—Cases.   I. Johnston,
Bryan M.   II. Title.
KF9084.A7L44   1988
347.73'9—dc19
[347.3079]   88-22027
                                                                          CIP

For Our Families

CONTENTS

PREFACE

We have taught an introductory course in dispute resolution at Willamette University College of Law for four years, and one summer session at the University of Bridgeport College of Law. The purpose of the course is to provide students with an overview of dispute resolution processes. Our biggest obstacle in teaching the course has been the lack of introductory material surveying the landscape of dispute resolution. We discovered during our first year, for example, that beginning students did not have the background to benefit from compilations of articles on dispute resolution written by experts for experts. That lack of background made a casebook approach to dispute resolution equally unsatisfactory. Our students taught us that they needed a basic introduction to dispute resolution processes before they could deal intelligently with commentaries, cases and policy analyses.

This book is our response. Our primary goal is to provide a clear description and definition of the basic terms associated with litigation, voluntary arbitration, court-annexed or mandatory arbitration, negotiation, and mediation. Readers then have a context for responding to questions raised by the examples of each process that follow the descriptions; evaluating emerging dispute resolution processes; and analyzing issues raised by the cases that conclude each chapter.

We endeavor to present the materials in this text in a straightforward manner. Following an introductory chapter that puts dispute resolution techniques in the context of adversary and inquisitorial principles, each chapter follows the same format: First is a definition of the dispute resolution process, its background, and situations in which it commonly is used. Second is an outline of how the process works. Third is an example of the process, derived from an actual case or composite of cases. The examples are followed by a series of questions to encourage discussion about the process and comparison with other processes. Fourth is an indication of the trends developing within each process. Each chapter ends with a series of cases that demonstrate judicial responses to each of the processes.

The book is designed for use in a variety of contexts. Like the Willamette College of Law, some schools now require students to take an introductory course in dispute resolution. We have used this book in draft form as the text in such a course, supplemented with videotapes, guest lectures and simulation exercises. Many law schools offer a course in legal processes. This book is appropriate in that course as well, particularly in light of the legal profession's current emphasis on alternatives to litigation. Some law schools seek to introduce students to dispute resolution as part of the course in civil procedure. This book can supplement a civil procedure casebook. Finally, the text is well suited to supplement the education given in business administration, public administration, social work and like programs. These professionals and their clients are frequent consumers of dispute resolution services, and need to understand the fundamental nature of each.

We gratefully acknowledge the assistance and suggestions of many people in the preparation of this book. Professor Christopher Simoni, now of the University of Texas College of Law, and Salem attorney Edward Harri read early drafts and made invaluable suggestions. Willamette law librarian Richard Breen and law cataloguing librarian Elysabeth Hall have kept us up to date with recent literature in the dispute resolution field. Ms. Hall also read with patience and care various chapters during the evolution of the text. We thank former Willamette students Jamie Sanders, Christopher Laia, and Steven Claussen for research assistance. Professionals in the dispute resolution field have given invaluable assistance, particularly in developing the examples that demonstrate each process. We note especially attorney/arbitrators Lynn Ashcroft, Eric Lindauer, and Sandra Gangle; mediator Vera Joslow Eden; attorney Edward L. Clark; and neighborhood dispute resolution coordinator Jan Alsever. Pamela Warden, Colleen Spedale and Magda Pena have assisted with production at different stages.

We save for last a special note of thanks to the students we have worked with in our dispute resolution courses at Willamette and the University of Bridgeport. It was they who prompted us to write the book, and they who have encouraged, suggested and nagged as the book has worked through its drafts. Some have been disappointed to learn that the practice of law is not what Perry Mason made it seem, but most have been eager to learn that the processes for resolving disputes are infinitely more varied and complicated than they may have thought.

Despite all the help we have received, we fear errors and omissions. We accept responsibility for them. If we have oversimplified any of the processes, it is not out of ignorance of their complexity and diversity. The text does not profess to be a substitute for more detailed analyses and evaluations of dispute resolution processes in the United States. Its goal is to lay the foundation upon which more sophisticated understandings can be built.

Salem, Oregon   Susan M. Leeson
1988   Bryan M. Johnston

1 INTRODUCTION

Human beings have disputed with one another for millions of years but never have devised a perfect mechanism for resolving their disputes. This book is about major dispute resolution processes available in the United States at the end of the twentieth century, and about emerging processes that either complement existing processes or may be alternatives to them. Some of the processes, such as litigation, court-annexed arbitration and court-annexed mediation, are associated with the formal justice system. Others, such as voluntary arbitration and voluntary mediation, are parts of private systems of dispute resolution. Each process has strengths and weaknesses. Each is capable of achieving some goals but not others. A rudimentary understanding of the processes is important to disputants and their advocates because the process used to resolve a dispute can be as important as the substantive outcome of the dispute.

The primary purpose of this text is to provide a general overview of litigation, arbitration, negotiation, mediation, and emerging processes such as med-arb, summary jury trials, and neighborhood justice programs. Each of these processes is elaborately detailed and intricate. Books and articles have been written about them and the skills required to be successful with them. The overview provided in this text is designed to provide a foundation for more advanced inquiry and to show how the processes are related to one another in the American legal system and culture.

In order to achieve this goal each chapter begins with a description of a dispute resolution process and how it works. Part of the description is a brief account of its historical origins. The historical information helps to clarify the assumptions underlying the process and the nature of the changes the process has undergone to adapt it to contemporary needs.

Each chapter also contains a section on the burdens of persuasion assigned by the process. Litigation, for example, assigns formal burdens of persuasion to disputants. Its starting premise is that the status quo is acceptable. A person who uses litigation to change the status quo, therefore, must assume the initial burden of persuading a judge or jury that the status quo is unacceptable and should change. Not all the processes examined in this text adopt litigation standards on burdens of persuasion, however. Understanding who carries the burden of persuasion is an important step towards understanding each of the processes and often is a major factor in the decision about which process to employ.

The role of the lawyer in each process also is a topic in each chapter. Although the lawyer's stereotyped role in American law is that of an advocate in a courtroom, the reality is much more complex and diverse. Some dispute resolution processes require a lawyer to act as decision-maker, negotiator, counselor, or facilitator as well. Success at these diverse roles requires special training, practice and skills.

Another important dimension of each chapter is a summary of trends associated with the dispute resolution process. Whether due to case overload in the formal judicial system or concern with the quality of dispute resolution for disputants, the major processes described in this text have not remained static. Some of the trends involve the blending of two existing dispute resolution processes, such as med-arb, a hybrid of mediation and arbitration. Others involve the development of new techniques for facilitating settlements prior to trial, such as the summary jury trial. Emergence of these new forms shows that creativity and innovation are alive and well in a legal system whose roots are thousands of years old.

In order to provide a better sense of how each dispute resolution process works, the text provides examples of how each was used in a particular situation. Each example is derived from an actual case or composite of cases. A series of questions follows each example to stimulate evaluation of the process, comparison with other processes, and assessment of its impact on the disputants and the larger social system.

Each chapter concludes with a series of cases selected to demonstrate how state and federal courts approach issues of dispute resolution. The cases help to highlight ongoing questions of public policy that surround each dispute resolution process. Attitudes of courts are crucial to the success of dispute resolution alternatives. Examination of the cases also helps to develop the critical analytical skills needed to make intelligent judgments about the dispute resolution forum most appropriate for particular parties and issues. Questions at the end of each case are designed to help develop analytical and evaluative skills.

Unlike most texts on dispute resolution, this book is not simply about alternatives to litigation. It is written from the perspective that litigation is and will remain an essential dispute resolution process because it offers advantages that no other process can offer. What is more, in the United States all other dispute resolution processes are understood in comparison to litigation. The importance of litigation in this text is emphasized by the fact that it is the first process examined. Knowing when to proceed with litigation and when to pursue an alternative is one of the keys to providing effective legal services to clients.

The Adversary and Inquisitorial Systems of Justice

A prerequisite to understanding and evaluating dispute resolution in America is understanding the adversary and inquisitorial systems of justice. America's formal judicial system subscribes to the adversary system; adversary principles are well established in American ideology and social interaction.[1] Other dispute resolution processes reflect elements of the inquisitorial system of justice, however, and a growing aspiration to move away from adversary relationships in law and culture.

The roots of the adversary system can be traced to seventeenth century social contract theory. According to social contract theorists such as John Locke, human beings are not by nature social.[2] They are endowed by nature with certain rights (specifically, life, liberty and estate which Locke calls by the general name "property") but are incapable of protecting those rights in their original "state of nature." They form civil society, government, and laws in order to protect their rights. Government and laws are seen as neutral adjudicators of the disputes that inevitably arise when human beings interact with one another and their rights come into conflict.

The adversary system reflects the assumptions of social contract theory: it assumes the existence of individual rights, that the persons in possession of those rights are in the best position to guarantee their protection, and that individuals or their advocates are capable of vindicating their rights. The adversary system also assumes the existence of an impartial, neutral arbitrator of rights. Not surprisingly, the adversary system has been called a "fight theory of justice."[3] The system works on the premise that justice is most likely to result from the clash of proofs between contesting parties. The parties are responsible for developing the legal theories they believe entitle them to prevail, marshalling evidence and witnesses in support of their contentions, exposing the weaknesses of their opponents' legal theories, and arguing persuasively to a neutral decision-maker why they should prevail in the dispute. Parties usually are represented by professional advocates (lawyers) who are specially trained to argue persuasively in the courtroom and to negotiate effectively on behalf of their clients.

The adversary system also has been characterized as a zero-sum game: one party wins and the other loses.[4] The determination of winners and losers is made by someone who is not a party to the dispute and who, ideally, has no personal stake in the outcome of the dispute.

An important feature of the adversary system is that the parties to a dispute are not responsible for resolving the dispute themselves. Their role is to make the best cases they can for themselves. The responsibility for resolving disputes belongs to a judge, jury, or some other neutral party. The decision-makers play passive roles in the adversary battle between or among disputants. They listen to arguments, consider evidence, scrutinize witnesses, and usually reach their decision outside the presence of the disputing parties. Once a final decision has been reached the disputing parties are bound to obey it. Failure to obey a judgment can result in sanctions including fines and jail.

Not all legal systems are based on adversary principles. Many European legal systems, for example, are grounded on inquisitorial rather than adversary principles. The inquisitorial approach has been characterized as a "truth seeking" system of justice.[5] It assumes that truth can be discovered best by specially trained judges who act both as investigators and decision-makers in a dispute. Parties to a dispute in an inquisitorial system play a passive role in the process compared to parties in an adversary system. They respond to questions posed by judges, who in turn rely on court-ordered investigations of the facts in dispute and the disputants. It is not uncommon for judges in an inquisitorial system to resolve disputes with an eye to what is socially desirable. Less emphasis is given to vindicating individual rights and more is placed on the needs of society and harmony between or among disputants. Split awards, as opposed to win-lose outcomes, are not uncommon.

Although the United States' judicial system is committed formally to adversary principles, there are many who for business, moral, or religious reasons believe that an adversary approach to dispute resolution is not desirable. These beliefs have led to the development of dispute resolution processes that reflect more inquisitorial premises. Some early colonists, for example, believed non-adversary mechanisms were more consistent with their religious principles. Hence they shunned litigation and relied heavily on mediation to resolve religious as well as secular disputes. The mediator was responsible for focusing the parties' attention on the religious principles that united them. That focus often helped the disputants to achieve their own resolution. Business persons have avoided litigation as well, but for more mundane reasons: lawsuits tend to shatter business relationships. The realities of the business world often tie parties together by contract for extended periods of time. Disputes over discrete portions of those contracts can arise which need to be resolved without the win-lose outcome of litigation. Private arbitration and negotiation are preferred by members of the business community whose disputes require no new declarations of law for resolution and for which judicial enforcement is not necessary.

Courts also can be seen to be moving away from adversary dispute resolution processes in some situations. Judges, for example, increasingly are hosting settlement conferences to help parties negotiate settlements to the disputes that have brought them to court. Some judges participate actively in settlement conferences, reminding the parties of the consequences of going to trial and the impact that a trial could have on their subsequent relationship. Courts also are experimenting with court-ordered mediation in marriage dissolution cases and in a narrow range of criminal cases.

Thus, while it is true that the United States is known primarily for subscribing to an adversary system of justice, some inquisitorial principles are woven into the fabric of dispute resolution in America. The theoretical premises of the two systems of justice provide a useful framework for understanding and evaluating the dispute resolution processes examined in the chapters that follow.

As noted earlier, litigation is the dispute resolution process examined first, the process that embodies adversary principles. Though by no means the oldest dispute resolution process in existence (mediation or arbitration have that honor), litigation is the process embedded in America's formal judicial system. It is the most formal of the dispute resolution processes as well, carefully regulated by publicly established rules and procedures. Because it is America's formal dispute resolution process, it is also the process against which all others are compared and evaluated.

Sources

B. Alper & L. Nichols, Beyond the Courtroom (1981).
Burger, *Isn't There a Better Way?*, 68 A.B.A.J. 274 (1982).
J. Frank, Courts on Trial: Myth and Reality in American Justice (1973).
Galanter, *Reading the Landscape of Disputes*, 31 U.C.L.A. L. Rev. (1983).
Gross, *Adversaries, Juries and Justice*, 26 Loy. L. Rev. 525 (1980).
S. Landsman, Readings on Adversarial Justice: The American Approach to Adjudication (1988).
National Institute for Dispute Resolution, Paths To Justice: (1983).
The Rand Corporation, Costs of the Civil Justice System (1983).
_____, Simple Justice (1983).

Endnotes

[1] An excellent overview and analysis of the adversary system is provided by S. Landsman, Readings on Adversarial Justice: The American Approach to Adjudication 1-74 (1988).

[2] Locke's argument is summarized in *An Essay Concerning the True Original, Extent and End of Civil Government*, in Social Contract (E. Barker ed. 1947).

[3] The phrase was suggested by Jerome Frank, Courts on Trial: Myth and Reality in American Justice 80-102 (1949).

[4] L. Friedman, A History of American Law (1985). Friedman contends that American law has been a zero-sum game since approximately the mid-nineteenth century. *See generally* Part III, Ch. 1, *Blood and Gold: Some Main Themes in the Law in the Last Half of the 19th Century.*

[5] J. Frank, *supra* note 3.

2 LITIGATION

Litigation is America's formal dispute resolution process, supervised by the judicial branch of government and supported by tax dollars. It begins with the filing of a lawsuit and ends with dismissal of the suit or enforcement of the judgment entered in the suit. Litigation seeks to answer three questions about a dispute: What are the facts? What is the relevant law? How does that law apply to the facts? Answers to these questions are sought through a process of pretrial, trial, and post-trial activities that occur in the context of rules of evidence and procedure. Lawyers, specially trained in law and procedure and licensed to practice before American courts, are the central figures in the litigation process.

Litigation embodies principles of the adversary system. With the exception of some administrative matters, courts do not initiate litigation activity. They respond to actions taken by disputants and make judgments based on disputants' presentations. Disputants are responsible for initiating litigation through the filing of complaints, submitting a variety of motions throughout the process, objecting to the introduction of certain of their opponents' evidence, persuading at trial or hearing, and filing appeals if they do not succeed at trial. The court's function consists of managing the process and rendering decisions.

Like all dispute resolution processes, litigation has several distinguishing characteristics. First, litigation can make law for society as a whole while resolving a particular dispute. Decisions of appellate courts establish precedents to be followed by trial courts confronted with similar facts in the future. Litigation is the only dispute resolution process that can establish rules for the resolution of subsequent disputes. Thus, if one of the disputants' goals is to clarify, modify or declare the law that governs particular facts, litigation must be used.

Second, litigation has the authority to compel participation. Once a lawsuit has been filed, properly invoking the court's authority, the individual sued must participate or risk the consequences of failure to mount a defense. Consequences can range from a default judgment (an award to the complaining party granting the action or amount requested) to a contempt citation (including an arrest warrant).

Third, litigation is conducted according to rigidly enforced procedural and evidentiary rules enacted by legislatures or adopted by courts. Rules of procedure govern the conduct of litigation; rules of evidence govern the proofs that may be considered by a judge or jury. Procedural errors, for example, can result in sanctions against the erring party, including dismissal. Failure to follow an evidentiary rule can result in crucial evidence not being considered at trial. Disputants have no voice in the formulation or enactment of the rules of procedure or the rules of evidence that govern a case; they control only the decision whether to attempt to invoke a particular rule.

Fourth, litigation is the only dispute resolution process with explicit enforcement powers. Courts may issue orders and invoke the police powers of their jurisdictions to require performance. Orders may range from compelling a person to appear as a witness to enforcing a judgment entered at the end of the litigation process. Failure to obey a court order can result in sanctions ranging from fines to imprisonment.

Finally, litigation is a public process. With rare exceptions its documents, records, and hearings are open to the public. Press coverage is not uncommon. Appellate decisions of state and federal courts are printed in a reporter system and distributed widely.

Litigation also is a public process in that it is supported by tax dollars. Although disputants typically are required to pay their own attorneys' fees and some court costs, they generally pay less to use the services of courts than it actually costs to run them. Taxpayer dollars support the facilities, judges, and other staff necessary to operate the judicial branch of government.[1]

Background of Litigation

1. The Court System

Disputes submitted to litigation are processed through elaborate systems of state or federal courts. Some disputes are processed through both systems. The existence of two separate court systems in the same geographic area in the United States is explained only by reference to history and the institution of federalism.

State constitutions drafted in 1776 and after provided for separation of government power among three branches. Although separating legislative, executive and judicial functions was a unique American invention, organization of the judicial branch in the states was influenced heavily by English law.[2]

The original states followed the English model and created a hierarchical set of trial and appellate courts. At the lowest level were courts of limited jurisdiction (jurisdiction confined to only certain types of disputes, such as probate or small claims). At the next level were trial courts of general jurisdiction, charged with handling most civil and criminal cases. Trial courts were designed to decide questions of fact and apply law. American colonists accepted the English principle that disputants are entitled to one review of the trial by an appellate court. Appellate review ensures that the trial process was not seriously flawed and that the trial court not only selected the correct law, but applied it properly.

Most states topped the judicial pyramid with a second appellate court, usually called the supreme court. These highest appellate courts were given considerable discretion over the cases they chose to review, since their review was to clarify the legal rules that were to apply throughout their judicial systems.

The United States Constitution of 1787 was modeled after the Constitution of the State of New York and, like it, created three branches of government, including an independent judiciary. Although the Constitution itself provided only for the United States Supreme Court, it gave Congress the power to create other courts as Congress saw fit and to determine the extent of the Supreme Court's appellate jurisdiction. Since the first Judiciary Act in 1789, Congress has created a series of "Constitutional courts" (established under Congress' Article III powers) and "legislative courts" (established under Congress'

Article I powers). Today, Article III courts include 97 district trial courts (at least one in each state as well as one in the District of Columbia and Puerto Rico), and thirteen courts of appeal (one for each of the twelve geographically organized circuits and a Court of Appeals for the Federal Circuit). Twelve of the courts of appeal are organized geographically and hear cases only from the district courts within their circuits. The Court of Appeals for the Federal Circuit hears appeals from all district courts in the country on such specialized federal matters as patent and copyright. Courts created under Congress' Article I powers include the United States Tax Court, the Court of Military Appeals, and the courts of the District of Columbia.

The U.S. Supreme Court is the final appellate court in the federal system. The court has original jurisdiction in a very limited number of cases, and considerable discretion over the cases it chooses to hear on appeal. The bulk of its caseload, therefore, are disputes it has agreed to hear. The Court provides guidance on the types of cases it will hear by rule,[3] and by stating in some of its opinions why the Justices agreed to hear that particular case.[4] In recent years the Court has denied or dismissed, or the parties have withdrawn, over 90 percent of the cases for which appeals or petitions for review were filed. Fewer than half the remaining 10 percent have resulted in written opinions.[5]

Since 1789, federal courts have existed in all the states. The United States Constitution gave Congress discretionary power to establish inferior courts within the geographic territory of states. The two systems operate almost completely separate from one another.

Federalism, the theory that states would remain viable and largely independent governing units despite the creation of the United States Government, is the explanation for the co-existence of two different court systems in the same territory. The federal government is a government of delegated powers; all powers not delegated to the federal government are retained by the states or by the people. Likewise, federal courts are courts of limited jurisdiction. To gain access to federal courts, disputants must show that the Constitution or an act of Congress gives them the right to litigate their dispute in federal court. Otherwise, it is assumed that a state court is the proper forum. State courts are presumed competent to resolve questions of federal statutory or Constitutional law as well as state law. Routes of appeal to federal courts exist should a disputant believe the state court misinterpreted or misapplied federal law.

Throughout American history some litigants have spent considerable time and money in the pretrial phase of litigation arguing whether their case should be tried in state or federal court. The perception that one system is more advantageous for a litigant than another could be based on a variety of conclusions. Rules of evidence and procedure, for example, may differ between the appropriate state court and the federal court. The amount of delay before trial may differ. Judicial selection techniques often differ. Federal judges, for example, are nominated by the President, confirmed by the Senate and serve life terms. State judges may be elected or appointed but tend to serve fixed, short terms. Such differences can make choice of forum an important consideration to parties.

2. *The Trial*

Just as the court system, through which litigation is processed, must be understood by reference to history, the trial itself, the most familiar aspect of the litigation process, is illuminated by historical reference. The modern trial is the descendant of several separate modes of trial and several hundred years of English court system development.

The early modes of trial were developed by the 12th century. At that time, the purpose of the trial was to allow a defendant who denied allegations against him to "prove" his case by use of a variety of methods of proof: compurgation, charter, record, witness, inquisition, ordeal or duel. Early decision-making was based on how well an accused could perform the task required by the method of proof selected. Each of the methods has contributed to today's trial.[6]

Compurgation required a party to bring forward a number of oath takers to swear in that party's favor. The oath takers all repeated the same oath. A simple mistake by any of the compurgators or the principal was considered evidence of the accused's guilt. One remnant of trial by compurgation is the modern trial requirement that all witnesses take an oath, or affirmation, to tell the truth before being allowed to testify.

Trial by charter required the accused to produce documents that had granted him certain rights, generally in property. The trial focused on proving the authenticity of those documents. Trial by record, on the other hand, required a party to prove what had happened in the court on some prior occasion. It required a witness present at the earlier proceeding to testify. Trial by charter and trial by record have been incorporated into the modern law of evidence. Establishing the authenticity of documents requires a proof reminiscent of trial by charter. Witnesses at prior judicial proceedings, however, no longer are required to testify as to what occurred at those proceedings. The records of earlier hearings are so accurate that rules of evidence now classify such records as "self-authenticating."

Trial by witness authorized men who knew something about the case, the parties, or both, to act as decision-makers, expressing their opinions about the appropriate outcome. Trial by inquisition sent a judge into the community in which the dispute occurred to select several men to act as decision-makers based on their knowledge of the dispute. Together, trial by witness and trial by inquisition evolved into parts of today's jury system, with the important modification that modern jurors know nothing about the case or the parties prior to commencement of the trial.

Trial by ordeal was a direct appeal to God to decide a case.[7] The ordeal itself was conducted under solemn religious ceremony; the uniformity of religious belief led to acceptance of the result. Chiefly, there were four forms of ordeal: by cold or hot water, by hot iron, or by morsel. The court determined the process to be followed based upon the class and status of the defendant. In trial by ordeal by hot water, for example, an accused would watch boiling water placed into a container. A rock on a cord would be lowered into the water to a depth determined by the severity of the accusation. The accused would plunge his arm into the water to retrieve the rock. His hand was then bandaged. The bandage was removed at the end of three days. If the wound had healed, the accused was deemed innocent; if it had festered, the accused was declared guilty.

Trial by duel was a form of high stakes appellate law. Unsatisfied by a result at some other mode of trial, a defendant could offer to support his proof by dueling with his accusor. If the offer was accepted by the judge, the parties would take a formal oath to follow a set procedure and a field of battle would be prepared. The defendant could acquit himself by surviving until sundown or by conquering his accusor. If the accusor prevailed within the day, he had to wage the duel again with other defendants similarly accused. Shortly after this mode developed, it became possible to substitute a "champion" for the actual party. Champions, of course, were selected for their ability to duel successfully.

While neither trial by ordeal nor trial by duel has survived, their influences still are felt in the aura of litigation.[8] Many perceive trials still to be by ordeal, the ordeal measured in financial and emotional rather than physical terms. Likewise, trial by duel or champions is reflected in the lawyer, cast as a party's champion, hired to fight the party's battle in the courtroom rather than in the open field.

How Litigation Works

Litigation occurs in five phases: pretrial, trial, post-trial, appeal, and enforcement.[9] A dispute travels as far through the process as a party insists. Each phase requires the accomplishment of specific tasks and presents new opportunities to resolve the dispute.

The pretrial phase is designed to answer questions concerning the appropriateness or scope of the legal issues in a case and to allow for discovery of factual information. The trial phase allows parties to present evidence to an impartial fact-finder. Both the post-trial and appeal phases allow parties to question the decisions made in the case during the earlier phases. Finally, the enforcement phase allows the prevailing party to invoke the court's power to obtain the relief ordered.

Throughout litigation answers are being sought to legal and factual questions. Legal questions concern such issues as whether the claim advanced is one that is cognizable under the law; the appropriateness of some evidence being considered by a jury; or whether the judge applied the law properly. Questions of fact, by contrast, concern the actions or events alleged to have occurred in the dispute.

1. *The Pretrial Phase*

The pretrial phase begins with the filing of a lawsuit and ends with motions made immediately prior to trial. Pretrial activity focuses on identifying the applicable law, narrowing the factual and legal issues that separate the parties, and learning about the strengths and weaknesses of the other side's case. Legal issues are addressed through motion practice; factual issues, through discovery.[10]

The pretrial phase formally begins with the filing of a complaint. The complaint outlines the legal theory plaintiff relies on, alleges that certain facts exist or have occurred, and that the law applied to these facts requires a finding for plaintiff. Upon receipt of a copy of the complaint and a summons from the court in which the complaint was filed, the defendant must file an answer, move against the complaint on legal grounds, or risk having an adverse judgment entered. The answer admits or denies the allegations contained in the complaint and presents any counterclaims defendant chooses to advance.

Pretrial motions may raise procedural matters, seek legal determinations, set case management matters, or request discovery rulings. A party may move to dismiss a case for improper service of summons and complaint, for example, or for filing after the time allowed to bring such a claim has expired. A motion for summary judgment requests the court to rule that no material issues of fact exist in the lawsuit and that as a matter of law the moving party is entitled to judgment. Motions also can seek continuances, schedule depositions, or handle other administrative details of the case. Motions for production can seek a court order requiring a party to produce evidence it has under its control.

Pretrial motion practice, like all of litigation, is an adversary process. The moving party (the party seeking some action by the court) must prove that it served the opposing party with a copy of the motion and notified the opposing party of the date, time, and location of the hearing on the motion. At the time set for hearing, the moving party is required to argue why the motion should be granted by the court. The opposing party's attorney can argue against granting the motion. If the opponent is silent, the motion generally is granted.

Discovery activity in the pretrial phase gives each party an opportunity to learn about the factual basis for the claim or defense of the opposing party or parties. Discovery rules, for example, allow parties to take depositions (sworn testimonies) from parties or witnesses, to submit written questions to an adverse party and receive written answers, or to request that a party make available relevant evidence for copying. Disagreements over discovery are resolved by a judge in response to the proper motion.

Over 90 percent of all lawsuits filed settle in the pretrial phase.[11] Information exchanged during discovery allows parties to better evaluate a case and the wisdom of continuing or defending it. Likewise, rulings from the court on various legal questions may effectively end a case. Some courts have developed procedures such as summary jury trials to increase settlement rates by providing parties with more information and limited assistance in their negotiations. Some of these trends are examined at the end of this chapter.

2. *The Trial Phase*

Trials follow a set chronological order:

(a) Selecting the fact-finder
(b) Opening statements
(c) Plaintiff's case
(d) Defendant's case
(e) Rebuttal cases
(f) Closing arguments
(g) Jury instructions (if a jury is used)
(h) Deliberation and verdict

(a) Selecting the Fact-Finder

Where trial by jury is provided for by constitution or statute, parties must decide during the pretrial phase whether a jury or judge is to be the trier of fact. In either event a judge conducts the trial and rules on questions of law. If the parties decide on a jury trial, citizens selected randomly, generally from voter lists, are called to serve as potential jurors. Some courts allow attorneys to question prospective jurors, while others leave questioning to judges. Counsel or the judge put questions to potential jurors to determine their suitability to hear the issues in the case. After potential jurors are questioned, those considered unacceptable can be removed. An unlimited number can be removed "for cause," such as being related to a party or to a witness or not being able to see well enough to evaluate exhibits. Another number, determined by the particular jurisdiction, can be removed by each side without explanation.[12]

(b) Opening Statements

After jury selection, a trial begins with attorneys for each side making opening statements. An opening statement is an explanation of a party's theory of the case, during which attorneys tell the trier of fact what evidence they intend to introduce. The rationale behind the opening statement is that evidence probably cannot be introduced logically or coherently during trial. Because an attorney may be required to call twenty witnesses and extract from each only a small portion of the overall case, it may be difficult for the trier of fact to understand each witness' contribution to the case. Opening statements provide jurors with blueprints of the cases the trial attorneys expect to build.

Verbal trappings of argument--conclusions, appeals to emotion, and analogies--are not allowed in opening statements. They are called "statements" specifically to distinguish them from closing arguments. It is common for trial attorneys, however, to try to persuade fact-finders during opening statements; the line between a descriptive statement and an argument frequently is blurred. A description of facts can be transformed by a skillful attorney into a persuasive explanation of why one position is correct and the other is not.[13]

(c) Plaintiff's Case

The plaintiff has the burden of establishing that the claim advanced in the complaint is valid. Assume, for example, a plaintiff automobile driver seeking to recover damages incurred when a truck failed to stop at a stop sign and struck plaintiff's car. Plaintiff could recover damages under the legal theory of negligence by demonstrating that the truck driver had a duty to stop; that the truck driver did not stop; and that, as a direct result, plaintiff was injured. Proving each of these elements to the degree of certainty required is plaintiff's burden. At the close of plaintiff's case, defendant could petition the court for an order dismissing plaintiff's case for failure to offer sufficient evidence, a question of law, on any one of the three elements of negligence.

A major strategic decision during plaintiff's case is choosing what evidence to offer.[14] Evidence may include demonstrative aids, such as charts, photographs or x-rays; physical evidence, such as a brake shoe, gun, or baggie of marijuana; documentary evidence, such as a contract or business record; and oral evidence, the testimony of witnesses. Evidence presented at trial can be considered by the trier of fact only if it is admitted under the rules of evidence. Whether evidence is admissible if challenged is a question of law to be resolved by the judge.

Most of the evidence in a trial usually comes from the testimony of witnesses. Witnesses are not free to speak at will; they may only respond to questions. Plaintiff's witnesses are questioned first on direct examination, by plaintiff's lawyer. The purpose of direct examination is to elicit testimony to support plaintiff's theory of the case. After plaintiff's attorney has finished direct examination, opposing counsel is allowed to conduct cross-examination. There are generally three approaches to cross-examination. First is to elicit testimony that supports defendant's theory of the case. Second is to elicit testimony detrimental to plaintiff's theory of the case. Third is to demonstrate why the witness should not be considered credible by the trier of fact.[15] After cross-examination, plaintiff may conduct redirect examination. The purpose of redirect examination is to give the attorney who called the witness an opportunity to allow the witness to explain any issues raised by the cross-examination.

(d) Defendant's Case

The defendant's case also is framed by the pleadings. If defendant has denied the facts plaintiff has alleged, for example, defendant's case attempts to demonstrate plaintiff's error. If defendant has pleaded a counterclaim, defendant stands in the position of plaintiff as to that claim and has the burden of establishing the elements to support the claim.

The questioning roles are now reversed. Defendant conducts direct and re-direct examination. Plaintiff conducts cross-examination.

At the close of defendant's case, both parties may make motions. Defendant, for example, could renew motions it made at the end of plaintiff's case, while plaintiff could ask the court to dismiss the claims of defendant for failure to offer evidence on a required element.

(e) Rebuttal Cases

Plaintiff is entitled to rebut the allegations raised in defendant's case. Plaintiff may seek to repair damage done by defendant's evidence, or may attack defendant's theory of the case. At this point, however, plaintiff may only introduce evidence that rebuts an attack made on plaintiff's case or that rebuts an allegation of support made for defendant's case.

At the discretion of the judge, defendant may be allowed to rebut plaintiff's rebuttal evidence, but defendant is limited to responding to evidence introduced in plaintiff's rebuttal case. Each step in the process thus narrows the scope of the next step. The purposes of narrowing the presentations are to prevent one side from introducing new evidence on issues when it is too late for the opposing party to rebut it, and to ensure that the trial eventually comes to an end.[16]

(f) Closing Arguments

Closing arguments are persuasive pleas to the trier of fact to adopt the theory of the case advocated by plaintiff or defendant. Plaintiff's attorney generally will describe the elements of the legal theory for the trier of fact and demonstrate that all elements have been proven, and that plaintiff therefore is entitled to relief. Defendant's attorney will argue that one or more elements of plaintiff's case have not been proven, or that the defense theory has been proven, and that plaintiff is therefore not entitled to relief.

Closing arguments give both parties' attorneys an opportunity to assist the trier of fact in deciding how to evaluate the evidence produced at trial. Counsel have broad latitude in closing arguments. They can discuss any reasonable inferences to be drawn from any evidence, either direct or circumstantial, in the case. They also can comment on the credibility of witnesses.

There are a few prohibitions in closing arguments, however. Attorneys cannot tell jurors to put themselves in a litigant's place. Arguments that appeal directly to the sympathy or prejudice of jurors also are improper. As in other phases of the process, attorneys are responsible for controlling one another's closing arguments. Judges interrupt arguments only when opposing counsel raise objections.[17]

(g) Jury Instructions (if a jury is used)

Before the end of a trial, attorneys present the judge with suggested jury instructions and present arguments about the relevant law. Because the determination of applicable law is a legal question, it is answered by the trial judge. Based on that determination, the judge instructs the jury about its responsibilities in deciding the case, including a description of the law they should apply. If the case concerned a driver who hit a pedestrian in a crosswalk, for example, the judge would explain the law of negligence and the jury would be charged with answering the factual questions in the case, then applying the law as given by the judge. Frequently judges present the jury with a list of factual questions it must answer in order to arrive at its verdict.[18]

(h) Deliberation and Verdict

The final step in a trial is reaching a verdict, the decision in the case. In reaching the verdict, the trier of fact is limited to considering the evidence presented at trial; it may not request additional evidence or conduct its own investigations. A judge acting as trier of fact may either render a verdict at the close of trial or reserve the case for later decision. If the trier of fact is a jury, it will retire to the jury room for deliberations. During deliberations, juries discuss the evidence presented, debate if necessary, and vote on the appropriate outcome. Deliberations last until a verdict is agreed on by the number required in that type of case or the judge accepts a jury's notification that they cannot reach a verdict. The trial of fact is over when the verdict is rendered.[19]

3. *The Post-Trial Phase*

Litigation activity after trial reverts once again to motion practice. These motions generally ask the trial judge to hold that there was something wrong with the fairness or administration of the trial. If necessary, the non-moving side has the opportunity to argue against the appropriateness of granting the motions filed. Post-trial motions generally focus on questions of law. A losing party may move for a new trial, for example, alleging that the judge committed prejudicial error while instructing the jury, or that one of the judge's legal rulings was incorrect.

The time allowed for the post-trial phase in most jurisdictions is short. It begins with the announcement of the verdict and ends some period of time after the signing of the final order by the court. Only a few motions, like those based on newly discovered evidence, may occur outside this time limitation.[20]

4. *The Appeal Phase*

The appeal phase involves courts at the top two levels of state and federal court systems. Appeal from a trial court to a first level court of appeals generally is a matter of right, while appeal from a court of appeals to a higher appellate court usually is a matter of discretion for the higher court.

Appellate practice differs from trial practice in several respects. At trial, juries or a single judge commonly are responsible for determining issues of fact. Judges alone, usually sitting in panels of three, hear legal issues on appeal. At trial, testimony is taken from witnesses. On appeal, there are no witnesses. Appellate judges read the briefs submitted by the parties, review some or all of the trial record depending on the issues appealed and the standard of review, and listen to oral arguments by counsel.

Oral argument occurs after the appellate court record (which includes the trial court record and all opening and responding briefs filed in the appeals court) is complete. Appellate arguments occur before an assigned panel of judges with each side having a specific time period in which to present its oral argument. Attorneys are given the opportunity to argue in support of the legal position asserted in their briefs, to rebut their opponents' briefs, or to answer questions from the judges.

Appellate briefs cite alleged trial errors and precedent. Absent precedent, the parties advance their theories of what the court's decision should be based upon arguments of public policy and fairness.

To get a broader perspective on issues in a case, appellate courts sometimes allow *amicus curiae* (friends of the court) to file briefs and to participate in oral argument. An appellate court's decision can answer not only the questions raised by the named parties in the suit, but any arguments raised by *amicus curiae*.

After argument, a case is taken under advisement by the appellate court. The court can request additional arguments, submission of supplemental briefs, or briefing of new or expanded issues. Generally, however, cases remain as submitted after oral argument. The panel may take weeks or months to file its decision, generally accompanied by a written opinion outlining the reasons for the decision. A decision that finds no error by the trial court will affirm that court's judgment. If the appellate court determines the trial court did err, it also will determine the appropriate response to the error. If the court finds the error harmless, it will affirm the trial court; if the court finds reversible error, it will return the case to the trial court with directions for the lower court. Each lower court is bound to follow the directions and announcements of the higher courts in its jurisdiction.[21]

Appellate courts apply different "standards of review" to cases, depending on the nature of the error or errors claimed by the appellant. The standard of review determines level of scrutiny an appellate court will give when reviewing the record of a trial. Three common standards are "abuse of discretion," "clear error," and "*de novo.*"

If an appellant argued that the trial court committed an error in the conduct of the trial, most appellate courts would apply an "abuse of discretion" standard of review. Appellant would have to show that the trial judge abused judicial discretion in the conduct of the trial in order to prevail on appeal. If the argument on appeal was that the trial court erred in its fact-finding function, most appellate courts would apply a "clear error" standard of review. Appellant would have to show that the finding of fact was clearly erroneous in order to have the trial court's decision reversed or the case remanded for further findings of fact. If the argument on appeal was that the trial court applied the wrong law or applied the law incorrectly, most appellate courts would apply a "de novo" standard of review, entitling the appellant to a review of the entire record of the trial by the appellate court.[22]

5. *The Enforcement Phase*

The final phase of litigation includes the steps taken to secure enforcement of the outcome in the suit. Most enforcement matters concern payment of a judgment. A judge, in response to a motion, can order a party to be deposed concerning assets or income, or order that property be sold or transferred, or order other steps taken to help satisfy the judgment. This step can be avoided by voluntary compliance with the judgment.[23]

Burdens of Persuasion in Litigation

For every question of fact submitted to a trier of fact in litigation, one of the parties carries the burden of persuasion. The party with the burden must produce a particular level of certainty in the mind of the trier of fact as to the existence or non-existence of that fact. The applicable burden applies to each element of a party's claim or defense. In an armed robbery case, for example, the law requires the attorney for the state to prove that the defendant, while armed with a weapon, did take from a person, something of value, without that person's consent, and that these acts occurred within the geographic area of the court's jurisdiction. Because it is a criminal case, the law would require that the trier of fact be convinced of each of these separate elements beyond a reasonable doubt before the state could prevail.

There are three burdens of persuasion in litigation: preponderance, clear and convincing, and beyond a reasonable doubt. Statutes or case law establish which burden needs to be met in a given situation.

"Preponderance" of the evidence is the least difficult burden of persuasion to satisfy. It is met by a party offering evidence that, when fairly considered, produces the stronger impression and is more convincing than the evidence offered against it. It is referred to as the greater weight of evidence or establishing that the facts are more likely than not to have occurred.[24] A preponderance is achieved when the balancing scales of believability tip slightly in one party's favor. It is the burden applied in most civil cases.

Proof by "clear and convincing evidence" generally means that the evidence offered in support of a party's position is enough, when considered with the evidence offered against it, to convince the decision-maker, a prudent person, of the correctness of that position. This standard requires the scales to be obviously and significantly tipped in favor of one party.[25] The clear and convincing standard is applied in matters such as civil commitment to a mental hospital or holding a person in contempt of court.

The most stringent and most difficult to define burden of persuasion is "beyond a reasonable doubt." It is not absolute certainty or proof beyond all possible or imaginary doubt, but proof beyond that doubt strong enough to cause a reasonable and prudent person to hesitate in carrying out important affairs.[26] Some courts had described it as "moral certainty."[27] It is the standard used in criminal prosecution.

The Role of the Lawyer in Litigation

Lawyers play several important roles in the litigation process. The most obvious role is to represent clients in the various phases of litigation. With varying degrees of client involvement, lawyers direct disputes through the phases of litigation. Lawyers also play important roles as legal advisors and counselors. Their advice and counsel can help prevent the need for litigation, or can focus on strategies to pursue while in litigation. Many lawyers aspire eventually to become judges, putting aside the responsibility of representing one of the parties to become the neutral decision-maker.

There is no legal requirement that a party to a lawsuit be represented by an attorney. A litigant appearing pro se ("for self") has full access to trial courts and access by permission to appellate courts. The overwhelming majority of litigants, however, choose to be represented by an attorney because of the complexity of the process and the need for legal training to be effective in the forum.

Knowledge of legal procedures and rules is a primary reason for disputants to employ lawyers to represent them in litigation. Failure to conform to a procedural rule, for example, can be fatal to the case. There are time, form, and delivery requirements for each document filed with a court. A single mistake in satisfying these requirements can result in losing the right to present a claim or defense. Likewise, ignorance of the rules of evidence can result in competent evidence not being introduced or improper evidence being admitted by an opponent for lack of objection.

Success in litigation also requires training in legal research. Determining which cases are relevant, and what weight to give to each in developing a legal theory, is a difficult task central to the lawyer's role in litigation. Knowledge of a particular statute or common law rule generally is only partial knowledge of the law. Law is an evolving body of rules that can best be understood by evaluating its application by various courts.[28]

Success in litigation also requires that parties be able to persuade the finder of fact. Being persuasive in a legal forum is an art that involves more than knowledge of substantive and procedural legal rules. It also requires the ability to make strategic choices in presenting a case and to implement those decisions effectively. In the pretrial phase, for example, lawyers are asked to make a variety of strategic suggestions to clients, including who to sue and in which court, which legal theories to follow, which discovery techniques to utilize and which motions to file. New strategic choices arise during the trial stage, such as which witnesses to call, which questions to ask, and in what order for maximum persuasive effect. At the appellate and enforcement stages additional strategic decisions must be made. Lawyers both advise clients on these decisions and seek to achieve the goals sought by each decision.

An important aspect of legal advice and counseling is to help clients decide whether other dispute resolution processes should be pursued in conjunction with litigation. The local court system may allow options for negotiation, mediation or arbitration. Knowing how to negotiate effectively and when to pursue settlement requires special skills and sophisticated knowledge of the legal system. Disputants usually look to lawyers throughout the process for guidance and assistance.

Success as a practicing lawyer generally is a prerequisite to becoming a judge. Most state court judges are elected. Gaining support of a bar association, usually an imperative for electoral success, typically requires years of experience as a practicing lawyer, service in the bar, and some level of political participation in the community. Federal judges are appointed, but the steps to achieving a judgeship are similar to running for office.[29] Rarely is a judge appointed to the bench who has not been a practicing lawyer or law professor, and who has not been involved with relevant bar associations and even the political process.

Example of Litigation

On December 24, 1982, Sara Goings, age 66, and her husband went to a shopping mall near their home. Their destination was Dollar Department Store, where they intended to purchase a gift for their grandson.

As they had expected, the Sharp Shopping Mall parking lot was packed. Dollar Department Store is located immediately adjacent to the parking lot. The Goings were able to park nearby, and enter Dollar through the northeast entrance.

Even for Christmas Eve the aisle they entered was unusually crowded. The candy department had a special sale table in that area, there was an Atari game display that was available for free play, and the garden shop, housewares, and sporting goods departments all met at a cashier in that aisle.

As the Goings made their way through this crowd, they were unable to walk side by side. Mr. Goings led the way and Mrs. Goings attempted to follow.

Mrs. Goings fell to the floor as she attempted to walk through the crowd. As Mr. Goings turned, he saw her lying on her side, the bottom of her shoe smeared with what appeared to be the remains of a smashed apple core. Another customer, Carolyn Rollins, came to Goings' assistance. Rollins had Goings almost standing before her husband was able to return to her. Rollins and Mr. Goings helped her from the main aisle to a bench in the sporting goods department, where she complained of pain in her left hip.

A salesperson joined the Goings and told them that she had called security. A few moments later, one of Dollar Department Store's security officers came to the scene. After taking some preliminary information, he authorized Goings to go to the local hospital for x-rays and emergency treatment.

Although released from the hospital within an hour, Goings' hip began to worsen. Two days after the fall, she saw her own doctor, who then ordered additional x-rays. He diagnosed the problem as a degenerative joint disease that had been dormant prior to the fall. He theorized the condition would not have made itself felt for another five to ten years if Goings had not fallen.

During the next year, Goings' condition worsened significantly. She was no longer able to work at the job she had had for 17 years, she was in almost constant pain, she was unable to sleep, she lost 35 pounds, she underwent physical therapy, consumed large quantities of pain relievers, and she was faced with the possibility of replacement surgery on her left hip.

Neither Mr. nor Mrs. Goings had ever sued anyone for anything prior to this time. They were reluctant to contact an attorney, but on the advice of a friend at their church contacted a lawyer who emphasized personal injury cases.

After investigating the facts and researching the law, it was clear to the attorney why Dollar Department Store had not attempted to negotiate this case within the past year. In order for Dollar Department Store to be found responsible for this injury, Goings would have to show that Dollar had notice of the dangerous condition. The applicable law required a store operator to have actual or constructive knowledge (in the exercise of reasonable diligence, should have known) of the fallen object. There was no evidence to support the contention that the department store knew of the apple core on the floor where Goings had fallen. The only evidence that supported the conclusion that Dollar had not acted with reasonable diligence was the opinion of the customer, Carolyn Rollins, that the core had been on the floor for awhile because of its color. The evidence that Dollar's actions or inactions brought it under the applicable law sufficiently to establish liability was at best questionable. At the conclusion of Goings' case, it would be unlikely that the court would determine that she had offered enough evidence to establish a "prima facie" case. Without a prima facie case (enough evidence to allow a reasonable juror to conclude that plaintiff had met its burden of persuasion), the judge would dismiss Goings' case.

According to Goings' attorney, however, there was a good argument that the law should be expanded. A minority of jurisdictions, including an adjacent state, had recognized a distinction between traditional store owners and major self-service stores like Dollar Department Store. If part of a store's method of operation was to rely upon customers serving themselves, and bringing items to a central cashier, some courts held the self-service retailer to a higher standard of care than small stores. If the self-service storekeeper's method of operation was such that the existence of an unsafe condition was reasonably foreseeable, liability could attach even without actual or constructive notice of the dangerous condition.

Several pieces of evidence suggested that Dollar Department Store should have realized that its method of operation was such that an unsafe condition was reasonably foreseeable. It had engineered a series of attractions--the Atari games, the candy sale, and the cashier location--in such a way as to create large crowds of people. No signs were posted requesting people not to bring food into the store. Dollar did not maintain an adequate labor force to check the floor area occasionally to insure its safety. It had not placed wastebaskets or trash containers in the passage-ways to decrease the possibility of littering. Employees had seen customers eating and drinking beverages in that area of the store on prior occasions. All these arguments would be helpful if the court was willing to expand the state's present theory of storekeeper liability.

Dollar's unwillingness to negotiate a settlement did not change once Goings' attorney entered the picture. The store steadfastly denied liability. Goings then authorized her attorney to file suit. Once the discovery process was significantly under way, and it became apparent to Dollar that Goings did intend to try the matter if the store was unwilling to settle, Dollar took a position in negotiations: Dollar was willing to pay a "nuisance" amount of $4,000 to terminate the suit.

Goings viewed Dollar's position as woefully inadequate and insensitive, and insisted that the matter be tried. Her attorney prepared to try the case under two theories. First, he would attempt to demonstrate that the apple core had been on the floor long enough that Dollar's employees should have been aware of it. Second, he would attempt to demonstrate that it was Dollar's method of operation that created the hazard and that the possible creation of the hazard was reasonably foreseeable from that method of operation.

Prior to trial, Dollar Department Store's attorneys made a motion for summary judgment alleging that there was no question of fact that should reach the jury. In order to make that motion, Dollar had to indicate that it did not, at least for the purpose of the motion, feel that there was a factual difference between the two sides. The trial court held that it was possible for Goings to convince the jury that the core had been there long enough, and that department store employees should have been aware of it. Thus, Goings' case would be allowed to go to trial. The court indicated that it felt it was a close call, but it was prepared to allow Goings to present her evidence to the court.

At the close of Goings' case, evidence had been introduced as indicated above. Dollar then made a motion for a directed verdict, claiming that under the state of the law Goings could not prevail unless there was enough evidence (a preponderance of the evidence) to convince the jury that it was more likely than not that the apple core had been on the floor long enough that the store reasonably should have known of its existence or that the store actually did know. The trial judge, after listening to arguments of both counsel, agreed with Dollar. Further, the trial court agreed that the only evidence on this subject, Carolyn Rollins' opinion, was not enough to allow the jury to so hold. The court directed the jury to enter a verdict for Dollar.

Within 30 days of the judge's signing the order dismissing the case, Goings appealed to her state's appellate court. She was required to meet certain procedural requirements to file the appeal, and to prepare a brief. Within 45 days of submission of her brief, Dollar Department

Store was required to respond. When both briefs were in front of the court, it had authority to request additional documents, to set the case for argument, or to affirm the lower court's opinion without issuing an opinion of its own. The appellate court chose to hear oral argument, then affirmed the lower court without writing an opinion.

Goings had one remaining option: She could petition the state's supreme court to review the action of the appellate court. She filed her petition for review in a timely fashion. The supreme court refused to review the lower court's holding. The law therefore would stay as it had been before Goings' case: a wronged plaintiff must demonstrate that a storekeeper had actual notice or should have known through reasonable diligence of the existence of a dangerous condition.

QUESTIONS

1. How would you characterize Goings' attorney's interest in this case? What were his options? Would you have recommended that Goings go to trial? Would you have recommended that she appeal?

2. How do you think Goings would feel about the legal system after her experience? Can you think of a better process for handling the facts in her case?

3. Is this the kind of case the public should subsidize by supporting the judicial system?

4. At trial, the judge refused to allow in evidence testimony that established that Dollar's security officer had authorized Mrs. Goings to go to the hospital, and that Dollar had paid the emergency treatment costs. Do you think the judge's ruling was fair?

Trends in Litigation

Common complaints about the litigation system focus on the time delay, cost in emotional and financial terms, and apparent insensitivity of the system.[30] In response to these criticisms, courts have developed several techniques to streamline the administration of litigation and to avoid trials. Court-annexed arbitration (considered in Chapter 4) perhaps is the most expansive. Other developments are considered below.

Rent-A-Judge

In the 1970s three lawyers in California were involved with a complex business dispute that the parties wanted to keep out of the public eye and to have resolved quickly, but which appeared destined to go to trial because negotiations had stalemated. The attorneys discovered an 1872 state statute that allowed the case to be tried by a referee selected and paid by the parties. Today, approximately ten states have statutes that allow this procedure, which is commonly referred to as "rent-a-judge."

Under "rent-a-judge" statutes, parties file a joint petition with the court in which the case has been filed (known as the presiding court) requesting that the case be tried before a "rented" judge of the parties' selection. Typically, "rented" judges are retired judges or magistrates who know the law and the procedural requirements of a formal trial in that jurisdiction. If the court agrees, the case is assigned to the "rented" judge.

The judge follows the jurisdiction's rules of evidence and procedure, and applies the jurisdiction's law in hearing the case. The judge submits findings of fact and conclusions of law to the presiding court. In some jurisdictions, the parties are given an opportunity to object to any findings or conclusions before the "rented" judge's opinion is submitted to the presiding judge and entered as the judgment of the court.

After the judgment is entered, parties retain the same rights of enforcement and appeal they would have if the case were tried in the presiding court. The parties must pay the judge's salary, which in 1986 ranged from an hourly fee of $50 to $100, or a daily fee of $300 to $750. Parties may be willing to share the cost of the judge because the procedure allows them to have their case tried quickly as opposed to having to wait their turn on the court docket, and they can select a judge with expertise in the subject matter of their dispute.

Statutes that permit "rented judges" differ in important ways. Some specify the kinds of cases that can be tried before "rented" judges, while others permit the entire gamut of civil cases to be handled through this procedure. Some statutes allow trials before "rented" judges to take place privately while others require public access.[31]

Example of "Rent-a-Judge"

Joan Reynoso is a popular TV news anchor at the local, non-network station, WDRP. She was hired to anchor the evening news at 5 O'clock and 11 O'clock. Her contract provided that she would have editorial responsibilities as well as delivering the news. Reynoso was inexperienced in television news when she was hired, although she brought eight years of radio broadcast experience to the position. Reynoso proved to be an outstanding interviewer when she was sent out on an investigative story one day when the regular reporter was ill. The production manager called on her increasingly to do interviews, as well as to edit and deliver the two news telecasts each weeknight. Reynoso did not object at first to the additional work because she was anxious to develop her skills and prove herself in this new medium. Within a few months, however, she felt that WDRP was taking advantage her.

When the production manager assigned her to her fourth interview in a week, Reynoso objected. The manager became angry and said he was sick and tired of having to "baby" temperamental TV personalities. He knew that Reynoso had applied to work at another local station, WLRB, affiliated with a major network. He was so irritated with Reynoso's refusal to do another interview, that he called the manager of WLRB and told her to think twice about hiring Reynoso because of her "difficult" personality and her aggressive style. A week later Reynoso received notice that her application to work at WLRB had been rejected because of what the production manager at WDRP said about her.

Reynoso contacted her attorney and decided to sue WDRP and its production manager for slander. An attorney for WDRP met with Reynoso's attorney. They agreed that the publicity of a trial would be detrimental to both sides and that the matter should be resolved as quickly as possible. The case could not come to trial for about 26 months because of the backlog on the civil docket in their jurisdiction. Reynoso's attorney consulted the statutes and found that the case could be tried by a "rented" judge.

When the two attorneys were satisfied that the dispute could not be resolved informally, they filed a petition with the presiding court requesting that the case be assigned to Judge Melvin

Warren, a retired circuit court judge. Judge Warren wrote a reference book on slander for the local bar soon after his retirement and remained active as a "rented judge" for a variety of civil cases. His fee was $500 per day. Reynoso and WDRP agreed to share the cost of Judge Warren's salary. The presiding judge assigned the case to Judge Warren, who met with the attorneys to determine a convenient time and place for the trial. The parties agreed to a discovery period of 60 days, to be followed by a trial in a conference room at a local convention center. The "rent-a-judge" statute in this jurisdiction allowed for a private trial at a time and place convenient to the parties. The parties agreed to share the cost of the room rental.

Judge Warren convened the trial according to the schedule agreed to by the parties following two hours of pre-trial motions. Both sides presented witnesses and evidence; a court reporter hired by them kept a verbatim stenographic record. Counsel for Reynoso and WDRP followed the rules of evidence and procedure of their jurisdiction and preserved objections to rulings by Judge Warren for possible appeal. The trial lasted three days. Judge Warren submitted findings of fact and conclusions of law to the parties two days after the trial. Reynoso's attorney objected to one of the findings of fact, so the trial was reopened for the purpose of hearing testimony on that point. Judge Warren did not change his findings of fact after the re-hearing. His findings and conclusions were then submitted to the presiding judge and were entered as a judgment for WDRP.

QUESTIONS

1. This proceeding was conducted in private, as the parties desired, in order to keep their dispute out off the public eye. Should parties who file cases in courts, which are public forums, be allowed to elect a process that sometimes prevents public access?

2. The "rent-a-judge" system is accessible only to those who can afford to pay the judge's salary. Is this fair? Do other litigants derive any benefits? How?

3. Do you see any policy problems with allowing "rent-a-judge" decisions to be appealed? With allowing those who can afford it to have their cases expedited?

Summary Jury Trial

The summary jury trial is a court-initiated technique that allows parties to have a shortened version of their case tried before an advisory jury. The technique was developed by federal court judges but is being used increasingly by state court judges as well. Based on the advisory jury's verdict, the parties have a better understanding of the risks of going to trial and often are able to negotiate a settlement.

The summary jury trial is recommended by a judge who has studied the pleadings, been advised by the lawyers that negotiations have stalemated, but thinks there may be a chance for a negotiated settlement if the parties have a more realistic understanding of how their case might appear to a jury. Each side is asked to present a shortened version of its case to a special panel drawn from the regular jury pool. The advisory jury can range from six to twelve in number, but six is the most common. The jury hears the lawyers' presentations, receives formal instructions from the judge on the relevant law, and then retires to deliberate on a non-binding verdict. Following announcement of the advisory verdict, lawyers are allowed to ask the jurors questions about what they considered the strengths and weaknesses of each side's presentation. The question-answer session allows lawyers and their clients to see how an actual jury might respond to their case. The session can provide useful information about how to prepare for trial, but more often it paves the way for settlement negotiations.

After the question-answer session, the advisory jury is dismissed. The parties meet with their lawyers to discuss the advantages and disadvantages of continuing with litigation. If the parties agree, their lawyers resume negotiations. Sometimes the judge who presided at the summary jury trial participates in the negotiations. If settlement is reached, the case is dismissed. If negotiation is not successful and the case goes to trial, neither the advisory jurors nor the judge who presided at the summary jury trial hears the case.[32]

Example of Summary Jury Trial

John Caruso is a twenty-five year old city employee. He also was a fitness buff who worked out at a local health spa routinely and rode his bike twelve miles to and from work each day. On his way home from work one evening, a car driven by George Garland backed out of its parking place, hit Caruso's bike and right leg, and threw him over the car onto the street. Caruso suffered a separated shoulder and a severely fractured ankle. The back-up lights on Garland's car did not work, which is why Caruso did not see him backing out in time to swerve out of the way.

Caruso was hospitalized for eight days with his injuries. Only a year before he had separated the same shoulder in another bicycle accident. The second injury did permanent damage and limited mobility in his shoulder by about ten percent. His ankle required surgery and traction and was in a cast for three months. The ankle required several weeks of physical therapy. Caruso's doctor was not sure whether the ankle would recover completely but estimated that it would be at least two years before it returned to normal. Caruso's injuries caused him to miss almost six months of work.

Caruso sued Garland for $750,700. Of that sum, $18,200 was for hospital and medical bills, and physical therapy. Another $12,500 was for lost wages. In addition, Caruso found that the loss of mobility in his shoulder and the pain in his ankle prevented him from returning to his landscape gardening job. He was forced to take an inside job with the city which, although it paid as well, was not as satisfactory to Caruso because he preferred to work outdoors and to be physically active on the job. With forty years left until retirement, Caruso claimed compensatory damages of $400,000 ($10,000 per year) to compensate for being forced into a desk job. He claimed an additional $320,000 ($8,000 per year) to compensate for the more limited routine he would be able to pursue at the health spa due to his shoulder injuries and his inability to ride his bike as much due to the ankle injuries.

Caruso's attorney and Garland's attorney were unsuccessful at negotiating a settlement. No one questioned Garland's liability because of his defective back-up lights. The sole question was the amount of damages Caruso deserved. Garland's insurance company was willing to pay all of Caruso's actual damages ($30,700), and an additional $80,000 in compensatory damages. Caruso insisted on receiving at least $400,000 in compensatory damages.

The judge to whom the case was assigned reviewed the pleadings and met in pretrial conference with the attorneys. The judge recommended a summary jury trial, to which the attorneys and their clients agreed. A panel of six jurors was selected and the process of the summary jury trial was explained.

Caruso's lawyer made a thirty-minute presentation of her client's case to the jury, explaining Caruso's injuries and the effect they had on his way of life. She portrayed him as an active young man committed to physical fitness prior to the accident, who had chosen his career to complement his lifestyle. Garland's lawyer also made a thirty-minute presentation, emphasizing that Caruso's pre-existing shoulder injury should be taken into account in determining damages, that he had suffered no loss of wages by being transferred to a desk job, and that there was not sufficient evidence of permanent ankle damage to warrant extensive compensatory damages for it. Garland's attorney also presented statistical evidence on the likelihood of Caruso suffering other injuries from biking during the next thirty years.

Following the presentations, attended by Caruso, Garland, and a representative of Garland's insurance company, the judge explained the law to the advisory jury, which then retired and deliberated on an advisory verdict. The jury returned an advisory award for Caruso for $30,700 in actual and $185,000 in compensatory damages. During the question-answer period jurors explained what they perceived to be the strengths and weaknesses of the arguments on both sides. They said they found Caruso to be a very "appealing plaintiff" whose way of life had been dramatically altered by an accident that was not his fault. They concluded, however, that Caruso was not entitled to more money because he might recover completely from his ankle injuries and at least be able to return to active cycling. They also felt that in this economy Caruso should not be compensated for having a job not quite to his liking, especially since his current job paid the same as his former job. Two members of the advisory jury were themselves unemployed and thought Caruso's argument bordered on selfishness.

Following the question-answer period, both attorneys consulted with their clients. Caruso expressed concern about whether another jury would be any more sympathetic to his argument about compensatory damages for his job. He also said he thought that his ankle was in fact getting better and that by the time of the actual trial his doctor might not be a helpful witness. Garland and his insurance representative, on the other hand, were worried by the fact that Caruso was such an appealing plaintiff. If he had a positive impact on the advisory jury by simply being in the room, they concluded that he would get even more sympathy if he testified at trial. They also were concerned about medical evidence of arthritis in Caruso's ankle which, if presented at trial, would help to establish a permanent injury and might affect the jury's view of appropriate damages. Both sides were therefore willing to try to negotiate again. The judge offered to meet with them if they wished, but the lawyers said they thought they should be able to work out the matter on their own.

After forty-five minutes of discussion, the attorneys reached an agreement that satisfied the parties. Garland and his insurance company agreed to pay Caruso $30,700 in actual damages immediately. They also agreed to a structured compensatory damages package in which Caruso would receive an additional $200,000 over a period of forty years. The judge was notified of the negotiated settlement and the case was dismissed.

QUESTIONS

1. If you were counsel for Caruso, would you have resumed negotiations or gone to trial following the summary jury trial? Would your perspective be different if you were counsel for Garland's insurance company?

2. Do you think it appropriate for judges to recommend and preside at a summary jury trial?

3. If a judge recommended a summary jury trial and you feared that the exercise might force you to reveal an important trial strategy, would you refuse to try the procedure?

Panel Evaluation

Another aid to negotiated settlements in some jurisdictions is the evaluation of a case by a panel consisting of a member of the plaintiff's bar, a member of the defense bar, and a judge. Pursuant to local rules, a case referred to panel evaluation is scheduled for a hearing. The parties make abbreviated presentations of their arguments and the evidence they would produce at trial. At the conclusion of the presentations, the panel retires to discuss the case. Upon its return, and in the presence of the parties, panel members comment on the perceived strengths and weaknesses of both sides' cases. The panel also announces a "verdict," sometimes a consensus on a given dollar amount or a range within which the panel thinks the case would be decided if it went to trial. The parties then return to negotiations, using the evaluation panel's comments and recommendations to help them arrive at a settlement.[33]

Example of Panel Evaluation

Joan Silberman was injured when her automobile was hit from behind by Lisa Barnes. Liability was clear: Barnes made admissions at the scene, and filed an accident report which indicated that she was inattentive while driving, had not noticed a turn signal, and ran into Silberman's car.

The case did not settle because of a dispute over damages. Silberman was employed as a maid at a motel and, with her family, pursued bow hunting as a hobby. Following the crash, she complained of severe cervical strain--whiplash--and an inability to lift her arms above her shoulders. The condition prevented her from performing some of the tasks necessary to her job and from enjoying her archery.

Silberman was discharged from medical treatment, with advice to continue to take aspirin for the pain and to apply hot packs in the evening. There were no objective findings by medical personnel about the severity or probable duration of her injuries.

Prior to coming to the panel evaluation, Barnes' last offer to settle was $4,000. Silberman's last offer was $15,000; the prayer for relief in her suit was $50,000.

Panel evaluation focused exclusively on the damages issue. Cervical strains are relatively common phenomena in the personal injury area. The attorneys and the judge on the panel were familiar with the amount of damages normally awarded in the jurisdiction for such injuries. A complicating factor to the normal amounts awarded was the impact the injury had on Silberman's employment and recreational activities. The panel concluded that the defendant was discounting the impact on employment and recreation too heavily, but that Silberman still was requesting too large a sum of money. The result of the panel evaluation was a recommendation that the case be settled for $8,000. Following the panel's opinion, the case settled for $7,250.

QUESTIONS

1. As a lawyer would you rather receive advice from a summary jury panel or a panel of lawyers and a judge?

2. Do you think it appropriate for courts to encourage negotiated settlements?

3. Who should attend panel evaluations? Explain.

Endnotes

[1] Lee, *The American Courts as Public Goods: Who Should Pay the Cost of Litigation?*, 34 Cath. U. L. Rev. 267 (Winter 1985).

[2] J. Goebel, History of the Supreme Court of the United States 13-46 (1971).

[3] Rules of the Supreme Court of the United States 17.

"1. A review on writ of certiorari is not a matter of right, but of judicial discretion, and will be granted only when there are special and important reasons therefor. The following, while neither controlling nor fully measuring the Court's discretion, indicate the character of reasons that will be considered:

(a) When a federal court of appeals has rendered a decision in conflict with the decision of another federal court of appeals on the same matter; or has decided a federal question in a way in conflict with a state court of last resort; or has so far departed from the accepted and usual course of judicial proceedings, or so far sanctioned such a departure by a lower court, as to call for an exercise of this Court's power of supervision.

(b) When a state court of last resort has decided a federal question in a way in conflict with the decision of another state court of last resort or of a federal court of appeals.

(c) When a state court or a federal court of appeals has decided an important question of federal law which has not been, but should be settled by this Court, or has decided a federal question in a way in conflict with applicable decisions of this Court.

2. The same general considerations outlines above will control in respect of petitions for writs of certiorari to review judgments of the United States Court of Appeals for the Federal Circuit, the United States Court of Military Appeals, and of any other court whose judgments are reviewable by law on writ of certiorari."

[4] *E.g., Patton v. Yount*, 467 U.S. 1025, 1031 (1984) (certiorari granted to consider the problem of "pervasive media publicity that now arises so frequently in the trial of sensational cases.")

[5] *See, The Supreme Court 1986 Term*, 101 Harv.L.Rev. 7, 236 (1987); *The Supreme Court 1985 Term*, 100 Harv.L.Rev. 1, 304 (1986); *The Supreme Court 1984 Term*, 99 Harv.L.Rev. 1, 322 (1985).

[6] *See generally* T. Plucknett, A Concise History of the Common Law (1956); Thayer, *Older Modes of Trial*, 5 Harv.L.Rev. 45 (1981).

[7] Tewksbury, *The Ordeal as a Vehicle for Divine Intervention* in Before the Law 334-336 (3d ed. 1984).

[8] J. Frank, *The Fight Theory Versus the Truth Theory* in Courts on Trial: Myth and Reality in American Justice 80-102 (1949).

[9] *See e.g.* J. Songteng, R. Haydock & J. Boyd, The Trialbook: A Total System for the Preparation and Presentation of a Case (Student ed. 1984).

[10] *See e.g.*, R. Haydock, D. Herr & J. Stempel, Fundamentals of Pretrial Litigation (1985).

[11] Galanter, *Reading the Landscape of Disputes: What We Know and Don't Know (And Think We Know) About Our Allegedly Contentious and Litigious Society*, 31 U.C.L.A. L. Rev. 4, 26 (1983-1984).

[12] *See e.g.* W. Wagner, Art of Advocacy: Jury Selection (1981).

[13] *See e.g.* A. Julien, Opening Statements (1985).

[14] Many works are available that suggest methods of accomplishing the strategic goals of trial counsel. *See generally* T. Mauet, Fundamentals of Trial Techniques (2d ed. 1988); P. Bergman, Trial Advocacy (1979); K. Hegland, Trial and Practice Skills (1978); J. Jeans, Trial Advocacy (1975); A. Morrill, Trial Diplomacy (1971).

[15] *See generally* I. Younger, The Art of Cross-Examination (Monograph, A.B.A. Section on Litigation, 1976); F. Wellman, The Art of Cross-Examination (1948); A. Cornelius, The Cross-Examination of Witnesses (1921).

[16] *See generally* F. Lane, Lane's Goldstein's Trial Techniques, Section 2201 (3d ed. 1984).

[17] *See e.g.* J. Stein, Closing Argument: The Art and the Law (1985).

[18] *See e.g.* G. Douthwaite, Jury Instructions on Medical Issues (1987).

[19] *See e.g.* R. Hastie, S. Penrod & N. Pennington, Inside the Jury (1985).

[20] *See* Sonsteng, Haydock & Boyd, *supra* note 9, at 367.

[21] *See generally* M. Houts & W. Rogosheske, Art of Advocacy: Appeals (1987); R. Stern, Appellate Practice in the United States (1981).

[22] *See e.g.* R. Martineau, Fundamentals of Modern Appellate Advocacy 131 (1985).

[23] *See e.g.* Smit, *Enforcement of Judgments in the United States of America,* 34 Am. J. Comp. Law 225 (supp. 1986).

[24] Black's Law Dictionary 1064 (rev. 5th ed. 1979).

[25] *Id.* at 227.

[26] *Id.* at 147.

[27] Oregon Jury Instructions for Criminal Cases 1006 (Oregon State Bar Supp. 1986).

[28] *See e.g. Rodgers v. Lincoln Towing Serv., Inc.* 771 F.2d 194 (7th Cir. 1985). (Seventh Circuit standards for imposing sanctions for failure to state a claim in civil litigation.)

[29] *See generally* American Bar Association Standing Committee on Judicial Selection, Tenure and Compensation, Model By-Laws for State and Local Bar Associations Respecting Appointment and Election of Judges (1968).

[30] *See* National Institute for Dispute Resolution, Paths to Justice: Major Public Policy Issues of Dispute Resolution (October, 1983).

[31] Coulson, *Rent-a-Judge: Private Settlement for the Public Good,* 66 Judicature 7 (1982). *Cf.* Gnaizda, *Rent-a-Judge: Secret Justice for the Privileged Few,* 66 Judicature 7 (1982); Note, *The California Rent-a-Judge Experiment: Constitutional and Policy Considerations of Pay-As-You-Go Courts,* 94 Harv. L. Rev. 1592 (1981).

[32] Lambros, *The Summary Jury Trial and Other Alternative Methods of Dispute Resolution: A Report to the Judicial Conference of the United States on the Operation of the Jury System* 103 F.R.D. 461 (1984).

[33] Addresses by Judge R. P. Jones, M. Bricker, S. English & R. Newell, *Third Annual Conference on Dispute Resolution* Willamette University College of Law (Oct. 24, 1986) (video tape available at Willamette's Center for Dispute Resolution Library).

Sources

American Bar Association, Model Code of Professional Responsibility (1980).

P. Bergman, Trial Advocacy (1979).

Black's Law Dictionary (5th ed. 1979).

Chayes, *The Role of the Judge in Public Law Litigation,* 89 Harv. L. Rev. 1281 (1976).

A. Cornelius, The Cross-Examination of Witnesses (1921).

Coulson, *Rent-a-Judge: Private Settlement for the Public Good,* 66 Judicature 7 (1982).

Council on the Role of Courts, The Role of Courts in American Society (J. Lieberman ed. 1984).

G. Douthwaite, Jury Instructions on Medical Issues (1987).

J. Frank, Courts on Trial: Myth and Reality in American Justice (1949).

Galanter, *Reading the Landscape of Disputes: What We Know and Don't Know (And Think We Know) About Our Allegedly Contentious and Litigious Society,* 31 U.C.L.A. L. Rev. 4 (1983-1984).

_____ *Why the 'Haves' Come Out Ahead: Speculations on the Limits of Legal Change,* 9 Law & Soc. Rev. 567 (1980-1981).

J. Goebel, History of the Supreme Court of the United States (1971).

Gnaizda, *Rent-a-Judge: Secret Justice for the Privileged Few,* 66 Judicature 7 (1982).

R. Hastie, S. Penrod & N. Pennington, Inside the Jury (1985).

K. Hegland, Trial and Practice Skills (1978).

M. Houts & W. Rogosheske, Art of Advocacy: Appeals (1987).

J. Jeans, Trial Advocacy (1975).

A. Julien, Opening Statements (1985).

Lambros, *The Summary Jury Trial and Other Alternative Methods of Dispute Resolution: A Report to the Judicial Conference of the United States on the Operation of the Jury System,* 103 F.R.D. 461 (1984).

F. Lane, Lane's Goldstein's Trial Techniques (3d. ed. 1984).

Lee, *The American Courts as Public Goods: Who Should Pay the Cost of Litigation,* 34 Cath. U. L. Rev. 267 (Winter 1985).

J. Lieberman, The Litigious Society (1981).

Marshall and Prentice, *Persuading Judges in Bench Trials,* Summer Litigation 11 (1977).

R. Martineau, Fundamentals of Modern Appellate Advocacy 131 (1985).

A. Morrill, Trial Diplomacy (1971).

National Institute for Dispute Resolution, Paths to Justice: Major Public Policy Issues of Dispute Resolution (1983).

Note, *The California Rent-a-Judge Experiment: Constitutional and Policy Considerations of Pay-As-You-Go Courts,* 94 Harv. L. Rev. 1592 (1981).

T. Plunknett, A Concise History of the Common Law (1956).

Rosenberg, Rient & Rowe, *Expenses: The Roadblock to Justice,* 20 Judges J. 16 (Summer 1981).

Smit, *Enforcement of Judgments in the United States of America,* 34 Am. J. Comp. Law 225 (supp. 1986).

J. Sonteng, R. Haydon, & J. Boyd, The Trialbook: A Total System for the Preparation and Presentation of a Case (Student ed. 1984).

Spansberg, *Basic Values and Techniques of Persuasion,* Winter Litigation 13 (1977).

J. Stein, Closing Argument: The Art and the Law (1985).

R. Stern, Appellate Practice in the United States (1981).

Thayer, *Older Modes of Trial,* 5 Harv. L. Rev. 45 (1981).

Trubek, Sarat, Felstiner, Kritzer & Grossman, *The Costs of Ordinary Litigation,* 31 U.C.L.A. L. Rev. 72 (1983).

W. Wagner, Art of Advocacy: Jury Selection (1981).

F. Wellman, The Art of Cross-Examination (1948).

I. Younger, The Art of Cross-Examination (Monograph, A.B.A. Section on Litigation, 1976).

National Hockey League

v.

Metropolitan Hockey Club, Inc.

427 U.S. 639 (1976)

Per Curiam.

This case arises out of the dismissal, under Fed. Rule Civ. Proc. 37, of respondent's antitrust action against petitioners for failure to timely answer written interrogatories as ordered by the District Court. The Court of Appeals for the Third Circuit reversed the judgment of dismissal, finding that the District Court had abused its discretion. The question presented is whether the Court of Appeals was correct in so concluding. Rule 37(b)(2) provides in pertinent part as follows:

> "If a party . . . fails to obey an order to provide or permit discovery . . . the court in which the action is pending may make such orders in regard to the failure as are just, and among others the following: * * *
>
> "(C) An order striking out pleadings or parts thereof, or staying further proceedings until the order is obeyed, or dismissing the action or proceeding or any part thereof, or rendering a judgment by default against the disobedient party."

This Court held in *Societe Internationale v. Rogers,* 357 U.S. 197, 212 (1958), that Rule 37:

> "should not be construed to authorize dismissal of [a] complaint because of petitioner's noncompliance with a pretrial production order when it has been established that failure to comply has been due to inability, and not to willfulness, bad faith, or any fault of petitioner. * * *

The District Court, in its memorandum opinion directing that respondents' complaint be dismissed, summarized the factual history of the discovery proceeding in these words:

> "After seventeen months where crucial interrogatories remained substantially unanswered despite numerous extensions granted at the eleventh hour and, in many instances, beyond the eleventh hour, and notwithstanding several admonitions by the Court and promises and commitments by the plaintiffs, the Court must and does conclude that the conduct of the plaintiffs demonstrates the callous disregard of responsibilities counsel owe to the

Court and to their opponents. The practices of the plaintiffs exemplify flagrant bad faith when after being expressly directed to perform an act by a date certain, viz., June 14, 1974, they failed to perform and compounded that noncompliance by waiting until five days afterwards before they filed any motions. Moreover, this action was taken in the face of warnings that their failure to provide certain information could result in the imposition of sanctions under Fed. R. Civ. P. 37. If the sanction of dismissal is not warranted by the circumstances of this case, then the Court can envisage no set of facts whereby that sanction should ever be applied." 63 F.R.D. 641, 656 (1974).

The Court of Appeals, in reversing the order of the District Court by a divided vote, stated:

> "After carefully reviewing the record, we conclude that there is insufficient evidence to support a finding that M-GB's failure to file supplemental answers by June 14, 1974, was in flagrant bad faith, willful or intentional." 531 F.2d 1188, 1195 (1976).

The Court of Appeals did not question any of the findings of historical fact which had been made by the District Court, but simply concluded that there was in the record evidence of "extenuating factors." The Court of Appeals emphasized that none of the parties had really pressed discovery until after a consent decree was entered between petitioners and all of the other original plaintiffs except the respondents approximately one year after the commencement of the litigation. It also noted that respondents' counsel took over the litigation, which previously had been managed by another attorney, after the entry of the consent decree, and that respondents' counsel encountered difficulties in obtaining some of the requested information. The Court of Appeals also referred to a colloquy during the oral argument on petitioners' motion to dismiss in which respondents' lead counsel assured the District Court that he would not knowingly and willfully disregard the final deadline.

While the Court of Appeals stated that the District Court was required to consider the full record in determining whether to dismiss for failure to comply with discovery orders, see *Link v. Wabash R. Co.*, 370 U.S. 626, 633-634 (1962), we think that the comprehensive memorandum of the District Court supporting its order of dismissal indicates that the court did just that. That record shows that the District Court was extremely patient in its efforts to allow the respondents ample time to comply with its discovery orders. Not only did respondents fail to file their responses on time, but the responses which they ultimately did file were found by the District Court to be grossly inadequate.

The question, of course, is not whether this Court, or whether the Court of Appeals, would as an original matter have dismissed the action; it is whether the District Court abused its discretion in so doing. Certainly the findings contained in the memorandum opinion of the District Court quoted earlier in this opinion are fully supported by the record. We think that the lenity evidenced in the opinion of the Court of Appeals, while certainly a significant factor in considering the imposition of sanctions under Rule 37, cannot be allowed to wholly supplant other and equally necessary considerations embodied in that Rule.

There is a natural tendency on the part of reviewing courts, properly employing the benefit of hindsight, to be heavily influenced by the severity of outright dismissal as a sanction for failure to comply with a discovery order. It is quite reasonable to conclude that a party who has been subjected to such an order will feel duly chastened, so that even though he succeeds in having the order reversed on appeal he will nonetheless comply promptly with future discovery orders of the district court.

But here, as in other areas of the law, the most severe in the spectrum of sanctions provided by statute or rule must be available to the district court in appropriate cases, not merely to penalize those whose conduct may be deemed to warrant such a sanction, but to deter those who might be tempted to such conduct in the absence of such a deterrent. Under the circumstances of this case, we hold that the District Judge did not abuse his discretion in finding bad faith on the part of these respondents, and concluding that the extreme sanction of dismissal was appropriate in this case by reason of respondents' "flagrant bad faith" and their counsel's "callous disregard" of their responsibilities. Therefore, the petition for a writ of certiorari is granted and the judgment of the Court of Appeals is reversed.

So Ordered.

QUESTIONS

1. At what phase of the litigation process was this case when the trial judge dismissed the case? Did the trial judge have other options? If so, what were they? If not, why not?

2. What issue(s) is the court reviewing in this case? What is the standard of review? Why?

3. Was dismissal warranted in this case? Was it necessary? Was the court sending a message to anyone but National Hockey's counsel in its decision?

Rodgers v. Lincoln Towing Service, Inc.

771 F.2d 194 (7th Cir.1985)

Cummings, Chief Judge.

Plaintiff Steve Rodgers filed the instant suit alleging numerous violations of his civil rights by the various defendants on October 6, 1983. Plaintiff filed an amended complaint on December 1, 1983, but on March 29, 1984, the district court granted a motion to dismiss for failure to state a claim filed by several of the defendants under Fed.R.Civ.P. 12(b)(6). 596 F. Supp. 13 (N.D.-) (N.D.Ill.1984). The trial court also assessed one-third of the defendant's attorney's fees and costs as sanctions against Rodgers' lawyers under Fed.R-.Civ.P. 11. Id. at 22. After the district court denied Rodgers' motion for reconsideration, Id.at 26, he filed the instant timely appeal. We have jurisdiction pursuant to 28 U.S.C. Section 1291, and we affirm.

For purposes of considering the dismissal of plaintiff's complaint under Rule 12(b)(6), we take the factual allegations of plaintiff's complaint as true. On the evening of October 7, 1982, Rodgers parked his car in the parking lot of Belton Corned Beef Center, on the north side of Chicago, Illinois. When he left the restaurant about an hour later, he found that his car had been towed by Lincoln Towing Service, Inc. ("Lincoln Towing"), a towing operation employed by restaurants and other establishments to remove illegally parked cars from their parking lots. Rodgers retrieved his car that evening, but only after paying a towing fee.

That evening, some unknown person threw paint on the side of Lincoln Towing's building. At about 1:00 a.m. on October 8, Rodgers received an anonymous phone call claiming to be from the police and informing him the police would be "coming to your house for throwing paint on the building." One week later, on October 15, Detective Philip Pagano of the Chicago Police Department telephoned Rodgers concerning the paint-throwing incident, told him he had been identified as the one who had thrown the paint, and requested him to come to the police station to "answer charges." Pagano told Rodgers to bring $100 with which to post bail in case a complaint was filed, and that if he did not come to the police station a warrant would be issued for his arrest.

Rodgers went to the police station on October 18 at 5:20 p.m. There he was questioned for ap-

proximately an hour by Pagano, Chicago Police Detective William McGarry, and two employees of Lincoln Towing, Steven Mash and Steven Eisgrau. Neither during this interview nor earlier during the phone call was Rodgers informed of any of his constitutional rights. Rodgers steadfastly maintained his innocence of the accusations.

While he was being questioned, Rodgers saw Mash and Eisgrau, who are personal friends of Pagano's, insisting that Pagano write up a complaint against Rodgers. Pagano did so, and Mash signed the complaint, at which time Rodgers was formally arrested. He was jailed for over ten hours, and until 5:00 a.m. the next morning, before being allowed to post bail, despite his informing Pagano and other police officers that he had sufficient funds to make bail. Rodgers was never informed of his constitutional rights, nor was he allowed to phone his attorney. Rodgers was acquitted of the charge in subsequent proceedings in state court. * * *

[Rodgers sued the towing company and the city of Chicago following acquittal on the criminal charges, alleging multiple violations of law. The trial court dismissed the complaint for failure to state a claim and imposed sanctions against Rodgers' lawyers. The appeal raised several claims that have been omitted here.]

Counsel's final arguments center on Judge Kocoras' assessment of Rule 11 sanctions. Fed.R. Civ.P. 11 provides in pertinent part:

> The signature of an attorney or party constitutes a certificate by him that he has read the pleading, motion, or other paper; that to the best of his knowledge, information, and belief formed after reasonable inquiry it is well grounded in fact and is warranted by existing law or a good faith argument for the extension, modification, or reversal of existing law * * *.
> If a pleading, motion or other paper is signed in violation of this rule, the court, upon motion or upon its own initiative, shall impose upon the person who signed it, a represented party, or both, an appropriate sanction, which may include an order to pay * * * a reasonable attorney's fee.

Rule 11 was amended in August 1983 to increase its effectiveness in deterring abuses. Most importantly, the previous requirement that the attorney against whom sanctions were imposed must have acted in bad faith was eliminated. "The new language is intended to reduce the reluctance of courts to impose sanctions * * * by emphasizing the responsibilities of the attorney and reinforcing those obligations by the imposition of sanctions." Fed.R.Civ.P. 11 advisory committee note (citation omitted). The standard used is an objective "one of reasonableness under the circumstances," *id.*, rather than a subjective one. Consequently, the plaintiff's reliance on *Suslick v. Rothschild Securities Corp.*, 741 F.2d 1000 (7th Cir. 1984), decided under the old Rule 11 with its bad faith requirement, is misplaced.

The assessment of attorney's fees in this case was well founded. A large part of Rodgers' complaint had no basis in law, and a majority of his allegations are conclusory ones, not factual ones, and so cannot withstand a motion to dismiss. Moreover, counsel has refused to recognize or to grapple with the established law of the Supreme Court and of this Circuit that defeats several of the claims at issue. For example, in arguing his Fourteenth Amendment liberty claim, counsel insists that *Logan v. Zimmerman Brush Co.*, 455 U.S. 422, 102 S.Ct. 1148, 71 L.Ed.2d 265 (1982) rather than *Parratt v. Taylor, supra*, controls, despite clear authority in this Circuit to the contrary. * * * Counsel does not even attempt to construct an argument regarding why the rule of Logan, rather than that of Parratt, should apply. Instead counsel asserts boldly that Logan does apply, and then moves on with the argument. The Fifth and Sixth Amendment claims and the Section 1985(3) claim were far-fetched to say the least. Equally far-fetched was Rodgers' Eighth Amendment claim, which evidently has not been appealed to this Court but with which the court below dealt.

Thus the circumstances warrant the imposition of sanctions. Counsel, however, has argued that the court below should have held a hearing on the issue of sanctions prior to imposing them. On the facts of this case, we do not agree. The Advisory Committee Notes observe:

The procedure [of imposing sanctions] obviously must comport with due process requirements. The particular format to be followed should depend on the circumstances of the situation and severity of the sanction under consideration. In many situations the judge's participation in the proceedings provides him with full knowledge of the relevant facts and little further inquiry will be necessary.

In the case at bar, the court below imposed sanctions of only $858.43, one-third of the attorney's fees and costs incurred by defendants, thereby crediting the possible merit of some of Rodgers' claims (596 F.Supp. at 26, 28). We agree with the district court that the complaint was overblown and that a hearing would have served no useful purpose. Plaintiff's counsel argue that they could have disclosed to the court at an *in camera* hearing all the information in their files on this case, including information protected by the attorney-client privilege, to show that their signing the amended complaint was justified. The court below, however, assessed sanctions for filing a complaint insufficient in several areas as a matter of law and in others for failing to include factual allegations that would indicate the claim might have merit. Counsel's file cannot correct the complaint's legal deficiencies. Nor could it supply necessary factual allegations, because privileged information would not be included in any complaint Rodgers might file. If the file contains unprivileged information that would rectify the factual deficiencies we have noted, plaintiff's counsel's failure to include those facts warrants the imposition of sanctions. The trial court has not based the sanctions on bad faith, which would require a hearing, see *Textor v. Board of Regents of Northern Illinois University*, 711 F.2d at 1395, but on counsel's incompetence in handling this matter by making "frivolous" and "worthless" claims "without first making a proper inquiry into the relevant law and facts" (596 F.Supp. at 28). The record fully supports the trial court's imposition of sanctions, a penalty which counsel had adequate opportunity to contest in its motion for reconsideration in the proceedings below and in its briefs and arguments to this Court. The district court's dismissal of the amended complaint for failure to state a claim and its imposition of sanctions for filing "a ponderous, extravagant, and overblown [amended] complaint that was largely devoid of a colorable legal basis" (*id.* at 22) are affirmed.

QUESTIONS

1. Rodgers thought that he had been harmed by the actions of the defendants. Why is he prevented from presenting his claims to a jury? Why sanction his attorney for attempting to zealously represent his client?

2. What is the policy behind Federal Rule 11? Did the policy change with elimination of the bad faith requirement? Can attorneys serve both as representatives and officers of the court?

3. Trace the procedural history of this case. Was Rodgers given sufficient opportunity to present his case? How many arguments was Rodgers allowed to make on the subject of sanctions? Does fairness suggest that Rodgers be given the *in camera* hearing opportunity to demonstrate the basis for the complaint?

Hodge and Hodge

77 Or. App. 538, 713 P.2d 1071 (1986), *rev'd*,
301 Or. 433, 722, P.2d 1235 (1986)

Rossmann, J.

In this dissolution action, the parties contest the custody of their four-year-old daughter. The trial court awarded custody to husband, and wife appeals. We affirm.

The court awarded custody to husband, because it found that he had been the daughter's primary parent and that it would be in her best interests to award husband custody with reasonable visitation rights to wife. Wife does not dispute those findings. Rather, she contends that custody should have been awarded to her, because of blood test results which show that husband is not the daughter's biological father. Husband argues that the blood test results are irrelevant and should not have been admitted, because he meets the criteria of ORS 109.070(1), which provides:

> "The child of a wife cohabiting with her husband who is not impotent or sterile at the time of conception of the child, shall be conclusively presumed to be the child of the husband, whether or not the marriage of the husband and wife may be void."

We agree with husband's argument. If he meets the requirements of ORS 109.070(1), then his paternity cannot be challenged legally by wife in this dissolution action, and the blood test results are irrelevant. * * *

The next issue, then, is whether husband meets the requirements of ORS 109.070(1). The only dispute is whether the parties were cohabiting at the time of the daughter's conception. Concerning cohabitation, the trial court placed the burden of proof on wife, found that the evidence was "evenly balanced" and thus ruled against wife on that issue.

Wife first contends that it was improper for the court to place the burden of proving non-cohabitation on her. We disagree. The party seeking to defeat the application of the conclusive presumption of ORS 109.070(1) must demonstrate that the statute does not apply. Thus, the trial court properly determined that the wife had the burden of persuasion on the issue of cohabitation.

Wife finally contends that the evidence on the issue of cohabitation was not "evenly balanced" because of the blood test results. That is a *non sequitur*. The blood test results do not tell us whether the parties were cohabiting during the time of conception. On our de novo review, we agree with the trial court that the evidence was "evenly balanced." Accordingly, wife did not meet her burden of persuasion on the issue of cohabitation, and the trial court properly found that husband met the requirements of ORS 109.070 (1).

Affirmed. Costs to husband.

QUESTIONS

1. Explain the nature of the dispute between the parties in this case. At what phase of the litigation process was the dispute resolved? If the wife's claim is correct, the man claiming custody of the child is not the child's biological father. Should the accuracy of her claim resolve the matter?

2. The Oregon Supreme Court reversed the court of appeals, holding, among other things, that because the husband sought to have ORS 109.071(1) applied, it was more appropriate to assign the burden of proof to him. Hence, he had to prove by a preponderance of the evidence that the couple was cohabiting at the time of conception. Because the trial court and the court of appeals found that the evidence on the question of cohabitation was "evenly balanced," the husband failed to meet his burden. Is the Supreme Court result more logical?

3. Litigation has been characterized as a fight theory of justice rather than a truth-seeking theory of justice. Does this case contribute to the accuracy of that assertion?

4. What standard of review does the Court of Appeals apply in this case? Why? When faced with a "conclusive presumption," how does a fact finder determine whether it applies?

People v. Natoli

70 Ill.App.3d 166, 387 N.E.2d 1096 (1979)

Simon, Presiding Justice.

The defendant, Joseph D. Natoli, appeals from his conviction in a jury trial of possession and delivery of a controlled substance (ethclorvynol), and his sentences of 1 to 3 years for delivery and 2 to 6 years for possession to run concurrently. He did not dispute his possession of the controlled substance, or that he delivered it to an informer, Kathy Krause, who was accompanied by an Elmwood Park police officer, Thomas Braglia, when she met with the defendant for the purchase. His defense was entrapment.

The defendant attacks his conviction on several grounds: * * * (ii) the prosecutor committed error in his closing argument when he called the defendant derogatory names, told the jury that the defendant's business was burglary and selling drugs, urged the jury to consider the defendant's prior burglary conviction for purposes other than determining his credibility, and suggested to the jury that the defendant was on parole and had violated his parole * * *.

The State concedes that prosecutorial errors occurred; its position is that the evidence of guilt is so overwhelming that the errors were harmless. The evidence against the defendant was strong, but he still was entitled to present his defense to a jury that would judge his credibility free from prejudice created by the trial tactics of the prosecutors. The defendant's explanation for his conduct was that the State's informer, Kathy Krause, telephoned him or his home approximately a dozen times on the day he met her and during the preceding 3 days, importuning him to supply her with drugs, and he did so only because he felt sorry for her. Prosecutorial errors detracted from the defendant's credibility when he took the stand to present this defense, and thus prejudiced him. As a reviewing court, we are unable to say with reasonable certainty how the jury would have viewed the defense of entrapment absent prosecutorial conduct designed to inflame the jury against the defendant and deny him a fair trial. Had the prosecutor engaged in only one impropriety, the error might more easily be excused as not substantially affecting the outcome of the trial. But in view of the combination of errors committed, it is pure speculation to say the jury would have reached the same conclusion had the errors not occurred. We believe that the defendant's conviction should be reversed, and that he should be retried on the charge of delivery. * * *

The next series of prosecutorial errors we note occurred in final argument. The prosecutor called attention to the defendant being on parole, and continued:

"That man, the parolee, and by the way, you know what parolee means. Parole, when you are released from the pen, comes from a French word which means 'word of honor'. You see what Mr. Natoli's word of honor is worth. He goes out and delivers dope."

This argument was improper and prejudicial. First, the words "That man, that parolee" in effect use the defendant's prior conviction to render him a bad person instead of simply to attack his credibility. Second, the emphasis upon the defendant's hearing violated his "word of honor" invited the jury to convict the defendant because he was a burglar and had violated the terms of his parole, rather than because he was guilty of the charges being tried.

Further, the prosecutor referred frequently to crime being the defendant's business. Some of his remarks were:

"[H]is business, ladies and gentlemen of the jury, is selling drugs." * * *

"The devil didn't make him sell drugs. That is his business." * * *

"He didn't come out rehabilitated. No, he goes right back out on the streets and says now I am not going to be a burglar anymore. I am going to be a dope dealer."

It is reversible error for a prosecutor to refer to a defendant as a habitual or professional criminal, or to suggest that the defendant's business or occupation is crime. *People v. Weathers*, 338 N.E.2d 880 (1975), the prosecutor asked the defendant whether he had any "occupation other than robbing people," and this was held to be reversible error. The court reasoned that the resolution of conflicting testimony revolved around credibility, and the prosecutor's question prevented the jury from evaluating the defendant's testimony dispas-

sionately--even though in that case the trial judge had sustained an objection and instructed the jury to disregard the question. Here, the reference to burglary and dealing in dope as the defendant's business, and to the defendant's decision not to be a burglar anymore, improperly diverted the jury from deciding the issue of entrapment on the evidence. In addition, the suggestion that the defendant had not been rehabilitated by his prior prison sentence but decided to become a dope dealer instead of a burglar, was an effort to use his burglary conviction to tell the jury that the defendant had a propensity to commit crime, an obviously improper implication.

Defense counsel failed to bring these defects in the prosecutor's argument to the trial court's attention through a timely objection; but they affected substantial rights of the defendant, and justice requires that we take note of them under the plain error rule. In applying the plain error rule we are mindful for the directives of our supreme court in *People v. Pickett*, 54 Ill.2d 280 (1973), that the rule is only a limited exception to the doctrine of waiver. However, in several instances in this case, as in McCray, the prejudice occurred when the prosecutor's statements were uttered, and could not have been cured even by a timely objection. * * *

A person is not guilty of an offense if his conduct is incited or induced by a public officer or employee for the purpose of obtaining evidence for the prosecution of that person. However, entrapment is not a defense if the public officer merely affords to such person the opportunity for committing an offense in furtherance of a criminal purpose which the person already has originated. In this case, the defendant's entrapment defense revolved around the credibility of his own testimony compared to that of informer Kathy Krause and Officer Braglia. The testimony of Krause and Braglia, if believed, was sufficient to prove beyond a reasonable doubt that the defendant was not entrapped, but rather acceded rapidly to Krause's request that he supply drugs. Thus, were it not for the errors noted above, reversing the defendant's conviction for delivery would not be warranted. However, because we are not convinced beyond a reasonable doubt that the jury, if not subjected to these errors, might not have found differently, this case must be remanded for a new trial.

QUESTIONS

1. Did Natoli deny performing the acts alleged in the case? What was his defense? How, if at all, was he prejudiced in presenting his defense?

2. Did the trial court in this case find the facts correctly? Did it apply the law correctly? Were there nonetheless errors committed in the case? Did the court have other options for correcting the errors?

3. The result of this case is that society is forced to pay the cost of a new trial. Is there any doubt in your mind as to the Natoli's guilt? Is it consistent or inconsistent with the adversary system to require society to pay for retrials of "obviously guilty" defendants?

State v. Rickey Jacobs

193 Cal.App.3d 375, 238 Cal. Rptr. 278 (1987)

Edwards, Associate Justice.

Defendant Rickey Jacobs was convicted by a jury of robbery, possession of stolen property, and removing the serial numbers from a firearm. In addition, defendant was convicted of misdemeanor violations of carrying a concealed weapon. The jury also found that defendant personally used a firearm in the commission of the robbery within the meaning of Penal Code sections 12022.5 and 1203.06, subdivision (a)(1).

* * *

Defendant appeals on the ground there was insufficient evidence for the jury to find he used a firearm within the meaning of Penal Code sections 12022.5 and 1203.06, subdivision (a)(1), and consequently the sentencing court erred in determining he was ineligible for probation and imposing the two-year enhancement.

On March 23, 1985, a man later identified to be defendant was looking at a black 1985 Mustang GT automobile on the lot of Fair City Ford in Pomona, California. Charles Szasz, a salesman for Fair City Ford, suggested that defendant test drive the Mustang.

Accompanied by Szasz, defendant drove the Mustang around the side streets of Pomona for a few minutes. Defendant then offered Szasz some cocaine. The offer was refused. A short while later, defendant explained to Szasz that he needed the Mustang to get to another location to see about a $10,000 cocaine deal, and that his wife and children were in danger. Szasz refused to allow defendant to take the Mustang for this purpose and suggested they return to the dealership car lot.

Defendant became adamant about his intentions and advised Szasz that he could either get out of the car now or go with defendant and risk getting shot. When Szasz refused to get out, defendant said "I have a gun and I don't want to use it." Szasz apparently did not believe defendant and indicated that he was going to take the key from the ignition. According to Szasz's testimony at trial, defendant then "reached over with his right hand and covered the ignition and reached in his jacket with his left hand and cocked what I thought or sounded like he cocked a gun in his jacket."

Szasz testified that he is familiar with guns and the sound of a revolver being cocked. He was positive defendant had a gun, although he never actually saw a firearm. Fearing for his life at this point, Szasz exited the Mustang and defendant drove off.

On April 1, 1985, a highway patrol officer observed defendant asleep in a parked black Mustang in the Highgrove area of Riverside County. The Mustang had New Mexico license plates which the officer determined to be stolen. Defendant was arrested for auto theft; a search of the interior revealed a .22 caliber magnum revolver located in the center console of the vehicle. The serial numbers had been removed but the gun was determined to be stolen.

At trial this gun was cocked by the deputy district attorney in the presence of witness Szasz who testified that the cocking noise was the same sound he heard when defendant threatened him in the Mustang.

Defendant claimed he was not the individual who stole the Mustang. He testified that during the evening hours of March 31, 1985, he was given a ride by an individual named Steve who was driving the black Mustang. They drove around until 2 a.m. the following day when Steve parked the vehicle and left to take care of some business. He never returned.

Defendant moved to the driver's seat and fell asleep. He awoke later that morning when the highway patrol officer arrived. Defendant testified he was not aware the revolver was in the car.

The Court is presented with two issues concerning the sufficiency of the evidence:

1. During the commission of the robbery was defendant armed with a firearm?

2. Did he use it?

In resolving these issues, the court is mindful of the basic standards of review that apply to this case. Whether the defendant was armed with and personally used a firearm are factual questions for the jury's determination. (*People v. Smith* (1980) 101 Cal. App. 3d 964, 967, 161 Cal. Rptr. 787.)

On appeal, "...the court must review the whole record in the light most favorable to the judgment below to determine whether it discloses substantial evidence... such that a reasonable trier of fact could find the defendant guilty beyond a reasonable doubt." (*People v. Johnson* (1980) 26 Cal. 3d 557, 578, 162 Cal. Rptr. 431, 606 P.2d 738.) The court must "presume in support of the judgment the existence of every fact the trier could reasonably deduce from the evidence. If the circumstances reasonably justify the trial court's findings, reversal is not warranted merely because the circumstances might also be reasonably reconciled with a contrary finding." (*People v. Redmond* (1969) 71 Cal. 2d 745, 755, 79 Cal. Rptr. 529, 457 P.2d 321.)

Implicit in the jury's verdict is a finding that defendant, in fact, had a gun at the time of the robbery. The evidence certainly supports this finding. Defendant told the victim he had a gun, the sound of cocking the hammer was heard by the victim who was familiar with such sounds, and a gun was subsequently discovered inside the stolen Mustang of which defendant was the sole occupant. Based upon this evidence, we find the jury reasonably found this fact to be true.

The more difficult question is whether the evidence supports a finding that defendant used the gun within the meaning of Penal Code sections 12022.5 and 1203.06, subdivision (a)(1). The California Supreme Court has given the following definition to the term "use" as contained in Penal Code section 12022.5. "Although the use of a firearm connotes something more than a bare potential for use, there need not be conduct which actually produces harm but only conduct which produces a fear of harm or force by means or display of a firearm in aiding the commission of one of the specified felonies." "Use" means, among other things, "to carry out a purpose or action by means of," to "make instrumental to an end or process," and to "apply to advantage." (*People v. Chambers* (1972) 7 Cal. 3d 666, 672, 102 Cal. Rptr. 776, 498 P.2d 1024.)

The *Chambers* court also held that, to give effect to the obvious legislative intent to deter the use of firearms, this term must be given a broad construction.

This definition has been followed in many opinions of the Courts of Appeal. Division One of our district reviewed and summarized the facts of those opinions and distinguished those factors which amount to the use of a firearm from those found to constitute mere possession during the commission of a specified felony. (*People v. Hays* (1983) 147 Cal. App. 3d 534, 195 Cal. Rptr. 252.)

Of the cases analyzed in *Hays*, those in which no use of a firearm was found involved the unintentional discharge of a weapon, or mere possession only, or a codefendant's use, or a holstered weapon. Those cases in which a firearm was found to be used were grouped into two categories: those in which the gun was aimed at the victim, intentionally fired or used to strike the victim; and those in which the gun was held or exposed in a menacing fashion accompanied by words threatening a more violent use. The actions described in the first category in themselves constitute the use of a firearm. Those in the second category require some type of display of the weapon, coupled with a threat to use it which produces fear of harm in the victim before there can be a use. Obviously, defendant's actions in this case did not fall within the first category. There is no evidence he aimed or discharged the weapon, or struck the victim with it. The jury's finding that he used a firearm would have to come within the second category.

Defendant does not argue that threats concerning the use of the gun were not made to the victim, or that these threats did not produce a fear of harm. Defendant only challenges the sufficiency of the evidence that the firearm was displayed. Admittedly, the victims in the cases reviewed in *Hays* visually observed the firearm being displayed, but none of these cases suggest that this is the only way a firearm can be displayed. We believe that to be consistent with the definition promulgated in *Chambers,* and to give the term a broad construction, a firearm is displayed when,

by sensory perception, the victim is made aware of its presence. Once displayed in such fashion, the threat of use sufficient to produce fear of harm becomes a use of that firearm proscribed by Penal Code sections 12022.5 and 1203.06, subdivision (a)(1).

The evidence in this case is sufficient to support the jury finding. The victim was made aware of the gun by defendant's statements. These statements were corroborated in the victim's mind when he heard the sound of the hammer being cocked. We cannot say that this was insufficient evidence of displaying a firearm. This fact, coupled with the threats and resultant fear of harm, amounted to a use of the gun.

The judgment of the lower court is affirmed.

QUESTIONS

1. Is the court in this case reviewing a question of law or a question of fact? If the court had concluded that the jury erred, what remedial action should it have ordered?

2. One of the issues in this case involves "use" of a gun. Would the result have been different if the statute had been more specific, e.g., "active use of a gun, such as pointing, firing, striking, or the like"? What standards should courts use when interpreting terms whose meaning is not clear?

Strandell v. Jackson County

838 F.2d 884 (7th Cir. 1987)

Ripple, Circuit Judge.

Mr. Tobin represents the parents of Michael Strandell in a civil rights action against Jackson County, Illinois. The case involves the arrest, strip search, imprisonment, and suicidal death of Michael Strandell. In anticipation of a pretrial conference on September 3, 1986, the plaintiffs filed a written report concerning settlement prospects. The plaintiffs reported that they were requesting $500,000.00, but that the defendants refused to discuss the issue. At the pretrial conference, the district court suggested that the parties consent to

a summary jury trial. A summary jury trial generally lasts one day, and consists of the selection of six jurors to hear approximations by counsel of the expected evidence. After receiving an abbreviated charge, the jury retires with directions to render a consensus verdict. After a verdict is reached, the jury is informed that its verdict is advisory in nature and nonbinding. The objective of this procedure is to induce the parties to negotiate a settlement. Mr. Tobin informed the district court that the plaintiffs would not consent to a summary jury trial, and filed a motion to advance the case for trial. The district court ordered that discovery be closed on January 15, 1987, and set the case for trial.

During discovery, the plaintiffs had obtained statements from 21 witnesses. The plaintiffs learned the identity of many of these witnesses from information provided by the defendants. After discovery closed, the defendants filed a motion to compel production of the witnesses' statements. The plaintiffs responded that these statements constituted privileged work-product; they argued that the defendants could have obtained the information contained in them through ordinary discovery. The district court denied the motion to compel production; it concluded that the defendants had failed to establish "substantial need" and "undue hardship," as required by Rule 26(b)(3) of the Federal Rules of Civil Procedure.

On March 23, 1987, the district court again discussed settlement prospects with counsel. The court expressed its view that a trial could not be accommodated easily on its crowded docket and again suggested that the parties consent to a summary jury trial. On March 26, 1987, Mr. Tobin advised the district court that he would not be willing to submit his client's case to a summary jury trial, but that he was ready to proceed to trial immediately. He claimed that a summary jury trial would require disclosure of the privileged statements, and ordered the parties to participate in a summary jury trial.

On March 31, 1987, the parties and counsel appeared, as ordered, for selection of a jury for the summary jury trial. Mr. Tobin again objected to the district court's order compelling the summary jury trial. The district court denied this motion. Mr. Tobin then respectfully declined to proceed with the selection of the jury. The district court informed Mr. Tobin that it did not have time available to try this case, nor would it have time for a trial "in the forseeable months ahead." Tr. of March 31, 1987 at 5. The court then held Mr. Tobin in criminal contempt for refusing to proceed with the summary jury trial. The district court postponed disposition of the criminal contempt judgment until April 6, 1987. On that date, the district court asked Mr. Tobin to reconsider his position on proceeding with the summary jury trial. Mr. Tobin reiterated his view that the court lacked the power to compel a summary jury trial, and maintained that such a proceeding would violate his client's rights. The district court entered a criminal contempt judgment of $500.00 against

Mr. Tobin. Mr. Tobin filed a notice of appeal that same day.

The district court filed a memorandum opinion setting forth its reasons for ordering a summary jury trial. *Strandell v. Jackson County,* 115 F.R.D. 333 (1987). The district court noted that trial in this case was expected to last five to six weeks, and that the parties were "poles apart in terms of settlement." *Id.* at 334. It further noted that summary jury trials had been used with great success in such situations.

In determining that it had the power to compel a summary jury trial, the court relied on a resolution adopted in 1984 by the Judicial Conference of the United States. The original draft of the resolution endorsed summary jury trials "with the voluntary consent of the parties." The final draft of the resolution, however, omitted this phrase.

The court then determined that Rule 16 of the Federal Rules of Civil Procedure permits a mandatory summary jury trial. The court pointed out that Rule 16(a) authorizes a court in its discretion to require attorneys "to appear before it for a conference or conferences before trial for such purposes as (1) expediting the disposition of the action . . . and . . . (5) facilitating the settlement of the case." Furthermore, Rule 16(c) provides that "[t]he participants at any conference under this rule may consider and take action with respect to . . . (7) the possibility of settlement or the use of extrajudicial procedures to resolve the dispute . . . and . . . (11) such other matters as may aid in the disposition of the action." The court admitted that "its discretion in this context is not unbridled." Mem.op. at 335. However, the court held that Rule 16 grants district courts "the power to order the litigants to engage in a process which will enhance the possibility of fruitful negotiations." Id.

The court also held that its obligations under the Speedy Trial Act, 18 U.S.C. Subsection 3161, et.seq., gave it additional authority for ordering a summary jury trial. The court noted that the Southern District of Illinois ranked second in the Seventh Circuit and fourteenth in the country for case filings per judgeship. Mem. op. at 336. The court said that the "ability of a court to use its best judgment to move its crowded docket must be preserved, where it involves a non-binding yet highly successful procedure." Id. at 336.

We begin by noting that we are presented with a narrow question: Whether a trial judge may require a litigant to participate in a summary jury trial to promote settlement of the case. We are not asked to determine the manner in which summary jury trials may be used with the consent of the parties. Nor are we asked to express a view on the effectiveness of his technique in settlement negotiations.

In turning to the narrow question before us-- the legality of compelled participation in a summary jury trial--we must also acknowledge, at the very onset, that a district court no doubt has substantial inherent power to control and to manage its docket. That power must, of course, be exercised in a manner that is in harmony with the Federal Rules of Civil Procedure. Those rules are the product of a careful process of study and reflection designed to take "due cognizance both of the need for expedition of cases and the protection of individual rights." That process, set forth in the Rules of Enabling Act, 28 U.S.C. Subsection 2072, also reflects the joint responsibility of the legislative and judicial branches of government in striking the delicate balance between these competing concerns. Therefore, in those areas of trial practice where the Supreme Court and the Congress, acting together, have addressed the appropriate balance between the needs for judicial efficiency and the rights of the individual litigant, innovation by the individual judicial officer must confirm to that balance.

In this case, the district court properly acknowledged, at least as a theoretical matter, this limitation on its power to devise a new method to encourage settlement. Consequently, the court turned to Rule 16 of the Federal Rules of Civil Procedure in search of authority for the use of a mandatory summary jury trial. In the district court's view, two subsections of Rule 16(c) authorized such a procedure. As amended in 1983, those subsections read:

> The participants at any conference under this rule may consider and take action with respect to * * *
>
> (7) the possibility of settlement or the use of extrajudicial procedures to resolve the dispute; * * *
>
> (11) such other matters as may aid in the disposition of the action.

Fed.R.Civ.P. 16(c)(7), (11).

Here, we must respectfully disagree with the district court. We do not believe that these provisions can be read as authorizing a mandatory summary jury trial. In our view, while the pretrial conference of Rule 16 was intended to foster set-

tlement through the use of extrajudicial procedures, it was not intended to require that an unwilling litigant be sidetracked from the normal course of litigation. The drafters of Rule 16 certainly intended to provide, in the pretrial conference, "a neutral forum" for discussing the matter of settlement. Fed.R.Civ.P. 16 advisory committee's note. However, it is also clear that they did not foresee that the conference would be used to "impose settlement negotiation on unwilling litigants . . ." Id.; ("As the Advisory Committee Note indicates, this new subdivision does not force unwilling parties into settlement negotiations."). While the drafters intended that the trial judge "explor[e] the use of procedures other than litigation to resolve the dispute,"--including "urging the litigants to employ adjudicatory techniques outside the courthouse,"--they clearly did not intend to require the parties to take part in such activities. Fed.R.Civ.P. 16 advisory committee's note (emphasis supplied). As the Second Circuit, commenting on the 1983 version of Rule 16, wrote: "Rule 16 . . . was not designed as a means for clubbing the parties--or one of them--into involuntary compromise."

Our interpretation of how Rule 16 was intended to be used with respect to settlement procedures is substantially reinforced by the drafters' commentary with respect to other parts of the rule. For instance, the last sentence of Rule 16(c), added in 1983, reads as follows: "At least one of the attorneys for each party participating in any conference before a trial shall have authority to enter into stipulations and to make admissions regarding all matters that the participants may reasonably anticipate may be discussed." Fed.R.Civ.P. 16(c). The drafters' notes describe it in the following terms:

> The last sentence of subdivision (c) is new. It has been added to meet one of the criticisms of the present practice described earlier and insure proper preconference preparation so that the meeting is more than a ceremonial or ritualistic event. The reference to "authority" is not intended to insist upon the ability to settle litigation. Nor should the rule be read to encourage the judge conducting the conference to compel attorneys to enter into stipulations or to make admissions that they consider to be unreasonable, that touch on matters that could not normally have been anticipated to arise at the conference, or on subjects of a dimension

that normally require prior consultation with and approval from the client.

Fed.R.Civ.P. 16 advisory committee's note (citation omitted). * * *

The use of a mandatory summary jury trial as a pretrial settlement device would also affect seriously the well-established rules concerning discovery and work-product privilege. These rules reflect a carefully-crafted balance between the needs for pretrial disclosure and party confidentiality. Yet, a compelled summary jury trial could easily upset that balance by requiring disclosure of information obtainable, if at all, through the mandated discovery process. We do not believe it is reasonable to assume that the Supreme Court and the Congress would undertake, in such an oblique fashion, such a radical alteration of the considered judgments contained in Rule 26 and in the case law. If such radical surgery is to be performed, we can expect that the national rule-making process outlined in the Rules Enabling Act will undertake it in quite an explicit fashion.

The district court, in explaining its decision to compel the use of the summary jury trial, noted that the Southern District of Illinois faces crushing caseloads. The court suggested that handling that caseload, including compliance with the Speedy Trial Act, required resort to such devices as compulsory summary jury trials. We certainly cannot take issue with the district court's conclusion that its caseload places great stress on its capacity to fulfill its responsibilities. However, a crowded docket does not permit the court to avoid the adjudication of cases properly within its congressionally-mandated jurisdiction. At this court said in *Taylor v. Oxford*, 575 F.2d 152 (7th Cir. 1978): "Innovative experiments may be admirable, and considering the heavy case loads in the district courts, understandable, but experiments must stay within the limitations of the statute." Id. at 154.

Because we conclude that the parameters of Rule 16 do not permit courts to compel parties to participate in summary jury trials, the contempt judgment of the district court is vacated.

QUESTIONS

1. Why was counsel held in contempt in this case? At what phase of the litigation process did this occur? What was the trial judge seeking to accomplish? As a result of this decision, what options are available to trial judges who wish to use summary jury trials in the Seventh Circuit?

2. Who controls the presentations at a summary jury trial? Can you figure out a way that counsel could have participated in the summary jury trial without disadvantage to his strategy if the case had gone to trial after the summary jury trial?

3. At least three district courts have concluded that trial judges do have authority to order summary jury trials. In *Williams v. Hall*, No. 84-149 (E.D. Ky. Apr. 5, 1988), the court "respectfully disagreed" with *Strandell*, citing the existence of a local rule authorizing the procedure. In *Arabian American Oil Company*, 119 F.R.D. 448 (M.D. Fla. 1988) the court found the procedure "a legitimate device" even though the defendant would have to travel from Greece to Florida to participate. In *Cincinnati Gas and Electric Co. v. General Electric Co.*, 117 F.R.D. 597 (S.D. Ohio 1987), the court claimed either an inherent power to order summary jury trials, or power under F.R.Civ.P. 16. Do any of these cases respond to the underlying issue in *Strandell*?

4. The summary jury trial is a relatively new development in the management of the litigation process. What public policy considerations should govern the use of the procedure?

Lockhart v. Patel

115 F.R.D. 44 (E.D.Ky. 1987)

Bertelsman, District Judge.

Unfortunately, the court finds it necessary in this case to discuss the question of its authority to order parties and their insurers to attend settlement conferences. Also involved is the propriety of sanctions for failure to attend.

This is a medical malpractice action in which the plaintiff, a teenager, lost the sight of one eye, allegedly due to the defendant doctor's negligence. In a summary jury trial an advisory jury awarded the plaintiff $200,000.

Following the summary jury trial, the court held several formal and informal pretrial and settlement conferences, both in person and by telephone. In a telephone conference on October 30, 1986, the attorney for the defendant doctor's liability insurance carrier, St. Paul Fire & Marine Insurance Company, advised the court that he had been authorized by that company's home office to offer $125,000 and no more and not to negotiate any further. At this time, the plaintiff's demand was $175,000.

Having had some success with settlement conferences in the past, the court directed the defense attorney to attend a settlement conference on November 3, 1986, and to bring with him the representative of the insurance company from the home office who had issued these instructions or one with equal authority. The court specifically and formally admonished defense counsel: "Tell them not to send some flunky who has no authority to negotiate. I want someone who can enter into a settlement in this range without having to call anyone else."

November 3 arrived, and so did the defense attorney. But the representative from St. Paul's home office did not. Instead, an adjuster from the local office appeared. She advised the court that her instructions from the officials at the home office were to reiterate the offer previously made and not to bother to call them back if it were not accepted.

When asked by the court whether there was some misunderstanding that it had stated a representative from the home office was required to attend, the adjuster replied, "I doubt if anyone from the home office would have come down even if in fact this is what you said." (Transcript page 5)

Measures in response to such clearly improper conduct seemed called for. At this point, the court made the appropriate oral findings, promptly followed by a written order, that "St. Paul had deliberately refused to obey the order of the court" and that "such disobedience was deliberately contemptuous, contumacious and purposely demonstrated disrespect and disregard for the authority of the court."

Accordingly, the court forthwith struck the pleadings of the defendant and declared him in default. The court further ordered that the trial set for the next day would be limited to damages only and that a hearing to show cause why St. Paul should not be punished for criminal contempt be held on December 12, 1986. Later that day, St. Paul settled with the plaintiff for $175,000.

December 12 arrived, and this time so did not one but several representatives from St. Paul's home office. The home office representatives through their counsel assured the court that it had all been a misunderstanding, not their fault indeed, but that of the local lawyer and adjuster. The court accepted these assurances at face value and permitted St. Paul to purge itself of contempt by providing a letter of apology from its Chief Executive Officer, assuring the court that it was not company policy to refuse to attend settlement conferences or take it on itself to disregard court orders. The letter was forthcoming and is attached hereto as an appendix.

This opinion is written, therefore, solely to discuss the authority of the court to hold meaningful settlement conferences and the propriety of the civil sanction imposed in the instance.

The authority of a federal court to order attendance of attorneys, parties, and insurers at settlement conferences and to impose sanctions for disregard of the court's orders is so well established as to be beyond doubt. 6 Wright & Miller, *Federal Practices & Procedure*, Section 1526 (1971); Moore's *Federal Practice*, ¶ 16.16.1, 16.22. F.R. Civ.P. 16 (f) specifically provides:

"(f) Sanctions. If a party or party's attorney fails to obey a scheduling or pretrial order, or if no appearance is made on behalf of a party at a scheduling or pretrial conference, or if a party or party's attorney is *substantially unprepared to participate* in the conference, or if a party or party's attorney fails to participate in good faith, *the judge, upon motion or his own initiative, may make such orders with regard thereto as are just, and among others any of the orders provided in Rule 37(b)(2)(B), (C), (D).* In lieu of or in addition to any other sanctions, the judge shall require the party or the attorney representing him or both to pay the reasonable expenses incurred because of any noncompliance with this rule, including attorney's fees, unless the judge finds that the noncompliance was substantially justified or that other circumstances make an award of expenses unjust." (Emphasis added)

Rule 16(f) was added to original Rule 16, along with several other amendments in 1983. Although the rule refers to "parties," it clearly would be meaningless if it did not also apply to a party's liability insurer.

The Advisory Committee Note to the Amendment states that the purpose of the addition of this subrule was to "reflect that existing practice, and to obviate dependence upon Rule 41(b) or the court's inherent power" to compel respect for the court's pretrial orders. The Committee Note cites several cases illustrating practice prior to the subrule's adoption.

"Furthermore," the Advisory Committee continues, "explicit reference to sanctions reenforces the rule's intention to encourage forceful judicial management."

The Note also makes clear that the striking of a party's pleadings is an appropriate sanction, as under F.R.Civ.P. 37. Further, the rule itself makes it clear that sanctions may be imposed on the court's own motion.

The reader is referred to the Advisory Note for decisions pre-dating the 1983 Amendment. Cases since the Amendment are few, perhaps because the text of the Rule is so clear as to require little interpretation. The court finds *G. Heileman Brewing Company, Inc., v. Joseph Oat Corp.,* 107 F.R.D. 275 (W.D.Wis. 1985), worthy of note, however. There, in circumstances virtually identical with those in the case at bar, the court stated:

"I do not accept the proposition that Rule 16 does not authorize a court to require the presence of parties with full authority to settle a case . . . The clear intention of the recent amendments to the Federal Rules is to provide courts with the tools that are required to manage their caseloads effectively and efficiently. One of those basic tools is the authority to conduct productive settlement conferences. *A settlement conference without all of the necessary parties present is not productive. Neither is a conference of persons who have no authority to settle.*

"By bringing their dispute to a court for resolution, the parties have invoked the use of an expensive public resource. It is a misuse of those resources for any party to refuse even to meet personally with the opposing party or its counsel to attempt to resolve their disputes prior to trial.

"It is no argument that it would have been futile for Joseph Oat or National Union Fire to appear by representatives with full authority to settle, simply because these corporations had decided that they would not settle on any terms other than full dismissal of the claims against Joseph Oat. It is always possible that exposure of the decisionmakers to the realities of a case will bring about a reevaluation of settlement posture on the part of those persons. *Thus it is appropriate for a judicial officer to require that, particularly in complex and protracted litigation, the decisionmakers be made aware of all aspects of the case and the anticipated costs of its prosecution and defense by being personally present before the court.*" (Emphasis added.)

107 F.R.D. at 277.

This court is in complete agreement with these observations. The normal caseload of a United States District Judge is now considered to be 400 civil cases. At this time, every judge in this district has half again that many, because of the extended illness of one of our judges. Although some of these cases are simple, many are complex. And in addition to this civil caseload the court is also expected to deal with the criminal docket, which for this court the averages about 40 cases per judge per year, some taking several weeks to try. The drafters of amended Rule 16 knew of the docket pressures to which our courts are subject, and knew that to process 400 cases you have to settle at least 350. That is why they encouraged "forceful judicial management," which is the only means of settling a high percentage of cases.

As I have observed in another place, the exigencies of modern dockets demand the adoption of novel and imaginative means lest the courts, inundated by a tidal wave of cases, fail in their duty to provide a just and speedy disposition of every case. These means may take the form of compulsory arbitration, summary jury trials, imposing reasonable limits on trial time, or, as here, the relatively innocuous device of requiring a settlement conference attended by the clients as well as the attorneys.

Of course, the court cannot require any party to settle a case, whether the court thinks that party's position is reasonable or not, but it can require it to make reasonable efforts, including attending a settlement conference with an open mind.

The court hopes that the sanctions imposed here will be sufficient to convince St. Paul and other similarly minded companies and individuals of this fact and prevent similar occurrences in the future.

QUESTIONS

1. Why was the defendant cited for contempt in this case? Did the defendant refuse to participate in the settlement conference?

2. Judge Bertelsman notes in the opinion that a court cannot require a party to settle a case. Was the trial court nonetheless attempting to compel settlement in this case? Explain.

3. The case of *G. Heileman Brewing Company, Inc. v. Joseph Oat Corp.* is quoted extensively in *Patel*. This 1985 decision stands for the proposition that F.R.Civ.P. 16 authorizes a district court to order parties with full authority to settle to appear at a settlement conference. When one party failed to appear at the settlement conference the court imposed sanctions. The *Heileman* case ultimately settled, but in the settlement agreement the sanctioned party reserved the right to appeal the sanction. The Seventh Circuit reversed the sanction (1988 WL 58980, 86-3118), holding that the court does not have the power to compel attendance of a party at a settlement conference. What effect might this ruling have on the development of this judicial activity?

3   VOLUNTARY ARBITRATION

Voluntary arbitration is the submission of a dispute to a neutral, non-governmental decision-maker (arbitrator). Parties surrender control of the outcome by submitting their dispute to arbitration, but can retain considerable control over the standards and procedures used by the arbitrator or arbitration panel in resolving the dispute. While available to parties in virtually all noncriminal disputes, voluntary arbitration is used most commonly to resolve disputes over the interpretation or performance of contracts.

Voluntary arbitration is distinguished from litigation in a variety of ways. First, it is private. It is conducted outside the public eye, at a time and in a location convenient to the parties. Second, the parties select their own decision-maker. The arbitrator need not be a judge or even a lawyer, although frequently parties employ retired judges or lawyers to arbitrate disputes. Parties may prefer to have an expert in the subject matter of their dispute serve as arbitrator, whether or not an attorney. They also may employ a panel of arbitrators rather than a single arbitrator.

Third, the parties retain much more control over the process of arbitration than they do over litigation. They can control such details as how arbitration will be invoked, whether the arbitrator's award will be advisory or binding, whether witnesses will be called and placed under oath, whether briefs will be submitted, and whether the record will remain open after the hearing for receipt of new evidence. These details generally are spelled out in an arbitration clause in a contract, or by a contract drafted after a dispute has arisen.

Fourth, arbitration gives the parties the option of selecting the standards the arbitrator will use in resolving a dispute. For example, an arbitration clause in a sales contract might state that the arbitrator is to reach a decision that is fair under the circumstances based on the evidence presented by the parties at the hearing. Some arbitration clauses instruct the arbitrator to rely on the customs of the trade or profession from which the dispute arises; others direct the arbitrator to follow applicable law. If the parties' contract is silent about the standards for resolving a dispute, arbitrators tend to rely on the standards set forth in the Commercial Arbitration Rules of the American Arbitration Association, a private dispute resolution organization that serves as a clearinghouse for arbitrators and mediators who assist in the resolution of a wide range of commercial, labor and public sector disputes.[1]

Finally, the parties pay all the costs associated with voluntary arbitration, including the arbitrator's fee and any other expenses. The taxpaying public bears none of the costs.

Background of Arbitration

Neutral third parties always have been used to resolve disputes. In that respect arbitration is as old as civilization, and was in use for centuries before the beginning of English common law. The Bible contains many examples of arbitration, including the famous case of King Solomon. The process is deeply rooted in the rabbinical tradition as a method for resolving disputes within that religious community.

Arbitration is well entrenched in the commercial world.[2] By the 18th Century, for example, businessmen preferred arbitration over courts to resolve disputes they could not resolve themselves.[3] Arbitration allowed the business community to resolve disputes using its own standards, rather than turning the disputes over to the judicial system whose precedent bound decisions did not reflect the flexibility considered appropriate in business.

Colonial Americans used arbitration in other contexts as well. George Washington, for example, included a provision in his will calling for arbitration of any conflict that might arise over the interpretation of his will and the distribution of his estate. In 1635, a Boston town meeting agreed that inhabitants would not sue one another. Disputes were to be settled "amicably by arbitration. . .without recourse to law and courts."[4] Bostonians were not alone in preferring arbitration to litigation. Other colonies had similar provisions.

While arbitration always has been used to resolve disputes informally, it was not until the 20th Century that arbitration statutes were passed in this country at the state and federal levels. The first appeared in New York in 1920. It provided the pattern for the Uniform Arbitration Act of 1955, adopted by the Conference of Commissioners on Uniform State Laws. Today most state statutes are modeled on the Uniform Arbitration Act. The New Jersey arbitration language is typical of modern state statutes:

> A provision in a written contract to settle by arbitration a controversy that may arise therefrom or a refusal to perform the whole or a part thereof or a written agreement to submit. . .any existing controversy to arbitration, whether the controversy arise out of the contract or otherwise, shall be valid, enforceable and irrevocable, except upon such grounds as exist at law or in equity for the revocation of a contract.[5]

This statute reflects a typical public policy favoring arbitration: once parties have agreed by contract to submit a dispute to arbitration, the arbitration clause typically cannot be revoked.

The first federal statutes on arbitration also were passed in the 1920s. The United States Arbitration Act, for example, was passed in 1925, making specifically enforceable arbitration clauses in all contracts (except contracts of employment) involving interstate commerce.[6] A year later the Railway Labor Act (later amended to include airlines) provided for arbitration of employment disputes between railroads and their workers as a means of keeping an industry viewed as essential to the nation's economic health from being torn by industrial strife.[7]

Public support for arbitration of other kinds of labor disputes grew rapidly during the 1930s and 1940s. The War Labor Disputes Act in 1943, for example, called for arbitration of labor disputes in industries substantially involved with the nation's defense.[8] In 1947, Congress passed the Taft-Hartley Labor-Management Relations Act, creating the National Labor Relations Board (NLRB), which was directed to arbitrate allegations of unfair labor practices by unions and management.[9] The public policy behind enactment of such statutes was to foster what Congress and the courts eventually were to call "industrial self-government" or resolution of labor-management disputes in private arbitration forums based on the contracts negotiated between labor and management during the collective bargaining process. Most states also have enacted statutes requiring arbitration of labor-management disputes, particularly those involving public sector employees such as teachers, police, and firefighters. Today over 90 percent of all collective bargaining agreements specify arbitration for the resolution of disputes.[10]

Arbitration in the labor-management context can take two forms. One is called interest arbitration, which occurs when the parties have reached impasse in the collective bargaining process. If they cannot agree to the terms of a contract through negotiation or mediation, an arbitrator can be called in to declare what the rights of the respective parties will be under the proposed contract. The second form is called grievance arbitration. It occurs when a dispute arises under an existing contract and the parties cannot agree about the meaning or significance of the terms.

The popularity of arbitration in the 20th Century has not been limited to industrial relations. It is common in patent, copyright, and trademark disputes.[11] The complicated, technical facts in such cases have encouraged the use of arbitration because the process allows the use of expert decision-makers. Arbitration also is used extensively in professional sports. Baseball owners and players, for example, use salary arbitration to determine many players' salaries for the coming season, as well as deciding grievances that arise under players' employment contracts. In football, players and owners recently arbitrated the issue of owners' ability to require players to submit to drug tests under existing employment contracts.

Arbitration is particularly common in international commercial disputes. Parties wish to avoid questions of which country's judicial system has jurisdiction over the dispute, and also are attracted by the ability to select an expert arbitrator. There has been significant growth in the number of organizations providing international arbitration services. The International Chamber of Commerce, the American Arbitration Association, and the state of Hawaii are among those competing for the international commercial dispute resolution business. Parties may employ the services of such organizations or may design their own arbitration process.

The 20th Century also has seen the growth of arbitration in consumer disputes.[12] When a consumer purchases a product or service, the sales contract frequently includes an arbitration clause. Stockbrokers, automobile manufacturers, moving companies, law firms, and health care organizations are examples of groups that commonly include arbitration clauses in their agreements with clients. Likewise, many insurance companies and their policyholders rely on arbitration to resolve uninsured motorist, extent of coverage, and other claims.

How Voluntary Arbitration Works

The foundation for managing most disputes arising out of the interpretation or performance of contracts is laid long before a dispute arises. Parties who want to include arbitration clauses in their contracts to retain control over the process and standards by which subsequent disputes are resolved confront those issues during the drafting stage. Questions frequently included in the negotiation of an arbitration clause include the following:

1. What provisions in the contract qualify for arbitration? Some clauses are general, calling for arbitration of "any difference or dispute arising under this contract."

Others specifically include or exclude matters that can be resolved through arbitration.

2. How will arbitration be initiated? What steps must a party take to invoke it? What responsibilities does each party have when arbitration is requested?
3. Who will serve as arbitrator? Sometimes the parties agree on the arbitrator during the contract drafting stage. More commonly, they agree on a process for selecting an arbitrator or arbitration panel.
4. What are the powers and duties of the arbitrator? The contract may specify such matters as how long the arbitrator has to render an award following the hearing, how the arbitrator will be paid, and whether the parties will exchange information and exhibits prior to the arbitration hearing.
5. What procedures will govern the arbitration hearing? For example, will each side be represented by counsel? Will witnesses be cross-examined? Will each side make opening statements and closing arguments? Will they submit briefs before or after argument? Will hearsay evidence be admitted?
6. Where will the arbitration hearing be held? Will a record be made of the hearing? In what form will the arbitration award be issued? What other administrative details need clarification?

If parties to a contract want an arbitration clause in their contract but do not wish to design the process themselves, they can agree to have any disputes resolved by the Commercial Arbitration Rules of the American Arbitration Association. A typical arbitration clause under such circumstances would read as follows:

Any controversy or claim arising out of or relating to this contract, or the breach thereof, shall be settled by arbitration in accordance with the Commercial Arbitration Rules of the American Arbitration Association, and judgment upon the award rendered by the Arbitrator(s) may be entered in any Court having jurisdiction thereof.[13]

If a contract calls for arbitration but the arbitration clause neither incorporates the Commercial Arbitration Rules by reference, nor specifies how the arbitrator or arbitration panel will be selected, many statutes provide for judicial appointment of the arbitrator. Once appointed, the arbitrator is assumed to have essentially the same authority as a judge to manage the process, except as limited by the arbitration clause itself.

Some disputes arise over contracts that lack arbitration clauses; many other civil disputes are not related to a contract. Parties who have not agreed beforehand to submit their dispute to arbitration can elect the process after a dispute arises. The parties' agreement to submit their dispute to arbitration is all that is required for the process to be invoked. Their submission agreement may take any of the forms suggested above.

Since arbitration is a private dispute resolution process controlled by the parties, no generalizations can be made applicable to all arbitrations. Several steps usually are followed, however. These steps provide a general overview of how the process operates.

The first step is for one of the parties to notify the other of its intent to submit a dispute to arbitration. This is called a "demand for arbitration" and typically is written. The demand outlines the dispute, the proposed remedy, and the amount of damages, if any, claimed. If the Commercial Arbitration Rules are followed, a copy of the demand also must be filed with the regional office of the American Arbitration Association. Usually the other party is required to reply in writing as well. Sometimes disputes can be resolved informally at this stage. One party may not realize that a dispute existed, for example, and may be willing to take steps to avoid the need for arbitration. Sometimes the party receiving the demand for arbitration will argue that the dispute is not arbitrable, either because the parties' contract does not provide for arbitration of that particular issue, or because arbitration of that issue is contrary to statute or public policy. Questions of arbitrability must be resolved through litigation.

If the parties agree after the exchange of the demand and reply that an arbitrable dispute exists, they must agree on the arbitrator or arbitration panel. The arbitration clause may indicate who will hear the dispute; more commonly, it will provide for a process of selecting the arbitrator or arbitration panel. The American Arbitration Association, the Federal Mediation and Conciliation Service (or their state equivalents), and the National Academy of Arbitrators are among those who provide lists of qualified arbitrators.

Once the parties have a list of prospective arbitrators, they select the person to hear their dispute. A typical procedure is for the parties to be furnished with a list of names, frequently five in number, and instructed to strike as many as four names they find unacceptable. The arbitrator then is chosen from the remaining names. If the parties prefer to have a panel of arbitrators, it is common for each party to select one member and for those selected to agree on a neutral third person to serve as chair.

Disputing parties frequently give the arbitrator authority to determine the time and place of the hearing, and to make other procedural decisions. Since arbitration is primarily a fact-finding process, preparation of evidence is a critical stage for the parties. It includes compiling relevant data and documents and preparing appropriate witnesses. Pre-hearing motions and discovery, similar in form to what occurs in litigation, often can be streamlined because of the arbitrator's expertise at fact-finding, or because of constraints imposed by the arbitration clause. Parties to voluntary arbitration frequently exchange information and witness lists at some point prior to the arbitration hearing.

The arbitrator or arbitration panel is responsible for the conduct of the hearing. In addition to the general tasks of convening the session and directing the flow of the procedure, the arbitrator has the task of maintaining control over the disputants and their representatives. The environment of the hearing frequently is not as formal as a trial, but must be one in which witnesses can speak and both sides can make their arguments.

Arbitration hearings are conducted like trials, in that each side is responsible for making the most persuasive argument it can for its position, showing weaknesses in the other side's position, and then turning resolution of the dispute over to the neutral decision-maker. Arbitration hearings even follow the basic outlines of a trial: each side makes a brief opening statement and usually a closing argument. Each side also presents witnesses and documents, and each has an opportunity to cross-examine opposing witnesses. Most lawyers thus have little difficulty adapting their courtroom skills to an arbitral forum.

In litigation it is common for parties to negotiate a settlement just prior to trial. So too in arbitration it is common for settlements to be reached just prior to the hearing. When the parties have compiled the information they will present at the hearing, they are in a better position to decide whether to submit their dispute to an arbitrator.

There are important differences between a trial and an arbitration hearing, however. First, arbitrators usually are given more discretion than judges in scheduling arbitration hearings, establishing procedural rules, granting postponements, issuing subpoenas, admitting evidence, and weighing evidence and testimony in arriving at a decision. Second, formal rules of evidence and procedure usually are not followed in arbitration hearings. Arbitrators are free to listen to hearsay testimony that would be excluded from trial if properly objected to by one of the parties. Arbitrators are assumed to have the ability to give appropriate weight to testimony offered. Third, the arbitrator is selected and paid by the parties. Fourth, arbitration hearings are not held in courtrooms. They can be held in the arbitrator's office or in any other location that is convenient and acceptable to the parties.

Arbitration hearings usually are less dramatic than jury trials. The purpose of the hearings is to clarify facts. The informality and location of an arbitration hearing and the expertise of the arbitrator help to eliminate much of the courtroom drama staged for the benefit of juries. Relaxed rules of procedure and straightforward presentation of evidence also contribute to the overall efficiency of arbitration.

Post-hearing procedures vary, depending upon the arbitration agreement and the arbitrator. Following the hearing, some arbitrators request that the parties submit briefs or memoranda that summarize their evidence and arguments. Some hearings may be reopened by the arbitrator or upon petition of the parties in order to submit additional evidence. In some situations, arbitrators retain jurisdiction over a dispute to insure that the award is implemented as intended.

The parties usually determine how long the arbitrator will have to issue a written award resolving the dispute. The typical length of time allowed is 30 to 45 days. Arbitrators frequently are given considerable discretion in fashioning an appropriate award in a case. Specific performance of contract terms, job reinstatement, and money damages are common forms of award. Arbitrators also may issue split awards unless the parties specify otherwise.

Awards issued in voluntary arbitration usually are the final word in a dispute. Over the years, state and federal courts have shown increasing unwillingness to review voluntary arbitration awards.[14] Occasionally appellate courts will vacate an award, but only if the appellant proves that the award was procured through fraud, corruption, or undue influence; that the arbitrator was corrupt or partial; that the arbitrator was guilty of misconduct in the handling of the proceeding; or that the arbitrator exceeded the authority granted by statute or by the agreement to arbitrate.[15] Vacation of an arbitration award means that the process must begin again, with a new arbitrator or arbitration panel.

Although courts are reluctant to review the appropriateness of awards, they demonstrate no reluctance to enforce the awards.[16] Statutes that authorize voluntary arbitration uniformly provide for judicial enforcement. Courts have the same power to enforce arbitration awards as they do judicial judgments.

Burdens of Persuasion in Voluntary Arbitration

It is difficult to generalize about the amount of proof required for a party to prevail in voluntary arbitration. For one thing, the parties may agree on a degree of proof. If their contract is silent on the degree of proof, it is up to the arbitrator to establish the standard that will be used. In labor arbitration, the degree of proof can depend on the nature of the issues or some practice of the parties. Some arbitrators borrow liberally from litigation language, going so far as to use criminal standards of proof in employee discharge cases where the employee is accused of dishonest or criminal behavior. The argument such rigorous standards is that discharge for dishonest or criminal behavior can make it virtually impossible for the employee to find subsequent employment.

Some arbitrators seek to avoid adopting the burdens of persuasion imposed by litigation. They prefer to speak of the "quantum of proof" that will be required to persuade the fact-finder. Other arbitrators refuse to apply any standards of proof, claiming that an arbitrator should rule in favor of the party whose evidence is most persuasive viewed as a whole.

The Role of the Lawyer in Voluntary Arbitration

Lawyers play three important roles in voluntary arbitration. First, they negotiate and draft contracts. Second, they represent parties in arbitration. Third, they serve as arbitrators.

The importance of the lawyer's role in drafting contracts cannot be overstated. Clear, precise writing of a contract is one of the best methods for avoiding disputes. Lawyers who draft contracts need to be skilled at negotiation, drafting, and helping their clients anticipate issues that should be covered by the contract. It is also at the drafting stage that parties need to decide whether arbitration will be used in the event of a dispute, what issues will be submitted to arbitration, and how the process will work. If a dispute arises between parties who are not bound by a contractual relationship, lawyers also play an important role in negotiating and drafting agreements for submitting the dispute to arbitration.

Although not all parties in voluntary arbitration choose to employ legal counsel, most do because voluntary arbitration usually is binding. Successful advocacy in the arbitral forum requires many of the same skills required for effective courtroom advocacy, despite the relative informality of an arbitration hearing. Hence most lawyers are comfortable representing clients in this forum.

Many lawyers serve as arbitrators. Parties and their representatives tend to prefer arbitrators who have had legal training. A lawyer, for example, might be considered better able to weigh hearsay evidence than most non-lawyers. Lawyers who want their names to appear on state or American Arbitration Association lists of arbitrators frequently must complete apprenticeship or training programs in order to be listed. In order to increase the likelihood of being selected by parties, they also must establish reputations for neutrality and fairness. Many lawyers combine traditional law practice with service as an arbitrator in voluntary arbitration, while others are drawn from law teaching to the field.

Trends in Voluntary Arbitration

All indications are that arbitration will remain a popular form of dispute resolution and that its use will expand as parties seek to avoid crowded court dockets and the glare of publicity associated with litigation.[17] There are some indications, however, that labor arbitration, traditionally a private system, may become more public and bound by precedent, just as the law did with the development of reporter systems.

Reporter systems have existed in the law since approximately the 13th Century; by the mid-19th Century complete reports of cases were available.[18] A major impact of reporters was to bind the law by precedent. Legal deference to decided cases (*stare decisis*) now is taken for granted.

Several labor law reporters are being published by private companies such as Commerce Clearinghouse and the Bureau of National Affairs. These reporters contain the written opinions and arbitration awards issued by labor arbitrators. The parties and the arbitrator must agree to publication, and the publisher must determine that the case was significant enough to include in the reporter. Most opinions in the reporter read like judicial opinions: following a summary of the facts and an explanation of the standards used to resolve the dispute, the arbitrator explains the award and the reasons leading to it. The reporter also contains lists of arbitrators and their qualifications.

The doctrine of *stare decisis* is beginning to appear in arbitration decisions. Some arbitrators have begun to cite reported cases as part of their rationale for reaching their decisions.[19] Not all arbitrators are sanguine about this development. They argue that a primary advantage of labor arbitration is privacy, and the opportunity for parties to decide by contract how their disputes should be resolved and the standards that should be used. Arbitrators, they claim, should resolve disputes based on the language of the contract, not by reference to other cases.

Example of Voluntary Arbitration

Velda Bruno was a senior typist for Midwest Phone Systems. On December 18, 1985, she was discharged from her job. Her discharge letter said that she had proved "unable to perform the word processing job for which she was hired." Bruno protested her discharge to the Communications Workers Union that represented Midwest Phone employees. Union and management representatives were unable to resolve the dispute informally. The union argued that Bruno was fired hastily and for insufficient reasons, after being transferred to a word processing job from a typing job where she performed satisfactorily. Midwest Phone argued that Bruno's job performance had been continuously substandard, that she had been disciplined regularly, and that the discharge was a logical consequence of her failure to improve her performance.

When attempts at informal resolution failed, the union sent a demand for grievance arbitration to Midwest Phone. The collective bargaining agreement between the Communications Workers and Midwest Phone provided for arbitration of disputes arising out of employee suspension or discharge by the company. Midwest Phone's reply to the demand made it clear that the two parties would be unable to resolve the dispute themselves. Attorneys for the company and the union met and drafted an agreement to govern the arbitration. Their "submission agreement" covered the following points:

1. *Parties.* Midwest Phone Systems and Communications Workers Union.

2. *Relevant contract provision.* Article 12, section 12.1(e) on "suspensions and dismissals" provides that "the Arbitrator shall determine whether the suspension or dismissal was for just cause, but the judgment of the Arbitrator may be substituted for that of the Company only if the Arbitrator finds that the Company acted without making a reasonable investigation or that it acted upon evidence that would not have led a reasonable person to take such action."

3. *Issue.* Was Velda Bruno discharged on December 18, 1985, for just cause? If not, what is the remedy?

4. *Arbitrator.* Alfred Wong was named arbitrator.

5. *Time and place of hearing.* The hearing was to be in the conference room of the Airport Holiday Inn in Minneapolis, Minnesota, beginning at 9:30 a.m., February 10, 1986.

6. *Report of the proceedings.* The parties agreed to share the cost of a stenographic record of the hearing.

7. *Procedures.* The hearing was to be closed to the public; witnesses were to be sworn; the order of presentation of evidence was established; each side was to make an opening statement and closing argument; each side was to offer rebuttal and surrebuttal evidence; all witnesses could be cross-examined and re-examined; each side would submit a post-argument brief to the arbitrator; and each side would provide the other with copies of exhibits ten days prior to the hearing. The parties also agreed that the arbitrator would be given authority to determine any other procedural issues that might arise at the hearing.

8. *Expense of arbitration.* Each party agreed to pay one-half of the arbitrator's expenses and fee.

9. *Decision of the arbitrator.* The arbitrator was to submit a signed copy of the decision and award as soon as possible following the hearing but no later than 45 days after the hearing.

The submission agreement was signed on January 13, 1986. The parties gave themselves a relatively short time to put together their cases. Prior to the hearing, Midwest Phone moved to compel production of personal notes that Bruno previously had given to the union and to a civil rights agency. Arbitrator Wong denied the motion on the grounds that the information should be regarded as a work product of the grievant, her union and its counsel, and hence was not subject to examination by Midwest Phone. Ten days before the hearing counsel for the union and the company exchanged copies of their exhibits.

The hearing commenced at 9:30 on February 10.

Company's case. The company put on its case first. It called five witnesses: the head of the personnel department and Bruno's first and second level supervisors at the different facilities where she worked. They testified that Bruno had been hired on October 8, 1983, as a senior typist assigned to the company's word processing center in the company's main building. Bruno passed the typing test given by the company, typing between 90 and 100 words per minute with two errors on an electronic typewriter. She worked with three other employees in a separate room, away from other clerical help and clients. After about three months on the job, her first supervisor testified, Bruno suffered a broken wrist and was unable to type for about two months. During that time she answered telephones at various offices in the company's buildings. When she returned to a typing job in March 1984 she was sent to another word processing center in a satellite facility. At the second center she was trained on Vydec word processing equipment, which displayed typewritten material on a cathode-ray tube, enabling typists to edit material before storing it on a floppy disk or printing it onto paper.

In April, Bruno met with her first level supervisor at the satellite facility, who informed her that her job performance was not satisfactory. Bruno was told that she had missed 31 percent of the due dates on her jobs and that she had not advised her supervisor early enough that she would not be meeting her deadlines. Bruno was given an opportunity for additional training prior to her six-month evaluation.

In June, Bruno received her six-month evaluation. Her typing evaluation was "satisfactory," but she received an "unsatisfactory" quantity rating on work produced. Bruno's supervisor said she apparently still found it easier to retype some jobs than to make corrections on the word processing equipment. She was given two months to improve her performance.

Bruno's supervisor testified that in August she still was not producing adequate quantities of work. The first level supervisor reported Bruno's lack of progress to the second level supervisor who informed Bruno that her performance would be subject to monthly evaluations and that if she did not improve within six months, she would be discharged.

By January 1985, Bruno's supervisors testified, her work had improved considerably. The threat of discharge was lifted. In February 1985, however, one of Bruno's jobs was returned because of improper formatting on a list of telephone extension numbers. Shortly thereafter, her first level supervisor testified, she neglected to index a job to facilitate future use of stored material. A few weeks later her supervisor discovered that the second page of a job had been stored on the same track as the first page, thereby erasing the first page. The company continued to have problems with Bruno. She would make some improvement, then lapse into errors. In June, for example, she stored four pages of material on a disk but could not locate them. Her first level supervisor found that she had written the wrong information on the index sheet, which is why she could not locate the work.

By July, Bruno and her first level supervisor were having serious communications problems. Her first level supervisor at the satellite facility testified that Bruno became so defensive about her errors that she tried to hide them and would not communicate candidly. The first level supervisor again notified the second level supervisor. In August, Bruno received the first warning notice from her second level supervisor: if her work performance did not improve she would receive a second warning in late October and would be terminated before the end of the 1985 calendar year.

Bruno's first level supervisor testified that after the first warning Bruno became even more defensive. In September, the company agreed to transfer Bruno to another work unit on the assumption that she might be able to perform more adequately under a different first-level supervisor. The new unit also used Vydec equipment. Bruno's first level supervisor in the new work unit testified that Bruno had severe problems operating the printers in that unit and that because of her problems her production never came up to acceptable levels. Bruno received her second warning letter in late October.

In mid-November, according to her supervisor's testimony, Bruno missed three job deadlines and improperly stored two jobs. The improper storage made it impossible for weekend typists to find and complete the jobs. In December, Bruno was discharged.

On cross-examination, Bruno's counsel elicited testimony that Bruno's job performance on her typing job before her broken wrist was well above average and that neither her supervisors nor her clients had anything negative to say about her work. Cross-examination also revealed that although the unit to which Bruno was assigned in September 1985 did use Vydec equipment, it was an updated version of the equipment Bruno had worked on previously. The printing system was almost entirely different, and storage and retrieval processes were substantially changed. The company's testimony lasted approximately a day-and-a-half.

Union's case. The union called only one witness, Velda Bruno. Bruno testified that she had been a typist for eighteen years at a local construction company before going to work for Midwest Phone. Prior to that she had been at home with her children for approximately fifteen years. During her tenure with the construction company she had consistently won merit promotions and pay increases. During that time she had worked on IBM Selectric typewriters and had learned to use electronic typewriters as well.

Bruno testified that she applied to work for Midwest Phone when the construction company went out of business. During her interview she was told that she would be required to work on the company's electronic typewriters and that she would be working in a separate typing unit with three other employees in the word processing center. Bruno also testified that in January 1984, three months after she was hired, she slipped on the ice on the way to work and broke her wrist. She was unable to type for two months. She was replaced by another typist and answered telephones until March 1984. When she was ready to resume her typing duties, Bruno testified, she was told that the company had been unable to find a temporary replacement for her while her wrist healed, that it had therefore hired a permanent replacement, and that she was being assigned to another word processing unit in a satellite building in another part of town. Bruno testified that she agreed to the transfer in order to keep her job, and that after she reviewed her contract with the company she realized that as a senior typist she was required to work on word processing equipment if asked.

When Bruno reported to her new job location she found that her hours would be 7:00 a.m. to 4:00 p.m. She received eight hours of training on the equipment. Bruno testified that her new typing duties involved primarily statistical typing, whereas her previous typing had been primarily manuscripts and letters.

Bruno admitted on both direct and cross-examination that she found the transition to her new job very difficult. Her new job required her to work in a large room with 30 other typists, on new equipment, doing very different work than she was accustomed to doing. She admitted that her production levels were lower than those of other employees and that she had trouble storing jobs on the Vydec equipment. Furthermore, she had trouble retrieving materials that had been stored by night and weekend typists. She testified that she found her first-level supervisor hard to work with and that she seemed to like to criticize Bruno's work in a loud voice in front of the other typists. Bruno said she became increasingly nervous about losing her job. When she received her first warning notice she was unable to sleep and finally requested a transfer, thinking that a different work unit might be better. She said the working conditions in the second unit were better and that she liked her new first level supervisor very much, but that it was difficult to adjust to the new Vydec equipment. Printers, for example were located in a separate room, rather than being connected to individual terminals. While that made the work place quieter, it did require typists to call up their jobs for printing and Bruno had difficulty learning the technique. As a result, her production rates dropped even further. She received no training in storage and retrieval on the new machines. She did receive a manual but could not understand it and was afraid she would be criticized if she asked too many questions.

On cross-examination Bruno was asked specifically about the jobs that had been returned to her, the material that she had lost through improper storage, and her failure to complete three jobs on time. She said that in each instance the jobs returned to her for correction had not been her original work product but that she could not prove that to her supervisor because the indexing cards on those jobs apparently had been lost. She said she felt terrible about the work she lost and that she thought it was the result of being new to the equipment and nervous about the possibility of losing her job. With respect to the jobs she failed to complete on time, Bruno explained that her work hours were 7:00 a.m. to 4:00 p.m. and that two of the jobs were called late because they were not done by her quitting time, even though she had been able to have them on her clients' desks by 8:00 a.m. the next day, their starting time. She said she received no complaints from her clients. The third late job had been marked "Rush" and on that day Bruno said she stayed late to get it done. Nonetheless, the job was called late because it was not ready at her regular quitting time.

Bruno's testimony and cross-examination took approximately three hours. Counsel for both sides then waived closing arguments, agreeing to summarize their arguments in the post-hearing briefs that were to be submitted to the arbitrator within five days of the hearing. The hearing was closed.

Arbitrator's award. Arbitrator Wong studied post-hearing briefs from each side (each approximately 25 pages long, summarizing its position based on the testimony) and reviewed some of the testimony given at the hearing. Approximately three weeks after the close of the hearing he delivered his opinion and award to the parties. The opinion addressed the issue submitted by the parties: "Was Velda Bruno discharged for just cause? If not, what is the appropriate remedy?" In a 27-page opinion Wong summarized relevant facts, including a chronological account of the events that led to Bruno's discharge, and a short statement of the positions of the parties. He included a short statement about the burden of persuasion and a statement that in his opinion, Midwest Phone had the burden of proving by a preponderance of the evidence that Bruno was discharged for just cause.

Wong concluded that although there were isolated instances of satisfactory performance on Bruno's part, her overall performance was not satisfactory and that Midwest Phone had just cause to take disciplinary action against her. Under the circumstances, however, discharge was not a reasonable penalty and should be set aside. Bruno had a good work record for eighteen years with another employer and for three months with Midwest Phone. However, Bruno did not successfully make the transition from typist on electric and electronic typewriters to the company's word processing equipment, a transition a senior typist was expected to be able to make according to the contract between the union and Midwest Phone. Hence, Wong concluded that Bruno should not be reinstated to the position of senior typist in the word processing center. Wong ordered a 30-day disciplinary suspension for Bruno without pay, and reinstatement with back pay and no interest as a typist at a reduced grade at one of the company's secretarial departments, assigned to tasks and equipment more commensurate with her former secretarial experience, training and background. In arriving at this conclusion, Wong cited as authority opinions from four other reported arbitration proceedings.

At the end of the month Arbitrator Wong submitted his bill to Midwest Phone and the union. The total included his travel and hotel expenses, stenographic assistance, research and $485 per day, his fee as an arbitrator. He spent a total of three days on the case. The company and the union each paid half of the bill, in addition to splitting the costs of renting the conference room.

QUESTIONS

1. According to Wong's opinion, which party was "wrong" in this case? Which party lost something as a result of his award?

2. What results would have been available if this case had gone to trial? Compare with the result reached in arbitration.

3. Having read the case, what suggestions would you have for changes in the arbitration clause at the next drafting stage if you were counsel for management? Counsel for the union?

4. Assume this case had been tried to a jury. What, if anything, would counsel have had to do differently to persuade a jury?

5. Compare Wong's statement of which party had the burden of persuasion in this case with the submission agreement. Did he follow the contract standards? What recourse would Midwest Phone Systems have?

Endnotes

1 *See* American Arbitration Association, Commercial Arbitration Rules (March 1, 1986).

2 J. Cohen, Commercial Arbitration and the Law 1-9 (1918).

3 Horwitz, *The Historical Foundation of Modern Contract Law,* 87 Harv. L. Rev. 917, 927 (1974).

4 J. Auerbach, Justice Without Law? 27 (1983).

5 N.J. Rev. Stat. *§* 2A:24-1 (1987).

6 Ch. 213, 42 Stat. 825 (1925) (codified as amended at 9 U.S.C. *§§* 1-14, 201-208 (1982)).

7 Ch. 347, 44 Stat. 136 (1926) (codified as amended at 15 U.S.C. *§§* 21, 45; 18 U.S.C. *§* 373; 28 U.S.C. *§§* 1291-1294; and 45 U.S.C. *§* 151-163, 181-188 (1982)).

8 Ch. 144, 57 Stat. 163 (1943) (omitted 1947).

9 Ch. 120, 61 Stat. 136 (1947) (codified as amended at 18 U.S.C. *§* 610 and 29 U.S.C. *§* 141-144, 151-167, 171-187, 504 (1982 & Supp. III 1985).

10 A. Cox, D. Bok & R. Gorman, Labor Law 518 (1981).

11 Federal law provides for arbitration in patent disputes. 35 U.S.C. 135d (supp. III 1985).

12 *See* Holiday, Kohl & Saig, *Alternatives to Civil Litigation of Consumer Disputes,* 65 Mich. B.J. 189-193 (1986); Murphy, *Voluntary Arbitration: An Alternate Means of Resolving Medical Malpractice Disputes,* 33 Med. Trial Tech. Q. 409-427 (1987).

13 R. Coulson, Business Arbitration: What You Need to Know 17 (1986).

14 *See* Hirshman, *The Second Arbitration Trilogy: The Federalization of Arbitration Law,* 71 Va. L. Rev. 1375-1378 (1985).

15 9 U.S.C. *§* 10 (1982).

16 *Wilco v. Swan,* 346 U.S. 427, 436 (1953).

17 Hirshman, *supra* note 14, at 1305-6.

18 L. Friedman, A History of American Law 621 (1985).

19 Rehmus, *Writing the Opinion,* in Arbitration in Practice 219-221 (1984).

Sources

American Arbitration Association, Commercial Arbitration Rules (March 1, 1986).

J. Auerbach, Justice Without Law? (1983).

Bureau of National Affairs, How Arbitration Works (4th ed. 1985).

_____, Practice and Procedures in Labor Arbitration (2d ed. 1981).

J. Cohen, Commercial Arbitration and the Law (1918).

A. Cox, D. Bok & R. Gorman, Cases and Materials on Labor Law (1981).

Coulson, *Arbitration in the Eighties: How to Make It Work for You,* 17 A.B.A. Forum 673 (1982).

R. Coulson, Business Arbitration: What You Need to Know (1982).

Horwitz, *The Historical Foundation of Modern Contract Law,* 87 Harv. L. Rev. 917 (1974).

M. Grossman, The Question of Arbitrability (1984).

Hirshman, *The Second Arbitration Trilogy: The Federalization of Arbitration Law,* 71 Va. L. Rev. 1305 (1985).

Holiday, Kohl & Saig, *Alternatives to Civil Litigation of Consumer Disputes,* 65 Mich. B.J. 189 (1986).

Murphy, *Voluntary Arbitration: An Alternate Means of Resolving Medical Malpractice Disputes,* 33 Med. Trial Tech. Q. 409 (1987).

D. Nolan, Labor Arbitration and Practice in a Nutshell (1981).

The Rand Corporation, Simple Justice (1983).

P. Staudohar, Grievance Arbitration in Public Employment (1977).

A. Zack, Arbitration in Practice (1984).

Steelworkers v. Enterprise Corp.

363 U.S. 593 (1960)

Opinion of the Court by Mr. Justice Douglas, announced by Mr. Justice Brennan.

Petitioner union and respondent during the period relevant here had a collective bargaining agreement which provided that any differences "as to the meaning and application" of the agreement should be submitted to arbitration and that the arbitrator's decision "shall be final and binding on the parties." Special provisions were included concerning the suspension and discharge of employees. The agreement stated:

"Should it be determined by the Company or by an arbitrator in accordance with the grievance procedure that the employee has been suspended unjustly or discharged in violation of the provisions of this Agreement, the Company shall reinstate the employee and pay full compensation at the employee's regular rate of pay for the time lost."

The agreement also provided:

". . . It is understood and agreed that neither party will institute *civil suits or legal proceedings* against the other for alleged violation of any of the provisions of this labor contract; instead all disputes will be settled in the manner outlined in this Article III--Adjustment of Grievances."

A group of employees left their jobs in protest against the discharge of one employee. A union official advised them at once to return to work. An official of respondent at their request gave them permission and then rescinded it. The next day they were told they did not have a job any more "until this thing was settled one way or the other."

A grievance was filed; and when respondent finally refused to arbitrate, this suit was brought for specific enforcement of the arbitration provisions of the agreement. The District Court ordered arbitration. The arbitrator found that the discharge of the men was not justified, though their conduct, he said, was improper. In his view the facts warranted at most a suspension of the men for 10 days each. After their discharge and before the arbitration award the collective bargaining agreement had expired. The union, however, continued to represent the workers at the plant. The arbitrator rejected the contention that expiration of the agreement barred reinstatement of the employees.

He held that the provision of the agreement above quoted imposed an unconditional obligation on the employer. He awarded reinstatement with back pay, minus pay for a 10-day suspension and such sums as these employees received from other employment.

Respondent refused to comply with the award. Petitioner moved the District Court for enforcement. The District Court directed respondent to comply. The Court of Appeals, while agreeing that the District Court had jurisdiction to enforce an arbitration award under a collective bargaining agreement, held that the failure of the award to specify the amounts to be deducted from the back pay rendered the award unenforceable. That defect, it agreed, could be remedied by requiring the parties to complete the arbitration. It went on to hold, however, that an award for back pay subsequent to the date of termination of the collective bargaining agreement could not be enforced. It also held that the requirement for reinstatement of the discharged employees was likewise unenforceable because the collective bargaining agreement had expired. We granted certiorari.

The refusal of courts to review the merits of an arbitration award is the proper approach to arbitration under collective bargaining agreements. The federal policy of settling labor disputes by arbitration would be undermined if courts had the final say on the merits of the awards. As we stated in *United Steelworkers of America v. Warrior & Gulf Navigation Co., ante,* p. 574, decided this day, the arbitrators under these collective agreements are indispensable agencies in a continuous collective bargaining process. They sit to settle disputes at the plant level--disputes that require for their solution knowledge of the custom and practices of a particular factory or of a particular industry as reflected in particular agreements.

When an arbitrator is commissioned to interpret and apply the collective bargaining agreement, he is to bring his informed judgment to bear in order to reach a fair solution of a problem. This is especially true when it comes to formulating remedies. There the need is for flexibility in meeting a wide variety of situations. The draftsmen may never have thought of what specific remedy should be awarded to meet a particular contingency. Nevertheless, an arbitrator is confined to interpretation and application of the collective bargaining agreement; he does not sit to dispense his own brand of industrial justice. He may, of course, look for guidance from many sources, yet his award is legitimate only so long as it draws its essence from the collective bargaining agreement. When the arbitrator's words manifest an infidelity to this obligation, courts have no choice but to refuse enforcement of the award.

The opinion of the arbitrator in this case, as it bears upon the award of back pay beyond the date of the agreement's expiration and reinstatement, is ambiguous. It may be read as based solely upon the arbitrator's view of the requirements of enacted legislation, which would mean that he exceeded the scope of the submission. Or it may be read as embodying a construction of the agreement itself, perhaps with the arbitrator looking to "the law" for help in determining the sense of the agreement. A mere ambiguity in the opinion accompanying an award, which permits the inference that the arbitrator may have exceeded his authority, is not a reason for refusing to enforce the award. Arbitrators have no obligation to the court to give their reasons for an award. To require opinions free of ambiguity may lead arbitrators to play it safe by writing no supporting opinions. This would be undesirable for a well-reasoned opinion tends to engender confidence in the integrity of the process and aids in clarifying the underlying agreement. Moreover, we see no reason to assume that this arbitrator has abused the trust the parties confided in him and has not stayed within the areas marked out for his consideration. It is not apparent that he went beyond the submission. The Court of Appeals' opinion refusing to enforce the reinstatement and partial back pay portions of the award was not based upon any finding that the arbitrator did not premise his award on his construction of the contract. It

merely disagreed with the arbitrator's construction of it.

The collective bargaining agreement could have provided that if any of the employees were wrongfully discharged, the remedy would be reinstatement and back pay up to the date they were returned to work. Respondent's major argument seems to be that by applying correct principles of law to the interpretation of the collective bargaining agreement it can be determined that the agreement did not so provide, and that therefore the arbitrator's decision was not based upon the contract. The acceptance of this view would require courts, even under the standard arbitration clause, to review the merits of every construction of the contract. This plenary review by a court of the merits would make meaningless the provisions that the arbitrator's decision is final, for in reality it would almost never be final. This underlines the fundamental error which we have alluded to in *United Steelworkers of America v. American Manufacturing Co., ante,* p. 564, decided on this day. As we there emphasized, the question of interpretation of the collective bargaining agreement is a question for the arbitrator. It is the arbitrator's construction which was bargained for; and so far as the arbitrator's decision concerns construction of the contract, the courts have no business overruling him because their interpretation of the contract is different from his.

We agree with the Court of Appeals that the judgment of the District Court should be modified so that the amounts due the employees may be definitely determined by arbitration. In all other respects we think the judgment of the District Court should be affirmed. Accordingly, we reverse the judgment of the Court of Appeals, except for that modification, and remand the case to the District Court for proceedings in conformity with this opinion.

It is so ordered.

QUESTIONS

1. How was the arbitration mechanism at issue in this case created? In what sense was arbitration in this situation "voluntary"? What are Enterprise Corporation's reasons for not wanting to proceed with or enforce the arbitration award?

2. Is the award granted in this case consistent with the remedy specified in the contract? If this case had gone through litigation, and the judge had not applied controlling precedent, what remedy would Enterprise Corporation have had? Is it fair to deny that remedy to parties in arbitration? What would be the consequence of making that remedy available?

3. What benefits are associated with arbitration in the workplace? Which, if any, of these benefits would be lost by allowing judicial review?

Bailey v. Bicknell Minerals, Inc.

819 F.2d 690 (7th Cir. 1987)

Easterbrook, Circuit Judge.

A depressingly large number of recent cases grows out of refusals to use or abide by the grievance-arbitration machinery of collective bargaining agreements. We attempt to discourage these refusals to say die (or even to say try) by awarding attorneys' fees. An arbitration clause in a collective bargaining agreement is supposed to ensure speedy resolution of disputes. Those who refuse to invoke the process or abide by the awards endanger the productivity of the workplace and divert judicial time from the disputes that courts are supposed to resolve. Today we consider a case filed by litigants who ignored the arbitral process.

In May 1982, Bicknell Minerals, Inc., a mining firm, signed a collective bargaining agreement with Local No. 1979A of the Progressive Mine Workers of America (the Union). It was supposed to last three years. In 1984, Bicknell asked the Union to accept lower wages. The Union's negotiators put a package of reductions before the members for a vote on August 9, 1984. The vote of the members present at the meeting was a tie; the Union's "pit committee" then accepted two votes by telephone, both favoring the reductions. The committee told Bicknell that the proposed agreement had been ratified, and Bicknell immediately put into effect the changes (expressed as an 11-page addendum to the collective bargaining agreement).

On August 19, Paul Bailey, the President of the Union, filed a grievance under the collective bargaining agreement, contending that because the acceptance of telephoned votes was irregular, Bicknell had not received authorization to implement the addendum. Bicknell rejected the grievance because, in its view, the Union is bound by its agents' declaration that the members had approved the proposal. Neither Bailey nor the Union asked for arbitration under the agreement, subsection 6.1 of which provides: "Whenever any dispute arises between the Company and the Union as to the meaning and application of the provisions of this Contract, or should any local trouble of any kind or character arise at the mine," the dispute will proceed through three steps followed by arbitration. Bailey instead pursued his complaint within the Union, which decided not to accept the telephonic votes and in December 1984, asked Bicknell to rescind the addendum. Bicknell refused. No employee filed a grievance from this decision or asked for arbitration. Instead Bailey and 22 other employees filed this suit under subsection 301, of the Labor Management Relations

Act, contending that the implementation of the addendum violated the collective bargaining agreement.

The parties consented to final disposition of the case by a magistrate. The magistrate granted Bicknell's motion to dismiss, concluding that the 23 employees had not exhausted the contractual grievance resolution machinery. The plaintiffs argued to the magistrate that the arbitration clause in the contract did not cover internal union disputes. The magistrate concluded, however, that the dispute here dealt with Bicknell's right to deviate from the terms of the 1982 agreement, and that an arbitrator could have ordered Bicknell to rescind the addendum. The arbitration clause in subsection 6.1 was exceedingly broad. Bicknell might have persuaded the arbitrator that the Union was bound by its representation on August 9, that the addendum had been ratified, but the arbitrator also could have decided otherwise. The magistrate recognized that there are exceptions to the requirement of exhaustion; for example, employees may file suit if the Union's failure to pursue arbitration was inconsistent with its duty of fair representation. But the plaintiff conceded that the Union did not breach its duty. * * *

On appeal the plaintiffs have abandoned their argument in the district court in favor of a new one: that Bicknell "repudiated" the agreement, which makes a request for arbitration futile and therefore allows a direct suit. Two things are wrong with this contention. First, it was not urged before the magistrate, and (with exceptions not material here) a civil litigant may not raise an issue for the first time on appeal. Second, it hopelessly misconceives the nature and basis of the "repudiation" doctrine. When one party to an agreement proclaims that it no longer considers the obligation to arbitrate binding, then a request for arbitration is futile; the other party need not waste time but may proceed straight to court. The "repudiation" doctrine is one of many dealing with anticipatory breach of contract. Yet there must be an anticipatory rejection of the arbitration clause; a failure to implement the (other side's version of the) substantive provisions of the agreement is not enough.

Bicknell did not say that it would refuse to arbitrate. The addendum negotiated in 1984 did not modify subsection 6.1 of the collective bargaining agreement although it modified many other sections. The plaintiff's contention amounts to the assertion that any breach of contract (here the refusal to pay the wages agreed on in 1982) is a "repudiation" of the commitment to arbitrate. But the purpose of the arbitration clause is to resolve disputes about contractual terms. In the plaintiff's eyes, every dispute would allow the complainant to bypass arbitration because the other side's failure to do as the complainant wishes "repudiates" the agreement. From this perspective, the circumstances that call for arbitration also make arbitration unnecessary. It is hard to see how a reasonably careful lawyer could miss the difference between repudiating the agreement to arbitrate (which excuses a demand for arbitration) and disagreeing about the continued effect of some substantive provision of the contract (which does not).

Plaintiffs also maintain that pursuing the grievance-arbitration machinery would have been futile because Bicknell enforced the addendum in bad faith. * * * Appellate courts have held repeatedly, in cases the plaintiffs do not discuss, that accusations of "bad faith" do not excuse an attempt to use the grievance-arbitration machinery. The employee must try the process and if "bad faith" thwarts its completion, only then may the employee file suit. * * *

The plaintiffs' obduracy--more accurately, the obtuseness of their lawyer--has prolonged a case that should not have been filed. The claims made on appeal were neither preserved in the district court nor plausible as original matters. Bicknell's brief in this court asked for an award of attorneys' fees under Fed.R.App.P. 28. The plaintiffs had an opportunity to file a reply brief demonstrating that their appellate arguments have substance or that an award of fees is inappropriate for some other reason. They elected not to file a reply brief. An award is appropriate here, * * * because the arguments are frivolous on an objective standard. They have consumed the resources of Bicknell and the time of the court, which leaves less time for other litigants whose claims belong here. Telling would-be litigants that the law is against them is an essential part of a lawyer's job. Plaintiffs' lawyer (who represented plaintiffs from the filing of the complaint through this appeal) should have told his clients this. We therefore order counsel for the plaintiffs to pay, out of his own pocket, the attorneys' fees reasonably incurred by Bicknell in defending against the appeal. Counsel for Bicknell have 15 days to file with the clerk of this court a statement (with itemization) of the fees reasonably incurred.

Affirmed, with sanctions.

QUESTIONS

1. Why is the union in this case so anxious to avoid arbitration? Following the court's ruling, is there any way for it to avoid arbitration in the future?

2. Judge Easterbrook notes that on appeal the union changed its argument. What argument did it make at trial? What argument did it make on appeal? Should the appellate court have allowed the new argument on appeal? Why or why not?

3. Why do you think the court of appeals imposed sanctions on Bailey's attorney? How could the attorney have avoided having sanctions imposed? What message does the court seek to convey by the imposition of sanctions in this case?

4. Does the imposition of sanctions in this case mean that Bailey has no remedy on the merits? Should the court have given Bailey guidance on how to proceed?

AMF Inc. v. Brunswick Corp.

621 F.Supp. 456 (E.D.N.Y. 1985)

Weinstein, Chief Judge.

In this case of first impression, AMF Incorporated seeks to compel Brunswick Corporation to comply with their agreement to obtain a non-binding advisory opinion in a dispute over the propriety of advertising claims. For reasons indicated below, the agreement to utilize an alternative dispute resolution mechanism must be enforced.

AMF and Brunswick compete nationally in the manufacture of electronic and automatic machinery used for bowling centers. In earlier litigation before this court, AMF alleged that Brunswick had advertised certain automatic scoring devices in a false and deceptive manner. Brunswick responded with counterclaims regarding advertisements for AMF's pinspotter, bowling pins and automatic scorer. In 1983 the parties ended the litigation with a settlement agreement filed with the court. Any future dispute involving an advertised claim of "data based comparative superiority" of any bowling product would be submitted to an advisory third party, the National Advertising Division ("NAD") of the Council of Better Business Bureaus, to determine whether there was experimental support for the claim.

Paragraph 9 of the agreement reads as follows:

If either party shall hereafter publish or disseminate any claim by advertisement or pro-

motional materials of any kind or nature, which expressly or impliedly refer to a comparative superiority of a bowling product manufactured, sold or distributed by either of them, as compared to a similar product manufactured, sold or distributed by the other, which claim shall expressly or impliedly be based on data, studies or tests (hereafter "data based comparative superiority") such claims shall be subject to the provisions of this paragraph . . .

Should either party make a claim to data based comparative superiority, the other may request that substantiation for the same be delivered to the agreed upon advisory third party, subject to the provisions of this agreement, whereupon the party who has made the claim shall promptly comply.

Both parties agree to submit any controversy which they may have with respect to data based comparative superiority of any of their products over that of the other to such advisory third party for the rendition of an advisory opinion. Such opinion shall not be binding upon the parties, but shall be advisory only . . .

NAD was created in 1971 the American Advertising Federation, American Association of Advertising Agencies, Association of National Advertisers, and the Council of Better Business Bureaus "to help sustain high standards of truth and accuracy in national advertising." It monitors television, radio, and print advertising, and responds to complaints from individual consumers, consumer groups, local Better Business Bureaus, competitors, professional and trade associations, and state and federal agencies. If NAD finds that the advertising claims are unsupported, and the advertiser refuses to modify or discontinue the advertising, the organization will complain to the appropriate governmental authority. Voluntary compliance with NAD's decisions has been universal. Reportedly no advertiser who has participated in the complete process of a NAD investigation and [National Advertising Review Board] appeal has declined to abide by the decision.

In March and April 1985, Brunswick advertised its product, Armor Plate 3000, in a trade periodical called *Bowler's Journal*. Armor Plate is a synthetic laminated material used to make bowling lanes. It competes with the wood lanes produced by AMF. "The wood lane. A relic of the past," claims the advertisement, under a sketch of a horse and buggy. It goes on to detail the advantages of Armor Plate; and, as indicated in the footnote to the advertisement, strongly suggests that research supports the claim of durability as compared to wood lanes.

> By replacing your worn out wood lanes with Armor Plate 3000, Brunswick's high tech laminated surface, what you're doing is saving money. Up to $500.00 per lane per year in lost revenue and upkeep.

> That's because today's high technology has helped make Armor Plate 3000 so tough and good looking that it seems to last forever.

AMF, disputing the content of the advertisement, sought from Brunswick the underlying research data referred to in the footnote. Brunswick replied that having undertaken the expense of research it would not make the results available to AMF. Thereupon AMF informed Brunswick that it was invoking Paragraph 9 of the settlement agreement and requested that Brunswick provide substantiation to an independent third party. Brunswick responded that its advertisement did not fall within the terms of the agreement. AMF now brings this action to compel Brunswick to submit its data to the NAD for nonbinding arbitration.

The agreement on its face covers the dispute. It provides, in relevant part, that:

> If either party shall [1] *hereafter* publish or disseminate any claim by advertisement or promotional materials of any kind or nature, which [2] expressly or *impliedly refers to a comparative superiority* of a bowling product manufactured, sold or distributed by either of them, as compared to a similar product manufactured, sold or distributed by the other, [3] which claim shall expressly or *impliedly* be *based on data, studies or tests* (hereafter "data based comparative superiority") [4] such *claims shall be subject to the provisions of this* paragraph . . .

The advertisement (1), was published after the agreement of June 30, 1983. It (2), impliedly refers to comparative superiority of a Brunswick bowling product over one of AMF. It is (3), impliedly based on data and tests. Thus (4), the dispute is subject to the agreement. * * *

AMF characterizes the settlement agreement as one subject to the Federal Arbitration Act, 9 U.S.C. Sec. 1 *et seq.* The Act provides for enforcement of agreements to "settle" disputes arising after the agreement was entered into. In relevant part it reads:

> A written provision in ... a contract evidencing a transaction involving commerce to *settle by arbitration* a controversy thereafter arising out of such contract or transaction, or the refusal to perform the whole or any part thereof ... shall be valid, irrevocable, and enforceable, save upon such grounds as exist at law or in equity for the revocation of any contract.

9 U.S.C. Sec. 2 (1982). The issue posed is whether "a controversy" would be "settled" by the process set forth in the agreement.

Brunswick argues that the parties did not contemplate the kind of arbitration envisaged by the Act because the opinion of the third party is not binding on AMF and Brunswick and the agreement cannot settle the controversy. Arbitration, Brunswick argues, must present an alternative to litigation; that is, it must provide "a final settlement of the controversy between the parties."

Arbitration is a term that eludes easy definition. One commentator has pointed out that "difficulty with terminology seems to have persisted throughout the entire development of arbitration." G. Taylor, Preface to E. Witte, Historical Survey of Labor Arbitration VI (1952). He suggests that arbitration has become "synonymous with 'mediation' and 'conciliation.' " *Id.* Case law has done little to sharpen the definition. See, e.g., *City of Omaha v. Omaha Water Co.,* 218 U.S. 180 (1910). ("An arbitration implies a difference, a dispute, and involves ordinarily a hearing . . . .").

The Federal Arbitration Act, adopted in 1925, made agreements to arbitrate enforceable without defining what they were. Contemporary cases provide a broad description of arbitration: "[a] form of procedure whereby differences may be settled." *Pacific Indemnity Co., v. Insurance Co., of North America*, 25 F.2d 930, 931 (9th Cir. 1928). At no time have the courts insisted on a rigid or formalistic approach to a definition of arbitration.

Case law following the passage of the Act reflects unequivocal support of agreements to have third parties decide disputes--the essence of arbitration. No magic words such as "arbitrate" or "binding arbitration" or "final dispute resolution" are needed to obtain the benefits of the Act.

The history of the Federal Arbitration Act indicates a strong desire by Congress to reject the centuries-old "jealousy" of the courts which hindered the enforcement of contracts to have a non-judicial person decide disputes which otherwise might require adjudication by courts. See H.R. Rep. No. 96, 68th Cong. 1st Sess. at 1 (1924). In the words of the House report:

> Arbitration agreements are purely matters of contract, and the effect of the bill is simply to make the contracting party live up to his agreement. He can no longer refuse to perform his contract when it becomes disadvantageous to him. *Id.*

As the Supreme Court pointed out in *Dean Witter Reynolds, Inc. v. Byrd*, 470 U.S. 213 (1985), compelling arbitration "successfully protects the contractual rights of the parties and their rights under the Arbitration Act." As "a matter of federal law, any doubts concerning the scope of arbitrable issues should be resolved in favor of arbitration . . . ." *Moses M. Cone Memorial Hospital v. Mercury Construction Corp.*, 460 U.S. 1, 24-25 (1983). * * *

The Second Circuit has set a standard of "fundamental fairness" in arbitration; rules of evidence and procedure do not apply with the same strictness as they do in federal courts. See *Bell Aerospace Co. v. Local 516, UAW*, 500 F.2d 921 (2d Cir. 1974).

Arbitration is a creature of contract, a device of the parties rather than the judicial process. If the parties have agreed to submit a dispute for a decision by a third party, they have agreed to arbitration. The arbitrator's decision need not be binding in the same sense that a judicial decision needs to be to satisfy the constitutional requirement of a justiciable case or controversy.

Under the circumstances of this case, the agreement should be characterized as one to arbitrate. Obviously there is a controversy between the parties--[are] there data supporting Brunswick's claim of superiority. Submission of this dispute will at least "settle" that issue, even though the parties may want to continue related disputes in another forum.

The mechanism agreed to by the parties does provide an effective alternative to litigation, even though it would not employ an adversary process. That the arbitrator will examine documents in camera and ex parte does not prevent recognition of the procedure as arbitration since the parties have agreed to this special practice in this unique type of dispute. Courts are fully familiar with the practice since prosecutorial and business secrets often require protection by ex parte and in camera proceedings during the course of a litigation.

In a confidential-submission scheme, such as the one agreed to here, adversarial hearings cannot take place. But this fact does not militate against application of the Act. Rather it supports arbitration since the special arbitrator may be more capable of deciding the issue than is a court which relies so heavily on the adversary process. Moreover, the particular arbitrator chosen by these parties is more capable than the courts of finding the faint line that separates data supported claims from puffery in the sometimes mendacious atmosphere of advertising copy. * * *

Untenable is the defendant's argument that there is an adequate remedy at law so that equity is without jurisdiction. Specific performance is available as a remedy where the remedy at law is not appropriate if such equitable relief will not force a "vain order." See, e.g., *Union Pacific Railroad Co. v. Chicago, R.I. & P.R. Co.*, 163 U.S. 564 (1896).

The agreement itself recognized that the legal process would not adequately address the parties' needs. Through their contract the parties have identified an "injury" sufficient to require the dispute resolution mechanism they thought most appropriate.

The alternative dispute resolution (ADR) procedure agreed upon in the settlement is designed to reduce the acrimony associated with protracted litigation and to improve the chances of resolving future advertising disputes. This form of ADR is designed to keep disputes of this kind out of court. * * *

General public policy favors support of alternatives to litigation when these alternatives serve the interests of the parties and of judicial administration. Here AMF and Brunswick agreed in June 1983 that a special ADR mechanism would serve them better than litigation. Such decisions are encouraged by no less an observer than the Chief Justice of the United States. In his words, ADR devices are often superior to litigation "in terms of cost, time, and human wear and tear." Remarks of Warren E. Burger, Chief Justice of the United States, at the Twin Cities Advisory Council of the American Arbitration Association, St. Paul, Minn., August 21, 1985.

As suggested by the "Plan for Court-Annexed Arbitration, United States District Court, Eastern District of New York," effective January 1, 1986, the specific policy of this court is to enforce ADR agreements. In most instances they reduce the need for court trials and save clients time and money.

A remedy at law would be inadequate since it could only approximate the skilled, speedy and inexpensive efforts available by way of specific performance. A law suit would deny AMF the practical specialized experience that the parties agreed to have available for an examination of data-based comparative advertising. A court decision and an NAD decision would have different effects on the parties' reputations within the bowl-

ing products industry. In short, a remedy at law falls short of providing many of the advantages of specific performance.

The new advertisement is not so explicit in denigrating the competitor's product as the former advertisements that were subject to the prior litigation. But for the readers--purchasers of bowling alleys--the effect is much the same. The current dispute is at least as important to the parties as the former one that resulted in litigation, a settlement, and an agreement on a process for resolving further disputes about advertising.

AMF's petition to compel the submission of data pursuant to Paragraph 9 of the settlement agreement of June 30, 1983 is enforceable under the Federal Arbitration Act and pursuant to this court's equity jurisdiction.

Brunswick shall submit its substantiation for the following claim: "Continuing independent research projects that Armor Plate 3000 will now last over 20 years before the possible need arises to replace a small lane area much like replacing a broken board in a wood lane" to the National Advertising Division of the Council of Better Business Bureaus, Inc., for an advisory opinion as provided for in Paragraph 9 of the Agreement of June 30, 1983.

So Ordered.

QUESTIONS

1. Do you think the parties in this case agreed to arbitrate future disputes regarding data based comparative superiority? What process did they agree to? Why is it important to resolve the issue whether the Federal Arbitration Act is applicable to this situation?

2. What benefits were the parties seeking to achieve with the "alternative dispute resolution mechanism" in this case? Are these benefits likely to be realized in a court proceeding? Why or why not?

3. Identify the public policy interests, if any, in upholding the agreement between AMF, Inc. and Brunswick Corporation.

United Paperworkers Intern. Union, AFL-CIO
v.
Misco, Inc.
108 S.Ct. 364 (1987)

Justice White delivered the opinion of the Court.

The issue for decision involves several aspects of when a federal court may refuse to enforce an arbitration award rendered under a collective-bargaining agreement.

Misco, Inc., (Misco, or the Company) operates a paper converting plant in Monroe, Louisiana. The Company is a party to a collective-bargaining agreement with the United Paperworkers International Union, AFL-CIO, and its union local (the Union); the agreement covers the production and maintenance employees at the plant. Under the agreement, the Company or the Union may submit to arbitration any grievance that arises from the interpretation or application of its terms, and the arbitrator's decision is final and binding upon the parties. The arbitrator's authority is limited to interpretation and application of the terms contained in the agreement itself. The agreement reserves to management the right to establish, amend, and enforce "rules and regulations regulating the discipline or discharge of employees" and the procedures for imposing discipline. Such rules were to be posted and were to be in effect "until ruled on by grievance and arbitration procedures as to fairness and necessity. For about a decade, the Company's rules had listed as causes for discharge the bringing of intoxicants, narcotics, or controlled substances on to plant property or consuming any of them there, as well as reporting for work under the influence of such substances. At the time of the events involved in this case, the Company was very concerned about the use of drugs at the plant, especially among employees on the night shift.

Isiah Cooper, who worked on the night shift for Misco, was one of the employees covered by the collective-bargaining agreement. He operated a slitter-rewinder machine, which uses sharp blades to cut rolling coils of paper. The arbitrator found that this machine is hazardous and had caused numerous injuries in recent years. Cooper had been reprimanded twice in a few months for deficient performance. On January 21, 1983, one day after the second reprimand, the police searched Cooper's house pursuant to a warrant, and a sub-

stantial amount of marijuana was found. Contemporaneously, a police officer was detailed to keep Cooper's car under observation at the Company's parking lot. At about 6:30 p.m., Cooper was seen walking in the parking lot during work hours with two other men. The three men entered Cooper's car momentarily, then walked to another car, a white Cutlass, and entered it. After the other two men later returned to the plant, Cooper was apprehended by police in the backseat of this car with marijuana smoke in the air and a lighted marijuana cigarette in the front-seat ashtray. The police also searched Cooper's car and found a plastic scales case and marijuana gleanings. Cooper was arrested and charged with marijuana possession.

On January 24, Cooper told the Company that he had been arrested for possession of marijuana at his home; the Company did not learn of the marijuana cigarette in the white Cutlass until January 27. It then investigated and on February 7, discharged Cooper, asserting that in the circumstances, his presence in the Cutlass violated the rule against having drugs on the plant premises. Cooper filed a grievance protesting his discharge the same day, and the matter proceeded to arbitration. The Company was not aware until September 21, five days before the hearing before the arbitrator was scheduled, that marijuana had been found in Cooper's car. That fact did not become known to the Union until the hearing began. At the hearing it was stipulated that the issue was whether the Company had "just cause to discharge the Grievant under Rule II.1" and "[i]f not, what if any should be the remedy.[1]

The arbitrator upheld the grievance and ordered the company to reinstate Cooper with backpay and full seniority. * * * In particular, the

---

[1] Rule II.1 lists the following as causes for discharge: "Bringing intoxicants, narcotics, or controlled substances into, or consuming intoxicants, narcotics or controlled substances in the plant, or on plant premises. Reporting for duty under the influence of intoxicants, narcotics, or controlled substances." App. to Pet. for Cert. 31a.

arbitrator found that the Company failed to prove that the employee had possessed or used marijuana on company property: finding Cooper in the backseat of a car and a burning cigarette in the front-seat ashtray was insufficient proof that Cooper was using or possessed marijuana on company property. The arbitrator refused to accept into evidence the fact that marijuana had been found in Cooper's car on company premises because the Company did not know of this fact when Cooper was discharged and therefore did not rely on it as a basis for the discharge.

The Company filed suit in District Court, seeking to vacate the arbitration award on several grounds, one of which was that ordering reinstatement of Cooper, who had allegedly possessed marijuana on the plant premises, was contrary to public policy. The District Court agreed that the award must be set aside as contrary to public policy because it ran counter to general safety concerns that arise from the operation of dangerous machinery while under the influence of drugs, as well as to state criminal laws against drug possession. The Court of Appeals affirmed, with one judge dissenting. The court ruled that reinstatement would violate the public policy "against the operation of dangerous machinery by persons under the influence of drugs or alcohol." * * *

Because the Courts of Appeals are divided on the question of when courts may set aside arbitration awards as contravening public policy, we granted the Union's petition for a writ of certiorari, and now reverse the judgment of the Court of Appeals.

The Union asserts that an arbitral award may not be set aside on public policy grounds unless the award orders conduct that violates the positive law, which is not the case here. But in the alternative, it submits that even if it is wrong in this regard, the Court of Appeals otherwise exceeded the limited authority that it had to review an arbitrator's award entered pursuant to a collective-bargaining agreement. Respondent, on the other hand, defends the public policy decision of the Court of Appeals but alternatively argues that the judgment below should be affirmed because of erroneous findings by the arbitrator. We deal first with the opposing alternative arguments.

A

Collective-bargaining agreements commonly provide grievance procedures to settle disputes between union and employer with respect to the interpretation and application of the agreement and require binding arbitration for unsettled grievances. In such cases, and this is such a case, the Court made clear almost 30 years ago that the courts play only a limited role when asked to review the decision of an arbitrator. The courts are not authorized to reconsider the merits of an award even though the parties may allege that the award rests on errors of fact or on misinterpretation of the contract. * * * As long as the arbitrator's award "draws its essence from the collective bargaining agreement," and is not merely "his own brand of industrial justice," the award is legitimate. * * *

The reasons for insulating arbitral decisions from judicial review are grounded in the federal statutes regulating labor-management relations. * * * The courts have jurisdiction to enforce collective-bargaining contracts; but where the contract provides grievance and arbitration procedures, those procedures must first be exhausted and courts must order resort to the private settlement mechanisms without dealing with the merits of the dispute. Because the parties have contracted to have disputes settled by an arbitrator chosen by them rather than by a judge, it is the arbitrator's view of the facts and the meaning of the contract that they have agreed to accept. Courts thus do not sit to hear claims of factual or legal error by an arbitrator as an appellate court does in reviewing decisions of lower courts. To resolve disputes about the application of a collective-bargaining agreement, an arbitrator must find facts and a court may not reject those findings simply because it disagrees with them. The same is true of the arbitrator's interpretation of the contract. The arbitrator may not ignore the plain language of the contract; but the parties having authorized the arbitrator to give meaning to the language of the agreement, a court should not reject an award on the ground that the arbitrator misread the contract. So, too, where it is contemplated that the arbitrator will determine remedies for contract violations that he finds, courts have no authority to disagree with his honest judgment in that respect. * * * [A]s long as the arbitrator is even arguably construing or applying the contract and acting within the scope of his authority, that a court is convinced he committed serious error does not suffice to overturn his decision. Of course, decisions procured by the parties through fraud or through the arbitrator's dishonesty need not be enforced. But there is nothing of that sort involved in this case.

B

The Company's position, simply put, is that the arbitrator committed grievous error in finding that the evidence was insufficient to prove that Cooper had possessed or used marijuana on company property. But the Court of Appeals, although it took a distinctly jaundiced view of the arbitrator's decision in this regard, was not free to refuse enforcement because it considered Cooper's presence in the white Cutlass, in the circumstances, to be ample proof that Rule II.1 was violated. No dishonesty is alleged; only improvident, even silly, factfinding is claimed. This is hardly sufficient basis for disregarding what the agent appointed by the parties determined to be the historical facts.

Nor was it open to the Court of Appeals to refuse to enforce the award because the arbitrator, in deciding whether there was just cause to discharge, refused to consider evidence unknown to the Company at the time Cooper was fired. The parties bargained for arbitration to settle disputes and were free to set the procedural rules for arbitrators to follow if they chose. * * * Here the arbitrator ruled that in determining whether Cooper had violated Rule II.1, he should not consider evidence not relied on by the employer in ordering the discharge, particularly in a case like this where there was no notice to the employee or the Union prior to the hearing that the Company would attempt to rely on after-discovered evidence. This, in effect, was a construction of what the contract required when deciding discharge cases: an arbitrator was to look only at the evidence before the employer at the time of discharge. As the arbitrator noted, this approach was consistent with the practice followed by other arbitrators. * * *

Under the Arbitration Act, the federal courts are empowered to set aside arbitration awards on such grounds only when "the arbitrators were guilty of misconduct . . . in refusing to hear evidence pertinent and material to the controversy. If we apply that same standard here and assume that the arbitrator erred in refusing to consider the disputed evidence, his error was not in bad faith or so gross as to amount to affirmative misconduct. Finally, it is worth noting that putting aside the evidence about the marijuana found in Cooper's car during this arbitration did not forever foreclose the Company from using that evidence as the basis for a discharge. * * *

The Court of Appeals * * * held that the evidence of marijuana in Cooper's car required that the award be set aside because to reinstate a person who had brought drugs onto the property was contrary to the public policy "against the operation of dangerous machinery by persons under the influence of drugs or alcohol." We cannot affirm that judgment.

A court's refusal to enforce an arbitrator's award under a collective-bargaining agreement because it is contrary to public policy is a specific application of the more general doctrine, rooted in the common law, that a court may refuse to enforce contracts that violate law or public policy. That doctrine derives from the basic notion that no court will lend its aid to one who founds a cause of action upon an immoral or illegal act, and is further justified by the observation that the public's interests in confining the scope of private agreements to which it is not a party will go unrepresented unless the judiciary takes account of those interests when it considers whether to enforce such agreements.

In the common law of contracts, this doctrine has served as the foundation for occasional exercises of judicial power to abrogate private agreements. * * *

As we see it, the formulation of public policy set out by the Court of Appeals did not comply with the statement that such a policy must be "ascertained 'by reference to the laws and legal precedents and not from general considerations of supposed public interests.' " The Court of Appeals made no attempt to review existing laws and legal precedents in order to demonstrate that they establish a "well defined and dominant" policy against the operation of dangerous machinery while under the influence of drugs. Although certainly such a judgment is firmly rooted in common sense, we explicitly held in *W.R. Grace & Co. v. Rubber Workers*, 461 U.S. 757, 766, 103 S.Ct. 2177, 2183, 76, L.Ed.2d 298 (1983), that a formulation of public policy based only on "general considerations of supposed public interests" is not the sort that permits a court to set aside an arbitration award that was entered in accordance with a valid collective-bargaining agreement.

Even if the Court of Appeals' formulation of public policy is to be accepted, no violation of that policy is to be accepted, no violation of that policy was clearly shown in this case. In pursuing its public policy inquiry, the Court of Appeals quite properly considered the established fact that traces of marijuana had been found in Cooper's car. Yet the assumed connection between the marijuana gleanings found in Cooper's car and Cooper's actual use of drugs in the workplace is tenuous at best and provides an insufficient basis for holding that his reinstatement would actually violate the public policy identified by the Court of Appeals "against the operation of dangerous machinery by persons under the influence of drugs or alcohol." A refusal to enforce an award must rest on more than speculation or assumption.

In any event, it was inappropriate for the Court of Appeals itself to draw the necessary inference. To conclude from the fact that marijuana had been found in Cooper's car that Cooper had ever been or would be under the influence of marijuana while he was on the job and operating dangerous machinery is an exercise in fact-finding about Cooper's use of drugs and his amenability to discipline, a task that exceeds the authority of a court asked to overturn an arbitration award. The parties did not bargain for the facts to be found by a court, but by an arbitrator chosen by them who had more opportunity to observe Cooper and to be familiar with the plant and its problems. Nor does the fact that it is inquiring into a possible violation of public policy excuse a court for doing the arbitrator's task. * * *

The judgment of the Court of Appeals is reversed.

Justice Blackmun, with whom Justice Brennan joins, concurring.

I join the Court's opinion, but write separately to underscore the narrow grounds on which its decision rests and to emphasize what it is not holding today. In particular, the Court does not reach the issue upon which certiorari was granted: whether a court may refuse to enforce an arbitration award rendered under a collective-bargaining agreement on public policy grounds only when the award itself violates positive law or required unlawful conduct by the employer. The opinion takes no position on this issue. * * *

QUESTIONS

1. Why did the Supreme Court grant certiorari in this case? What does the Court's explanation reveal about the purpose of Supreme Court review?

2. On what grounds did the arbitrator in this case order Cooper reinstated? What policy argument did the company argue to the district court? What factual finding is implicit in that argument? Should a district court review the factual findings of an arbitrator? Why or why not?

3. Does this case stand for the proposition that under no circumstances will the Supreme Court vacate an arbitration award on the grounds that the award is contrary to public policy? Why or why not?

4. Is there, or should there be, a public policy that prevents the enforcement of arbitration awards that order one party to perform illegal acts? Is there, or should there be, a public policy that prevents the enforcement of arbitration awards that harm the public? For example, should a court enforce an arbitration award of a 15% salary increase to police officers in a community that will have to increase taxes to implement the award? When would such public policies come into play? Who should determine their contents?

Commonwealth Coatings Corp.

v.

Continental Casualty Co.

393 U.S. 145 (1968)

Mr. Justice Black delivered the opinion of the Court.

At issue in this case is the question whether elementary requirements of impartiality taken for granted in every judicial proceeding are suspended when the parties agree to resolve a dispute through arbitration.

The petitioner, Commonwealth Coatings Corporation, a subcontractor, sued the sureties on the prime contractor's bond to recover money alleged to be due for a painting job. The contract for painting contained an agreement to arbitrate such controversies. Pursuant to this agreement petitioner appointed one arbitrator, the prime contractor appointed a second, and these two together selected the third arbitrator. This third arbitrator, the supposedly neutral member of the panel, conducted a large business in Puerto Rico, in which he served as an engineering consultant for various people in connection with building construction projects. One of his regular customers in this business was the prime contractor that petitioner sued in this case. This relationship with the prime contractor was in a sense sporadic in that the arbitrator's services were used only from time to time at irregular intervals, and there had been no dealings between them for about a year immediately preceding the arbitration. Nevertheless, the prime contractor's patronage was repeated and significant, involving fees of about $12,000 over a period of four or five years, and the relationship even went so far as to include the rendering of services on the very projects involved in this lawsuit. An arbitration was held, but the facts concerning the close business connections between the third arbitrator and the prime contractor were unknown to petitioner and were never revealed to it by this arbitrator, by the prime contractor, or by anyone else until after an award had been made. Petitioner challenged the award on this ground, among others, but the District Court refused to set aside the award. The Court of Appeals affirmed and we granted certiorari.

In 1925, Congress enacted the United States Arbitration Act, 9 U.S.C. §§ 1-14, which sets out a comprehensive plan for arbitration of controversies coming under its terms, and both sides here assume that this Federal Act governs this case. Section 10 * * * sets out the conditions upon which awards can be vacated.[1] The two courts below held, however, that subsection 10 could not be construed in such a away as to justify vacating the award in this case. We disagree and reverse. Section 10 does authorize vacation of an award where it was "procured by corruption, fraud, or undue means" or "[w]here there was evident partiality . . . in the arbitrators." These provisions show a desire of Congress to provide not merely for any arbitration but for an impartial one. It is true that petitioner does not charge before us that the third arbitrator was actually guilty of fraud or bias in deciding this case, and we have no reason, apart from the undisclosed business relationship, to suspect him of any improper motives. But neither this arbitrator nor the prime contractor gave to petitioner even an intimation of the close finan-

---

[1] "In either of the following cases in the United States court in and for the district wherein the award was made may make an order vacating the award upon the application of any party to the arbitration—

"(a) Where the award was procured by corruption, fraud, or undue means.

"(b) Where there was evident partiality or corruption in the arbitrators, or either of them.

"(c) Where the arbitrators were guilty of misconduct in refusing to postpone the hearing, upon sufficient cause shown, or in refusing to hear evidence pertinent and material to the controversy; or of any other misbehavior by which the rights of any party have been prejudiced.

"(d) Where the arbitrators exceeded their powers, or so imperfectly executed them that a mutual, final, and definite award upon the subject matter submitted was not made.

"(e) Where an award is vacated and the time within which the agreement required the award to be made has not expired the court may, in its discretion, direct a rehearing by the arbitrators."

cial relations that had existed between them for a period of years. We have no doubt that if a litigant could show that a foreman of a jury or a judge in a court of justice had, unknown to the litigant, any such relationship, the judgment would be subject to challenge. * * * It is true that arbitrators cannot sever all their ties with the business world, since they are not expected to get all their income from their work deciding cases, but we should, if anything, be even more scrupulous to safeguard the impartiality of arbitrators than judges, since the former have completely free rein to decide the law as well as the facts and are not subject to appellate review. We can perceive no way in which the effectiveness of the arbitration process will be hampered by the simple requirement that the arbitrators disclose to the parties any dealings that might create an impression of possible bias.

While not controlling in this case, subsection 18 of the Rules of the American Arbitration Association, in effect at the time of this arbitration, is highly significant. It provided as follows:

"Section 18. Disclosure by Arbitrator of Disqualification - At the time of receiving his notice of appointment, the prospective Arbitrator is requested to disclose any circumstances likely to create a presumption of bias or which he believes might disqualify him as an impartial Arbitrator. Upon receipt of such information, the Tribunal Clerk shall immediately disclose it to the parties, who if willing to proceed under the circumstances disclosed, shall, in writing, so advise the Tribunal Clerk. If either party declines to waive the presumptive disqualification, the vacancy thus created shall be filled in accordance with the applicable provisions of this Rule."

And based on the same principle as this Arbitration Association rule is that part of the 33d Cannon of Judicial Ethics which provides:

"33. Social Relations.

. . . [A judge] should, however, in pending or prospective litigation before him be particularly careful to avoid such action as may reasonably tend to awaken the suspicion that his social or business relations or friendships, constitute an element in influencing his judicial conduct."

This rule of arbitration and this canon of judicial ethics rests on the premise that any tribunal permitted by law to try cases and controversies not only must be unbiased but also must avoid even the appearance of bias. We cannot believe that it was the purpose of Congress to authorize litigants to submit their cases and controversies to arbitration boards that might reasonably be thought biased against one litigant and favorable to another.

Reversed

Mr. Justice White, with whom Mr. Justice Marshall joins, concurring.

* * * The Court does not decide today that arbitrators are to be held to the standards of judicial decorum of Article III judges or indeed of any judges. It is often because they are men of affairs, not apart from but of the marketplace, that they are effective in their ajudicatory function. Cf. *United Steelworkers v. Warrior & Gulf Navigation Co.*, 363 U.S. 574 (1960). This does not mean the judiciary must overlook outright chicanery in giving effect to their awards; that would be an abdication of our responsibility. But it does mean that arbitrators are not automatically disqualified by a business relationship with the parties before them if both parties are informed of the relationship in advance, or if they are unaware of the facts but the relationship is trivial. I see no reason automatically to disqualify the best informed and most capable potential arbitrators.

The arbitration process functions best when an amicable and trusting atmosphere is preserved and there is voluntary compliance with the decree, without need for judicial enforcement. This end is best served by establishing an atmosphere of frankness at the outset, through disclosure by the arbitrator of any financial transactions which he has had or is negotiating with either of the parties. In many cases the arbitrator might believe the business relationship to be so insubstantial that to make a point of revealing it would suggest he is indeed easily swayed, and perhaps a partisan of that party. But if the law requires the disclosure, no such imputation can arise. And it is far better that the relationship be disclosed at the outset, when the parties are free to reject the arbitrator or accept him with knowledge of the relationship and continuing faith in his objectivity, than to have the relationship come to light after the arbitration, when a suspicious or disgruntled party can seize on it as a pretext for invalidating the award. The judiciary should minimize its role in arbitration as part of the arbitrator's impartiality. That role is best consigned to the parties, who are the architects of their own arbitration process, and are far better informed of the prevailing ethical standards and reputations within their business. * * *

Mr. Justice Fortas, with whom Mr. Justice Harlan and Mr. Justice Stewart join, dissenting.

* * * The facts in this case do not lend themselves to the Court's rulings. The Court sets aside the arbitration award despite the fact that the award is unanimous and no claim is made of actual partiality, unfairness, bias or fraud.

The arbitration was held pursuant to provisions in the contracts between the parties. It is not subject to the rules of the American Arbitration Association. it is governed by the United States Arbitration Act. * * *

Both courts below held, and petitioner concedes, that the third arbitrator was innocent of any actual partiality, or bias, or improper motive. There is no suggestion of concealment as distinguished from the innocent failure to volunteer information.

The third arbitrator is a leading and respected consulting engineer who has performed services for "most of the contractors in Puerto Rico." He was well known to petitioner's counsel and they were personal friends. Petitioner's counsel candidly admitted that if he had been told about the arbitrator's prior relationship "I don't think I would have objected because I know Mr. Capacete [the arbitrator]."

Clearly, the District Judge's conclusion affirmed by the Court of Appeals for the First Circuit, was correct, that "the arbitrators conducted fair, impartial hearings; that they reached a proper determination of the issues before them, and that plaintiff's objections represent a 'situation where the losing party to an arbitration is now clutching at straws in an attempt to avoid the results of the arbitration to which it became a party.' "

I agree that failure of an arbitrator to volunteer information about business dealings with one party will, prima facie, support a claim of partiality or bias. But when there is no suggestion that the nondisclosure was calculated, and where the complaining party disclaims any imputation of partiality, bias, or misconduct, the presumption clearly is overcome. * * *

Arbitration is essentially consensual and practical. The United States Arbitration Act is obviously designed to protect the integrity of the process with a minimum of insistence upon set formulae and rules. The Court applies to this process rules applicable to judges and not to a system characterized by dealing on faith and reputation for reliability. Such formalism is not contemplated by the Act nor is it warranted in a case where no claim is made of partiality, of unfairness, or of misconduct in any degree.

QUESTIONS

1. Why does the majority set aside the arbitration award in this case? Given the facts presented in the case, do you think the majority or dissent reaches the correct conclusion? Why?

2. Why does the majority believe that arbitrators should not be held to the same standard of ethics as judges? Despite this opinion, could Congress impose the same standards on arbitrators and judges if it chose to?

3. What ethical standards would Justices White and Marshall impose on arbitrators? How do their views differ from the views expressed by the majority?

Scherk v. Alberto-Culver Co.

417 U.S. 506 (1973)

Mr. Justice Stewart delivered the opinion of the Court.

Alberto-Culver Co., the respondent, is an American company incorporated in Delaware with its principal office in Illinois. It manufactures and distributes toiletries and hair products in this country and abroad. During the 1960's Alberto-Culver decided to expand its overseas operations, and as part of this program it approached the petitioner Fritz Scherk, a German citizen residing at the time of trial in Switzerland. Scherk was the owner of three interrelated business entities, organized under the laws of Germany and Liechtenstein, that were engaged in the manufacture of toiletries and the licensing of trademarks for such toiletries. * * * In February 1969 a contract was signed in Vienna, Austria, which provided for the transfer of the ownership of Scherk's enterprises to Alberto-Culver, along with all rights held by these enterprises to trademarks in cosmetic goods. The contract contained a number of express warranties whereby Scherk guaranteed the sole and unencumbered ownership of these trademarks. In addition, the contract contained an arbitration clause providing that "any controversy or claim [that] shall arise out of this agreement or the breach thereof" would be referred to arbitration before the International Chamber of Commerce in Paris, France, and that "[t]he laws of the State of Illinois, U.S.A. shall apply to and govern this agreement, its interpretation and performance."

The closing of the transaction took place in Geneva, Switzerland, in June 1969. Nearly one year later Alberto-Culver allegedly discovered that the trademark rights purchased under the contract were subject to substantial encumbrances that threatened to give others superior rights to the trademarks and to restrict or preclude Alberto-Culver's use of them. Alberto-Culver thereupon tendered back to Scherk the property that had been transferred to it and offered to rescind the contract. Upon Scherk's refusal, Alberto-Culver commenced this action for damages and other relief in a Federal District Court in Illinois, contending that Scherk's fraudulent representations concerning the status of the trademark rights constituted violations of Sec. 10(b) of the Securities Exchange Act of 1934, 48 Stat. 891, 15 U.S.C. Sec. 78j (b), and Rule 10b-5 promulgated thereunder, 17 CFR Sec. 240.-10b-5.

In response, Scherk filed a motion to dismiss the action for want of personal and subject-matter jurisdiction as well as on the basis of *forum non conveniens*, or, alternatively, to stay the action pending arbitration in Paris pursuant to the agreement of the parties. Alberto-Culver, in turn, opposed this motion and sought a preliminary injunction restraining the prosecution of arbitration proceedings. On December 2, 1971, the District Court denied Scherk's motion to dismiss, and, on January 14, 1972, it granted a preliminary order enjoining Scherk from proceeding with arbitration. * * *

The United States Arbitration Act, now 9 U.S.C. Sec. 1 *et seq.*, reversing centuries of judicial hostility to arbitration agreements, was designed to allow parties to avoid "the costliness and delays of litigation," and to place arbitration agreements "upon the same footing as other contracts...." Accordingly, the Act provides that an arbitration agreement such as is here involved "shall be valid, irrevocable, and enforceable, save upon such grounds as exist at law or in equity for revocation of any contract." 9 U.S.C. Sec. 2. The Act also provides in Sec. 3 for a stay of proceedings in a case where a court is satisfied that the issue before it is arbitrable under the agreement, and Sec. 4 of the Act directs a federal court to order parties to proceed to arbitration if there has been a "failure, neglect, or refusal" of any party to honor an agreement to arbitrate. * * *

In this case, in the absence of the arbitration provision considerable uncertainty existed at the time of the agreement, and still exists, concerning the law applicable to the resolution of disputes arising out of the contract.

Such uncertainty will almost inevitably exist with respect to any contract touching two or more countries, each with its own substantive laws and conflict-of-laws rules. A contractual provision specifying in advance the forum in which disputes shall be litigated and the law to be applied is, therefore, an almost indispensable precondition to achievement of the orderliness and predictability essential to any international business transaction. Furthermore, such a provision obviates the danger that a dispute under the agreement might be submitted to a forum hostile to the interests of one of the parties or unfamiliar with the problem area involved.

A parochial refusal by the courts of one country to enforce an international arbitration agreement would not only frustrate these purposes, but would invite unseemly and mutually destructive jockeying by the parties to secure tactical litigation advantages. In the present case, for example, it is not inconceivable that if Scherk had anticipated that Alberto-Culver would be able in this country to enjoin resort to arbitration he might have sought an order in France or some other country enjoining Alberto-Culver from proceeding with its litigation in the United States. Whatever recognition the courts of this country might ultimately have granted to the order of the foreign court, the dicey atmosphere of such a legal no-man's-land would surely damage the fabric of international commerce and trade, and imperil the willingness and ability of businessmen to enter into international commercial agreements. * * *

For all these reasons we hold that the agreement of the parties in this case to arbitrate any dispute arising out of their international commercial transaction is to be respected and enforced by the federal courts in accord with the explicit provisions of the Arbitration Act.

QUESTIONS

1. Does arbitration offer particular strengths in the transnational arena? Compare this case with *AMF v. Brunswick*. Lacking an arbitration clause in *AMF*, what law would be applied to resolve the dispute?

2. What would have happened in this case if Scherk had appeared in court in Illinois ready and willing to proceed with a suit against Alberto-Culver? What would have happened to the arbitration clause if Scherk had done so?

3. If the parties in this case proceed with arbitration, in keeping with the Court's opinion, where might they turn to seek enforcement of the award?

4. Does this case stand for the proposition that in international agreements arbitration clauses need not be drawn with as much precision as in domestic cases? Explain.

4 COURT-ANNEXED ARBITRATION

Court-annexed arbitration is the assignment by a court of selected cases to arbitration as a precondition to or substitute for a trial. The court that assigns a case supervises the arbitration program and establishes qualifications for arbitrators. Some jurisdictions appoint the arbitrator to hear cases; some allow parties to name their own arbitrator or to select one from a list of arbitrators qualified to serve. If the arbitrator's award is acceptable to the parties, the award is filed with the court and is entered as the court's judgment in the case. If either party finds arbitration unacceptable, the recourse is to demand a trial de novo. In some jurisdictions, the party demanding a trial de novo can face monetary sanctions if its position following trial is not substantially better than it was following arbitration. As in voluntary arbitration, the parties usually are responsible for paying the arbitrator's fee, but the fee is established by statute or court rule.

Most jurisdictions that have court-annexed arbitration programs assign only civil cases involving relatively small dollar amounts: $15,000 to $50,000 is common in state programs while $75,000 to $100,000 ceilings apply in federal courts.[1] Significantly, the overwhelming majority of cases filed in state courts involve claims of less than $10,000; many cases filed in federal courts are under the $100,000 ceiling.[2] Court-annexed arbitration thus is capable of resolving a significant number of civil cases filed in American courts.

Three primary modifications distinguish court-annexed arbitration from voluntary arbitration. First, cases assigned to court-annexed arbitration remain on the court's docket and hence under the assigning court's jurisdiction. If parties object to the case being sent to arbitration, they can petition the court to allow the case to proceed to trial. Similarly, if parties want their civil dispute to be resolved by court-annexed arbitration rather than by trial, they can petition the court to assign the case even if by dollar amount or subject matter it would not qualify for assignment under that jurisdiction's rules. The decision to assign a case to arbitration remains with the court.

A second important difference between court-annexed and voluntary arbitration is that the substantive law of the jurisdiction in which the case was filed governs the resolution of the dispute. Parties in court-annexed arbitration cannot select the standards by which their dispute will be resolved. Most jurisdictions with court-annexed programs do permit less formality at arbitration hearings, including relaxed rules of evidence and procedure, but the substantive law of the jurisdiction remains the standard by which the dispute is resolved.

The final important difference between court-annexed and voluntary arbitration is that arbitrators generally must be certified by the court they serve. Courts typically require court-annexed arbitrators to be lawyers or retired judges with at least a minimum of practice experience; some require arbitrators to have specialized knowledge of the cases they will hear, be they personal injury, contract, or domestic relations disputes.

States or federal district courts that adopt court-annexed arbitration programs do so for a variety of reasons. Court-annexed arbitration is a method of diverting cases from overcrowded dockets.[3] Each case that can be resolved through court-annexed arbitration is removed from the court's docket, making room for other cases that require a trial. Court-annexed arbitration is viewed as more economical: parties pay less in transactional costs, and taxpayers pay less in providing a forum for the dispute. A third reason for court-annexed arbitration is that it allows disputes to be resolved more quickly than if they were to await trial.

Party satisfaction with the adjudicative system generally is enhanced with court-annexed arbitration.[4] First, parties like the relative speed with which disputes are resolved. Second, arbitration hearings are less intimidating than trials. Hearings typically are held in the arbitrator's office rather than in a formal courtroom, making witnesses more comfortable. Third, hearings are more understandable to the participants because rules of evidence and procedure are relaxed. Interviews with disputants whose cases have been arbitrated indicate a generally high level of satisfaction with the process because they had an opportunity to present their arguments to the arbitrator without being thwarted by the incomprehensible maze of procedural rules and objections.[5]

Background of Court-Annexed Arbitration

The nation's first court-annexed arbitration program began by court rule in 1952 in Pittsburgh, Pennsylvania. On its own initiative the court identified types of civil cases that would be reviewed for assignment to court-certified arbitrators. Between 1952 and 1987 the District of Columbia and twenty-two states (Arizona, California, Colorado, Connecticut, Delaware, Florida, Georgia, Hawaii, Illinois, Michigan, Minnesota, Nevada, New Hampshire, New Jersey, New Mexico, New York, North Carolina, Ohio, Oregon, Pennsylvania, Vermont and Washington) adopted some form of court-annexed arbitration program.[6] Proposals for court-annexed arbitration are pending in several other states. Today it is most common for state programs to be initiated by legislatures which pass statutes either requiring or permitting local courts to adopt court-annexed arbitration programs and to develop rules for their implementation. The California court-annexed arbitration statute of 1976 provides a common explanation for legislative action in this area:

> The legislature finds and declares that litigation involving small civil claims has become so costly and complex as to make more difficult the efficient resolution of such civil claims, that courts are unable to efficiently resolve the increased number of cases filed each year, and that the resulting delays and expenses deny parties their right to a timely resolution of minor civil disputes. The Legislature further finds and declares that arbitration has proven to be an efficient and equitable method for resolving small claims, and that courts should encourage or require the use of arbitration for such actions whenever possible.[7]

Most statutes spell out the broad outlines of court-annexed arbitration programs, leaving local courts with the responsibility to develop detailed rules. The California statute, for example, specifies that arbitration proceedings are to be simple and economical, that hearings should be private, and urges members of the California bar to volunteer their services without compensation when possible. The Judicial Council of the State of California adopted rules to implement and administer the statute.[8]

Federal court-annexed arbitration programs began in 1978 with three federal district courts: the Northern District of California, the Eastern District of Pennsylvania, and the District of Connecticut. (The Connecticut program was discontinued in 1981.) In 1988, mandatory programs were in effect in ten district courts: the Central District of California, the Eastern Districts of New York and Pennsylvania, the Middle Districts of North Carolina and Florida, the Western Districts of Missouri, Oklahoma, Texas and Michigan, and the District of New Jersey.[9] In 1984, Congress appropriated $500,000 to start court-annexed programs in other federal district courts; several are considering experimenting with the technique. Federal programs have been initiated by local court rule, under authority of the Federal Rules of Civil Procedure which give trial judges authority to develop techniques for managing their caseloads.[10]

How Court-Annexed Arbitration Works

Court-annexed arbitration statutes and programs follow a variety of models. Some, like Michigan, follow a mediation model. Others, like Connecticut, follow a litigation model. Most court-annexed arbitration programs fall somewhere between these two.

Under the Michigan court-annexed arbitration statute, any tort action filed can be assigned to arbitration on motion of the parties or by the court on its own initiative. The case is heard by a panel of three arbitrators. The arbitrators listen to the parties' lawyers deliver fifteen minute summaries of their arguments. Neither side is allowed to call witnesses. Following the presentations, the arbitrators meet informally with the attorneys to help them attempt to negotiate a settlement of the case. If negotiation succeeds, the case is withdrawn from the court's docket. If the attorneys are unable to settle the case with the help of the arbitration panel, the panel is responsible for deciding how much, if anything, in the way of damages should be awarded to the plaintiff. The panel's opinion is entered as its award. If a party is not satisfied with the panel's award, it can demand a trial *de novo* within forty days; if neither side demands a trial, the award is filed with the court and is entered as the court's judgment in the case. The Michigan statute creates a risk for a party who demands a trial *de novo* following a unanimous award by the arbitration panel: it must pay a penalty if it does not improve its position at trial by ten percent relative to the arbitration panel's evaluation of the merits of the case.[11]

The Michigan statute's reliance on the mediation model is demonstrated by its efforts to facilitate agreement before the panel imposes an outcome. After allowing both sides to summarize their positions, the panel assists in negotiation efforts between or among the parties. Only if the panel fails to help the parties achieve settlement does it render an opinion. Often the parties accept the panel's opinion because they believe it is a good indication of the result they would receive if they were to take the case to trial.

Connecticut statutes provide a good example of the litigation model of court-annexed arbitration. Arbitration hearings are conducted by court certified lawyer-arbitrators. Hearings are held in courtrooms provided by the court. They are conducted according to the same rules of evidence and procedure that would be used at trial. Witnesses are sworn, and a complete stenographic record of proceedings is kept. The arbitrator's salary is paid from court funds. A party requesting a trial must show that the arbitrator acted arbitrarily or capriciously, or that the award was procured by corruption or other undue means.[12]

An outside observer probably would have difficulty distinguishing between a court-annexed arbitration hearing and a trial in Connecticut. The primary observable difference is that the arbitrator does not wear a robe. For all practical purposes, lawyer-arbitrators do the jobs of small claims court judges.

The design of most court-annexed arbitration programs places them somewhere between the extremes reflected by the Michigan mediation model and the Connecticut litigation model. The location of other programs between these two models depends on their levels of formality, adherence to procedural rules, and recommended levels of involvement by arbitrators in party negotiations. Programs tend to be structured according to the following framework:

1. Filing and Assignment

The first step is for a plaintiff to file a complaint in court, just as though the case were to be litigated. The defendant must file an answer within the time specified by the rules of civil procedure. Upon receipt of the defendant's answer, court personnel review the documents filed by each party to determine the issues and whether the case qualifies for court-annexed arbitration. This also is the stage at which the parties can request that their case be assigned to arbitration. If the case is deemed appropriate for arbitration, the court clerk notifies the parties that it is being assigned. The parties have a period of time in which to object to arbitration; objections usually are stated on a form provided by the court and are submitted to the presiding judge for review. If no objections are filed, or the court rejects a party's objections, the case is sent to arbitration.

2. Selection of the Arbitrator; Pre-hearing Procedures

In some jurisdictions the parties select the arbitrator from a list of court-certified arbitrators. In other jurisdictions an arbitrator is appointed by the court, with the provision that either party can have the arbitrator removed and another appointed.

Following selection of an arbitrator, a date is set for the arbitration hearing. Some programs require the arbitrator to set the hearing date at the time the case is assigned. Other programs allow the parties to agree on a date. Most programs also provide for a limited discovery period, after which the parties are to provide each other with witness lists and exhibits.

3. Arbitration Hearing

Most court-annexed arbitration hearings follow the basic outlines of a non-jury trial but are less formal. In some jurisdictions the court provides a hearing room, though not necessarily a courtroom. In others, the arbitrator and the parties agree on an appropriate location. Many court-annexed arbitration hearings are held in the arbitrator's office. Jurisdictions also differ over whether rules of evidence and procedure are followed strictly or are merely guides; whether a stenographic record is kept; and whether witnesses are required to take an oath. The goal of all programs is to provide a forum that is conducive to fairness, and that gives the parties an opportunity to present their side of the case.

4. Award

Following the arbitration hearing arbitrators are required to submit their awards within a time specified by local rules. Some rules require a decision within a week of the hearing. The decision is submitted to the court, where it is entered as the court's judgment in the case if neither party demands a trial *de novo*. Once the judgment is entered, it is a fully enforceable court order.

5. *Trial De Novo*

A party dissatisfied with an award or the hearing process can demand a trial *de novo*. The demand must be made to the presiding court. The trial court hears the case as though it had not already been to arbitration. No evidence of the prior arbitration is admissible. The only use that can be made of testimony given at the prior arbitration hearing is to impeach a witness at trial. For example, if a witness in an arbitration hearing concerning an automobile crash testified that the traffic light was green at the time of the collision, and at the subsequent trial testified that the traffic light was red, the testimony from the arbitration hearing could be used at trial to impeach the witness' credibility.

Most court-annexed arbitration programs attach certain disincentives to demanding a trial *de novo*. Generally, the party demanding the trial must improve its position by at least ten percent relative to the arbitration award, or risk paying penalties that can include court costs and even the other party's attorney's fees for the trial. The purpose of sanctions is to provide an incentive for the parties to put on their best cases in the court-annexed forum and to accept the decision of the arbitrator. The threat of sanctions discourages parties from using the court-annexed proceeding as a discovery device for the subsequent trial. Such sanctions, coupled with the uncertainty of the result of a trial and a high level of satisfaction with arbitration awards, assure that requests for trials *de novo* are relatively few.[13]

Burdens of Persuasion in Court-Annexed Arbitration

Cases assigned to court-annexed arbitration remain under the jurisdiction of the court in which they were filed; the laws of that jurisdiction therefore are applied in the arbitration hearing. As a result, arbitrators impose the same burdens of proof on the parties in court-annexed arbitration proceedings that would be imposed at trial. The most common burden of proof in civil cases is "preponderance of the evidence." A plaintiff suing a defendant for negligence, therefore, would be required to make the same "preponderance of the evidence" showing negligence in court-annexed arbitration as would be required at trial. That showing always is made to an arbitrator trained in the law; juries never are used in court-annexed arbitration.

While the actual burden of proof is the same in court-annexed arbitration as it is at trial, relaxation of evidentiary and procedural rules can make it easier or harder for a party to prove or defend a case against certain allegations. For example, hearsay evidence might be allowed in an arbitration hearing while it could be ruled inadmissible upon objection at trial. It is assumed in court-annexed arbitration that lawyer-arbitrators will be competent to evaluate evidence and testimony. If a party thinks the arbitration hearing was procedurally flawed or that the result was substantively in error, the remedy is to demand a trial *de novo*.

The Role of the Lawyer in Court-Annexed Arbitration

Lawyers play two important roles in court-annexed arbitration. First, they perform their traditional representative function. Representing a client in an arbitration forum requires the same skills as those required in representing a client at trial. Reduced formality and relaxed procedures do not alter the risks of non-persuasion. The lawyer's representative task remains convincing the decision-maker of the correctness of a client's position.

Second, lawyers serve as arbitrators in court-annexed programs. The ability to conduct hearings in accordance with local rules, coupled with adequate knowledge of the applicable law, requires arbitrators to be trained in the law. The difficulty of grasping the law and applying it correctly to diverse facts has led several jurisdictions to impose length of practice and subject matter of practice requirements on lawyers. A common requirement, for example, is five years of practice in the subject matter of the case assigned to arbitration.

Trends in Court-Annexed Arbitration

If existing court-annexed arbitration programs continue to be successful in achieving the dual goals of judicial efficiency and party satisfaction, use of the technique undoubtedly will be expanded in both state and federal courts. Many states and federal district courts already are considering adopting court-annexed arbitration programs.

In addition to increasing numbers of court-annexed programs throughout the country, it also is likely that jurisdictional ceilings will be made higher or eliminated altogether. Many states already have raised the ceilings. The court-annexed arbitration program in Hawaii, for example, now takes cases with damage claims up to $150,000.[14]

Some jurisdictions are considering ways other than amounts in controversy to determine which civil cases qualify for court-annexed arbitration. Other criteria under consideration include number and complexity of issues, number of parties, and the desirability of having arbitrators with specialized expertise hear certain cases. Debate undoubtedly will continue over the standards to use for determining which cases should be referred to arbitration and which should remain on the court's docket for trial.[15]

Some observers believe that another trend in court-annexed arbitration will be its use in marriage dissolution cases. Delaware already provides for court-annexed arbitration in family law cases.[16] Court-annexed arbitration allows couples seeking a divorce to present their arguments about property settlement, child and spousal support, and visitation rights in a less formal setting than a trial and with more privacy than they would have at trial.

Example of Court-Annexed Arbitration

On May 31, 1985, ABC Construction Company filed a complaint in the county circuit court against George and Emma Hagerson for $13,328, plus interest, attorney fees and costs. The complaint stated that Emma Hagerson had given ABC a promissory note for $13,328 on January 3, 1985, as down payment on a house she and George purchased from the company. The complaint stated that the Hagersons had repudiated the note and were not going to pay.

On June 5, 1985, the Hagersons filed their answer, claiming that on April 19, 1985, ABC Construction had accepted back the deed to the property they had purchased and hence owed the company nothing. Court personnel reviewed the complaint and answer to determine the appropriateness of arbitration. The court's arbitration program allowed civil cases under $25,000 to be assigned to arbitration.

On June 15 the case of *ABC Construction Company v. George and Emma Hagerson* was found suitable for arbitration. Attorneys for both sides were sent an "Order Assigning Case to Arbitration and Notice to Select Arbitrator." The attorneys were asked to stipulate to an arbitrator of their choice or to select one from a list of five names listed under "Proposed Arbitrators" on the order. Counsel also were provided with a form entitled "Objection to Arbitration" which they could submit to the court if they or the parties objected to the proceeding. Grounds listed for objecting to arbitration included: that the claim exceeded $25,000, relief other than a money judgment was being sought, or other reasons supplied by the parties. Neither side filed an objection.

Counsel for ABC Construction and the Hagersons agreed by telephone in late June to have Pat Smith serve as their arbitrator. Smith's name was on the list of proposed arbitrators. She was a local attorney who had practiced for eight years in that county and who served occasionally as judge pro-tempore in the municipal court. The attorneys also agreed on dates that would be acceptable for the arbitration hearing. They agreed on two days in October 1985 and four days in November that were acceptable. That would give them approximately three months to complete discovery and prepare for the hearing. Each filled out a form provided by the arbitration office listing available hearing dates and predicting the number of hours required for a hearing.

When the arbitration office received the information from the two attorneys it notified Smith that she had been appointed arbitrator in the case. Included with the appointment notice she received were copies of the complaint and answer, the list of acceptable dates for a hearing, the predictions of how long the hearing would take, and the "Arbitration Award/Settlement" and time forms that she would be required to submit to the court following the hearing.

Under this jurisdiction's program, disposition of the case now was under Smith's control. She arranged a conference call with the attorneys to discuss the case and a hearing date. The three agreed to a hearing date of October 5, 1985 and agreed to hold it in the conference room of Smith's law office. Each side also was asked to send the arbitrator $150, its half of the maximum of $300 Smith could earn for serving as the arbitrator in this case. If her fee turned out to be less than $300, she would refund appropriate amounts to each side. Finally, Smith asked both attorneys to supply her with exhibits and witness lists within fifteen days prior to the hearing.

Attorneys for ABC Construction and the Hagersons completed discovery and submitted the information requested by Smith. They met on October 3 to try to settle the case informally. It was clear that each side thought it should prevail and that there was no room for compromise.

The arbitration hearing began at 9:30 a.m. on October 5 at Smith's office. The conference room was arranged like an informal courtroom. Smith sat at a table facing tables where the parties and their counsel were seated. Witnesses were asked to testify sitting in a chair next to the arbitrator's table. Smith explained to the parties how the hearing would be conducted. All witnesses would be sworn and the same rules of evidence and procedure would be followed as would be at trial. Smith would rule on objections as raised. However, no stenographic record of the hearing would be kept. Smith asked if either side objected to witnesses being present in the conference room throughout the hearing. Neither objected.

The only witnesses to testify for the plaintiff were Robert Waldo, president of ABC Construction and the person who dealt with the Hagersons on the property transaction, and Beth Waldo, his wife and secretary. Emma Hagerson was the only witness for the defense.

ABC's case. Robert Waldo testified first. He said he had first met with the Emma Hagerson in October 1984 to discuss the sale of a home that his company had on the market. He said he talked with her at least three times between October 1984 and January 3, 1985, when they finalized the sale. He said that the Hagerson's primary problem with the purchase was that they had no money for a down payment. ABC finally agreed to sell them the property if they would execute a promissory note to him in the sum of $13,328 for the down payment, to be paid in monthly installments of $200 plus interest. They executed the note on December 31, 1984. Waldo then drafted a contract of sale for the remaining balance due on the house. Beth Waldo typed the contract. Under the contract, house payments were to be $314 per month. The Hagersons took possession of the house in mid-January 1985. Robert Waldo testified that he received two house payments, no payments on the promissory note, and no third house payment. Beth Waldo testified that she contacted Emma Hagerson by telephone and was informed that George Hagerson was living and working in Alaska. Beth Waldo set up an appointment between her husband and Emma Hagerson for April 3 to see if they could negotiate a settlement to the payment problem. Robert Waldo testified that he offered the Hagersons a series of alternatives to foreclosing on the house, including lowering the interest rate and extending the payment period. He said Emma Hagerson refused.

On April 19, according to Robert Waldo, Emma Hagerson came to his office and said she was giving him the house back. She had the appropriate papers drawn up and presented them to him. According to Waldo, Hagerson told him, "Now we're even. I don't owe you anything and you don't owe me anything."

ABC's attorney introduced the contract of sale and the promissory note as evidence. The contract of sale included a provision stating, "This is an absolute conveyance. This agreement is not to include the note dated December 31, 1984, in an amount of $13,328."

On cross-examination, Robert Waldo was asked what steps he had taken to make sure that Emma Hagerson understood the terms of the contract and her obligations under the promissory note. Waldo said he had advised her to consult with an attorney before signing the papers but did not know if she had done so.

Hagerson's case. Emma Hagerson testified that she and her husband had purchased a house from ABC Construction Company on January 3, 1985 and that they had given ABC Construction a promissory note for $13,328 as a down payment. She further testified that she lived in the house alone for approximately two months while her husband was working in Alaska. In February, she said that her husband was told that he would be receiving a drastic cut in pay. He told her they would have to do something about the financial obligations they had. Hagerson testified that it was soon clear to her that they would not be able to keep the house. She met with Robert Waldo on April 3 and told him there was no way she would be able to continue to make payments. She asked him if he would take the house back and was assured that he would. She said Waldo told her that if he took the house back the "slate would be wiped clean." She decided that was the best solution to the problem and had the necessary papers drawn up. She presented the papers to Waldo on April 19 with the assumption that she owed him nothing and he owed her nothing.

Hagerson testified that in late April and again in May she received phone calls from Beth Waldo telling her that her payments on the promissory note were past due and that ABC Construction might be forced to take legal action if Hagerson did not meet her obligations. Hagerson said she told Beth Waldo that she owed the construction company nothing. Hagerson said she had been assured by Robert Waldo when she gave him the papers on April 19 that everything had been resolved.

According to Hagerson, Robert Waldo called her early in May and demanded payment on the promissory note. She told him she had no intention of paying him another cent.

On cross-examination Hagerson was asked if she had gotten legal advice on the contract of sale. She said that she did not feel that she could afford the $50 or so it would have cost her but that she did explain the contract to a second year law student who lived next door to her and felt confident that she understood its terms. On re-direct examination, Hagerson testified that the oral assurances she had received at her meeting with Robert Waldo early in April were what led her to have the papers drawn up to give the house back to him.

The hearing lasted approximately two hours. Under the rules of this jurisdiction's court-annexed arbitration program, Smith had to issue an award within seven days.

Arbitration award. Smith did research on the case and issued her award two days later, finding in favor of ABC Construction Company. She awarded the company $13,328, the amount of the promissory note, plus interest from December 31, 1984 to the date of judgment, plus attorney fees. Smith spent a total of eight and a half hours on the case, including reviewing the files, discussing the case with counsel during the telephone conference, reviewing documents and exhibits, conducting the hearing, researching the issue and drafting the award. Her total fee was $250. She returned $25 each to counsel for ABC and the Hagersons. ABC Construction's attorney fees amounted to $1,071, including a little over seventeen hours of attorney time, secretarial and paralegal assistance, filing, service and arbitration fees. The total award in favor of ABC Construction Company came to $16,279.90.

The Hagersons had twenty days to decide whether to demand a trial *de novo*. Emma Hagerson still felt that she had been misled by Robert Waldo and wanted to take the case to trial. After discussing the matter more with her attorney, she concluded that the time and risks involved in a trial were not worth it. The case would not come to trial for approximately eleven months and her husband was urging her to come to Alaska where they would attempt to make a "fresh start." They discussed by telephone declaring bankruptcy and starting over.

On October 27, after the twenty days for appeal had lapsed, the presiding judge of the circuit court signed an order entering Smith's award as the court's judgment in the case of *ABC Construction Company v. Hagerson.* Entry of the judgment removed the case from the court's docket.

QUESTIONS

1. If you had been counsel for either side would you have objected to this case going to arbitration? Why or why not?

2. If you were counsel for the Hagersons, would you prefer to try this case to a person with legal training or to a jury? Why? Would your response differ if you were counsel for ABC Construction Company? Why?

3. Do you think court-annexed arbitration hearing should be held in lawyers' offices or other private locations? Why or why not?

Endnotes

1 The range is $2,000 in Louisiana to an unlimited amount in tort actions in Michigan. A recent study by the National Center for State Courts, State By State Profiles (1987); Levin & Golash, *Alternative Dispute Resolution in Federal District Courts,* 37 U. Fla. L. Rev. 29, 32-33 (1985).

2 Disputes Processing Research Program, The Costs of Ordinary Litigation 15, 21 (1983).

3 Federal Judicial Center, Evaluation of Court-Annexed Arbitration in Three Federal District Courts 8-21 (1983).

4 Simoni, Wise & Finigan, *Litigant and Attorney Attitudes Toward Court-Annexed Arbitration: An Empirical Study* 39, 45-48 (Willamette University 1988, to be published in Santa Clara L. Rev.)

5 Nejelski & Zeldin, *Court-Annexed Arbitration in Federal Courts: The Philadelphia Story,* 42 Md. L. Rev. 787 (1983).

6 National Center for State Courts, *supra* note 1.

7 Cal. Civ. Pro. Code § 1141.10 (West 1982).

8 Ca. R. Ct. (State) 1600-1617.

9 Walker, *Court-Ordered Arbitration Comes to North Carolina and the Nation,* 21 Wake For. L. Rev. 901, 902 n. 3 (1986); telephone interview with Barbara Myerhoffer, Research Division of the Judicial Center (May 3, 1988).

10 F. R. Civ. P. 39(c), 40, 42.

11 Mich. Comp. Laws Ann. §§ 600.4951-100.4969 (West 1987).

12 Conn. Gen. Stat. Ann. §§ 52-549n-52-549z (West 1988).

13 Wise, Simoni and Finigan, *supra* note 4, at 19-21.

14 National Center for State Courts, *supra* note 1, at 9.

15 Sander, *Alternate Methods of Dispute Resolution: An Overview,* 37 Fla. L. Rev. 1, 14-15 (1985).

16 National Center for State Courts, *supra* note 1, at 6.

Sources

Action Commission to Reduce Costs and Delay, Description of Major Characteristics of the Rules for Selected Court-Annexed Mediation/Arbitration Programs (1983).

Disputes Processing Research Program, The Costs of Ordinary Litigation (1983).

Federal Judicial Center, Evaluation of Court-Annexed Arbitration in Three Federal District Courts (1983).

Hensler, *What We Know and Don't Know About Court Administered Arbitration,* 69 Judicature 270 (1986).

Institute for Civil Justice, Court-Annexed Arbitration: The National Picture (1985).

_____, Introducing Court-Annexed Arbitration: A Policymaker's Guide (1984).

Levin and Golash, *Alternative Dispute Resolution in Federal Courts,* 376 U. Fla. L. Rev. 29 (1985).

National Center for State Courts, State By State Profiles (1987).

Nejelski & Zeldin, *Court-Annexed Arbitration in Federal Courts: The Philadelphia Story,* 42 Md. L. Rev. 787 (1983).

Sander, *Alternate Methods of Dispute Resolution: An Overview,* 37 Fla. L. Rev. 1 (1985).

Simoni, Wise and Finigan, *Litigant and Attorney Attitudes Toward Court-Annexed Arbitration: An Empirical Study* (Willamette University 1988, to be published in Santa Clara L. Rev.)

Walker, "Court-Ordered Arbitration Comes to North Carolina and the Nation," 21 Wake For. L. Rev. 901 (1986).

Kimbrough v. Holiday Inn

478 F. Supp. 566 (1979)

Ditter, District Judge.

In this case, defendants present a challenge to an experimental program instituted by the Department of Justice to test the feasibility of compulsory arbitration in civil suits. Plaintiffs, husband and wife, brought this diversity action seeking damages in an amount less than $50,000 for personal injuries allegedly suffered by the wife during an assault when she was a business visitor at defendants' hotel. Defendants demanded a jury trial as permitted by Fed.R.Civ.P. 38(b). Pursuant to Local Rule 49, however, the case was referred to arbitration. Defendants now move to prohibit arbitration and to vacate the order of referral.

Through the addition of Local Rule 49, this court adopted a compulsory, nonbinding arbitration system on February 1, 1978, for a trial period of one year. It did so as part of a Department of Justice experiment, the express purpose being to test a plan which will "broaden access for the American people to their justice system and to provide mechanisms that will permit the expeditious resolution of disputes at a reasonable cost." Basically, this arbitration system provides that certain types of cases with money damages of $50,000, or less shall be automatically referred to arbitration, an arbitration hearing held in 30 days in most cases, and an award entered. Unless a party demands a trial de novo within 20 days after the entry of the award, the arbitration panel's decision becomes a final, nonappealable judgment. To discourage frivolous appeals, Local Rule 49 imposes upon the party who demands a trial de novo and fails to obtain a more favorable judgment, exclusive of interest and costs, the amount of the arbitration fees and imposes upon the defendant interest on the award from the time it was filed.

Defendants contend that by making arbitration a mandatory prerequisite to jury trial, Local Rule 49 violates the parties [sic] right to a trial by jury, * * * and denies litigants equal protection of the laws.

Defendants first argue that application of Local Rule 49 will violate their right to trial by jury as at common law, a right guaranteed by the Seventh Amendment and by 28 U.S.C. 2072. As early as 1897, the Supreme Court noted that the aim of the Seventh Amendment "is not to preserve mere matters of form and procedure, but substance of right." *Walker v. Southern Pacific Railroad*, 165 U.S. 593, 596 (1897). The high court has consistently held that:

> The command of the Seventh Amendment that 'the right of trial by jury shall be preserved' . . . does not prohibit the introduction of new methods for determining what facts are actually in issue, nor does it prohibit the introduction of new rules of evidence. Changes in these may be made. New devices may be used to adapt the ancient institution to present needs and to make of it an efficient instrument in the administration of justice. Indeed, such changes are essential to the preservation of the right. The limitation imposed by the amendment is merely that enjoyment of the right of trial by jury be not obstructed, and that the ultimate determination of issues of fact by the jury be not interfered with. *Ex parte Peterson* 253 U.S. 300, 309-310. * * *

The leading case upholding the constitutional validity of a compulsory arbitration system is the Pennsylvania Supreme Court's pronouncement in *Smith's Case* 381 Pa. 223 (1955).

In *Smith's Case*, a challenge based on the Pennsylvania Constitution, Article I, § 6, which provides that trial by jury shall be as heretofore, and the right thereof remain inviolate, was brought against a local rule of court authorizing compulsory arbitration pursuant to a Pennsylvania legislative enactment providing for such arbitration in all cases involving claims less than $1000. The court in *Smith's Case* construed the Pennsylvania constitutional mandate of trial by jury to be consistent with the U.S. Supreme Court's interpretation of the Seventh Amendment in *Hof*, and held that "[t]he only purpose of the constitutional provision is to secure the right of trial by jury before rights of person or property are finally determined. All that is required is that the right of appeal for the purpose of presenting the issue to a jury must not be burdened by the imposition of onerous conditions, restrictions or regulations which would make the right practically unavailable." 381 Pa. at 230-31 (emphasis in original). The court also emphasized that the burden imposed on parties by compulsory arbitration was far outweighed by the benefits of a speedy, less expensive, and more efficient trial system. *Id.* at 229-30.

While conceding that court-mandated arbitration is in general constitutional, defendants seize upon the exception noted in *Smith's Case* and claim that Local Rule 49 creates a burdensome, onerous condition to jury trials, i.e., since the arbitration limits are so high, $50,000, there must be a full scale trial at the arbitration level to protect the parties' interests.

Challenges strikingly similar to those presented by the defendants in the instant case were recently rejected by the Pennsylvania Supreme Court in *Parker v. Children's Hospital of Philadelphia*, 483 Pa. 106 (1978). Parker deals with a section of the Pennsylvania Health Care Services Malpractice Act, 40 P.S. § 130l.10l et seq. (Supp. 1979-80), which requires compulsory arbitration prior to jury trial in malpractice cases where health care providers are defendants. In upholding the constitutionality of this provision, the court reaffirmed *Smith's Case* in emphasizing that arbitration as a condition precedent approaches unconstitutional proportions only when substantial restrictions are placed on the right to jury trial. *Parker* rejected defendants' contention that arbitration would penalize appeals since the statute provides for imposition of all costs of both arbitration and trial, including expert witness expenses on the losing party if the court finds that an appeal was arbitrary and capricious. 483 Pa. 106 (1978). In *Parker*, it was also argued that malpractice cases are so complex and expensive to try that an arbitration system which would in effect require two trials is unduly burdensome. This position parallels the defendants' contention in the instant case that claims of $50,000 are so substantial as to necessitate two trials. The Pennsylvania Supreme Court rejected this duplicity argument by pointing out that the assumption of a need for a second trial to obtain a fair result is totally unsupported. 483 Pa. 106 (1978). The purpose of arbitration is to provide a swift, fair, less expensive means of dispute-resolution and every indication is that appeals from arbitration awards should be minimal. Defendants in *Parker* and in the instant case have attempted to show through statistics that present performance of arbitration is unsuccessful. I agree with the *Parker* court's analysis in that deference should be given to the arbitration rule in according a reasonable time period to test the system's effectiveness. 483 Pa. 106 (1978).

The conditions for appeal de novo do not outweigh the benefits of arbitration in providing an efficient alternative for dispute-resolution. The *Parker* court summed up the issue by remarking that:

Where the reason for the postponement of the right results from the effort on the part of the state to achieve a compelling state interest and the procedure is reasonably designed to effectuate the desired objective, it cannot be said that there has been a constitutionally impermissible encroachment upon that right. The acceptance in this jurisdiction of arbitration as a viable, expeditious, alternative method of dispute-resolution is no longer subject to question. . . . Nor does the fact that the arbitration here is compulsory rather than voluntary, detract from its usefulness for this purpose. *Smith's Case*, supra. We are therefore satisfied that the precondition of compulsory arbitration in cases of this type does not present the type of 'onerous' restriction which we referred to in *Smith's Case*. 483 Pa. 106 (1978).

The analysis used in *Parker* to reject Seventh Amendment and due process challenges has been consistently applied by courts to uphold statutes requiring submission of claims to medical malpractice review panels prior to jury trial. * * * [Th]e wealth of case law indicates the growing recognition that arbitration is a useful tool to promote greater efficiency in litigation and that pretrial review in no way infringes upon constitutional rights of litigants.

Furthermore, arbitration provides a valuable service by promoting speedy and inexpensive dispute-resolution. Litigants have the opportunity to test the validity of their claims very shortly after they are filed. Certainly, this limits the time and expense of discovery prior to arbitration. In the normal course of trial without arbitration, voluminous resources can be expended in discovery which is of marginal advantage at trial. The pendency of arbitration forces counsel to focus their attention on the basic elements of the case. Aside from the ultimate award, if arbitration reveals that no claim exists, settlement will become a viable possibility. At the very least, arbitration helps counsel streamline their case and direct their additional discovery in profitable areas.

I conclude that the arbitration system created by Local Rule 49 does not impose conditions so burdensome or so onerous that it interferes with the rights guaranteed by the Seventh Amendment. * * *

In analyzing the arbitration rule in terms of equal protection, defendants generally concede that the government can classify as long as such distinctions are rationally related to a legitimate governmental interest and are not so arbitrary and capricious that persons similarly situated will be treated unequally. *Shapiro v. Thompson*, 394 U.S. 618 (1969).

Defendants argue that Local Rule 49 violates equal protection in several respects: a pilot program inherently treats litigants in this district differently from those in similar districts, the imposition of interest falls only on defendants who appeal from arbitration awards, and the classification of claims for arbitration based on amount in controversy and subject matter jurisdiction are arbitrary and bear no rational relationship to a legitimate governmental interest.

Admittedly, federal arbitration is an experimental program implemented in three districts nationwide. Each program has its own unique characteristics. This means that litigants in three federal districts arbitrate prior to trial while other litigants nationally do not, and that the procedures in each of those three districts vary. However, the allegedly "unequal treatment" in the government's plan has a rational basis far outweighing any possible equal protection violation. The local arbitration rule is a first step to develop a fast, efficient, and inexpensive system of dispute-resolution on a national scale. Reform can proceed one stage at a time. See *Williamson v. Lee Optical Co.*, 348 U.S. 483 (1955). Unfortunately, the price of planned progress may be temporary disparity. Here, such disparity is minimal. Additionally, defendants' equal protection argument based on geographic scope ignores the implicit authorization in Fed.R.Civ.P. 83 for district courts to make local rules which by their very nature will differ among districts.

The second equal protection challenge centers on this interest and cost provision of Local Rule 49(7)(d):

> If the party who demanded a trial de novo fails to obtain a judgment in the district court, exclusive of interest and costs, more favorable to him than the arbitration award, he shall be assessed the amount of the arbitration fees and, if he is a defendant, he shall pay to the plaintiff interest on the arbitration award from the time it was filed, at the current legal rate of interest.

On its face, Local Rule 49 imposes costs on plaintiffs or defendants who appeal from arbitration awards but only taxes interest on defendants who appeal. Generally, cost provisions have been upheld as a valid deterrent for frivolous appeals and as a means to promote swift, efficient dispute-resolution. Similarly, Local Rule 49 implemented a system of costs and interest which rationally discourages meritless appeals. It is logical that taxing interest on defendants can best serve the system. More often than not, a plaintiff who loses an arbitration case will have no financial award from which to appeal. In that situation, allowing--or disallowing interest--is nonsense. Where plaintiff appeals from an award which he regards as inadequate and the second judgment is less than the arbitration award, plaintiff still should not be required to pay interest on the award. Plaintiff will have been penalized by both the lower recovery and the loss of interest which otherwise would have run from the time the arbitration award was entered. Conversely, these reductions will benefit the defendant and help repay the necessary costs of two trials. In contrast, requiring a defendant who loses an appeal from an arbitration award to pay interest is logical because plaintiff was deprived of the use of the money awarded to him while defendant appealed and lost. Since the interest provision of Local Rule 49 is rational it does not offend equal protection requirements.

Finally, defendants allege that the arbitration classification for the amount in controversy and subject matter jurisdiction do not bear a rational relationship to a legitimate governmental interest. They contend that the goals of arbitration promoting speedier administration of justice and efficient use of resources are not necessarily fostered by arbitrating $50,000 claims which mandate extensive preparation for the initial arbitration and frequently are appealed. The Pennsylvania Supreme Court has rejected a similar challenge based on the jurisdictional amount in Smith's Case, 381 Pa. 223 (1955). There, the court commented:

> [i]t is, however, too well established to require extended discussion or citation of authorities that all that the Constitution demands is that the basis for classification be reasonable and founded upon a genuine and not merely artificial distinction, the test being, not wisdom, but good faith in classification. Statutory distinctions based on the amount involved in the litigation have been regularly upheld. *Id.* at 233.

In fact, a jurisdictional limitation of $20 exists on the face of the Seventh Amendment's guarantee of the right to jury trial. Since jurisdictional categories abound throughout civil procedure and are universally upheld as rational, I find no equal protection problem with Local Rule 49's amount in controversy provision.

Defendants further contend that the subject matter categories are not areas necessarily suited to arbitration. Attorney General Griffin Bell's statement demonstrates that the categories were chosen after careful study and analysis:

> The [experimental arbitration bill] sets forth specific categories of cases which would automatically be referred to arbitration before trial. These cases were identified on the basis of three criteria. The first criterion is that the cases involve claims for money damages only. In such cases, often the only dispute is over the amount of money owed by one party to the other. In contrast, pleas for equitable relief would probably mean increased complexity and could require the continuing supervision of the court. Such cases would be inappropriate for arbitration.

> The second criterion is that cases referred to arbitration be limited to those in which the claim does not exceed $50,000. In cases with claims in the hundreds of thousands or millions of dollars, the cost of a subsequent trial and of any disincentives for demanding such a trial are very small, relative to the claim itself. It is our belief, based upon the experience in the states that, where larger amounts are involved in the suit, the likelihood of one litigant or another requesting a trial de novo is greatly increased. In addition, cases involving hundreds of thousands of dollars or more could very well be of such complexity that they would require arbitration proceedings of greater length than the speedy proceedings intended to be produced by the bill. As a result, suits over $50,000 are not mandatorily referred, but the parties to a money damage law-

suit of any amount may consent to arbitration under the procedures set forth in the bill.

> The final criterion is that the cases present predominantly factual issues, rather than complex legal questions, constitutional claims, or novel issues of law which may establish important precedents. These matters are the province of the federal judiciary. With cases involving arbitration, referral under the bill is to occur only after the disposition of pretrial motions, which will allow for the pre-arbitration resolution by the district court judge of many legal issues.

> By applying the foregoing three criteria to the federal civil docket, we have concluded that money damage tort and contract cases are the groups of cases that are most suitable for arbitration.

Statement of Griffin Bell before the Committee on the Judiciary Concerning Arbitration on April 14, 1978.

Although contending that these categories lack a rational basis, defendants offer little support for their assertion and suggest no alternative subject matter areas more suitable for arbitration. Defendants argue that the addition of more federal judges or resources would be the least restrictive means for promoting a fast and efficient trial system. However, there is no assurance that additional resources would remedy the problem, and certainly it would not provide an inexpensive alternative to trial. I conclude that the subject matter categories survive the test of rationality and do not infringe upon the equal protection clause.

In view of the foregoing analysis, I find that Local Rule 49 does not violate the Seventh Amendment or the Equal Protection Clause, nor is it inconsistent with section 2072 of Title 28 and the Federal Rules of Civil Procedure. Defendants' Motion to Prohibit Arbitration must be denied and an arbitration hearing should be scheduled as a matter of course.

QUESTIONS

1. Why did the parties object to court-annexed arbitration in this case? Do you think the real problem is lack of a jury or not wanting their case to be treated as an "experiment"? Given the underlying facts, what advantages would there be to trying the case to a jury? What advantages to trying it to an arbitrator? Might parties and attorneys have different views on this question?

2. Summarize Judge Ditter's argument about why the prerequisite of court-annexed arbitration does not deny the right to a jury trial. Are you persuaded by the argument?

3. Summarize Judge Ditter's argument on the equal protection claim. Do you agree or disagree? Should all litigants subject to a court's jurisdiction be subject to the same procedures?

4. Judge Ditter appears to apply cost-benefit analysis in resolving this case, and appears to conclude that the benefit to the public of court-annexed arbitration outweights the cost, if any, to the parties, of the process. Is this a correct reading of the case? What role should cost-benefit analysis play in the evaluation of alternatives to litigation?

Demirgian v. Superior Court

187 Ca.App.3d 372, 231 Cal.Rptr. 698 (1986)

Johnson, Associate Justice.

Petitioner, Sarkis Demirgian, and his mother, Virginia Demirgian, filed a complaint against Donald Leach, the real party in interest. The complaint alleged petitioner and his mother were injured on November 5, 1983, when their automobile was struck by a vehicle driven by Mr. Leach. On November 14, 1984, petitioner and Mr. Leach settled their case and entered into a settlement contract. Later petitioner was allowed to file a supplemental cause of action alleging Mr. Leach breached this settlement contract.

The superior court ordered both counts to mandatory arbitration. At the arbitration hearing, the arbitrator ruled in favor of petitioner's mother on her personal injury count and ruled in favor of petitioner on his second cause of action for breach of the settlement contract.

Mr. Leach did not file a request for a trial de novo on either Virginia Demirgian's personal injury award or petitioner's breach of settlement contract award. However, Virginia Demirgian requested a trial de novo on her personal injury award.

Petitioner filed a motion for order entering judgment on his arbitration award. Mr. Leach then filed an opposition to petitioner's motion since petitioner's mother had requested a de novo trial. The trial court denied petitioner's motion for order entering judgment on his arbitration award. Petitioner then filed a writ of mandate with this division of the Court of Appeal which we denied.

The California Supreme Court, however, granted Mr. Demirgian's petition for review and ordered us to issue an alternative writ.

The issue before us is whether all parties to a multi-party mandatory arbitration are automatically required to retry their cases in the court even if only one of the parties requests a trial de novo. The decision of the superior court appears to answer this question in the affirmative. Petitioner concedes this general rule may be appropriate where the parties' claims are interdependent. But, he argues, it is not appropriate here because petitioner's claim is distinct from and unaffected by his co-plaintiff's claim. Moreover, to apply the rule here runs counter to the policy reasons behind the Judicial Arbitration Act. We agree.

Any person who has recently participated in our court system or any person even remotely familiar with the judicial process is aware of the ever increasing caseloads facing our courts. In Los Angeles County, for example, a 1982 report concluded it took over three years for a civil case to come to trial. "For justice to be effective, not only must the law be fair, but also the machinery developed to administer the law must dispense justice inexpensively and quickly without sacrificing fairness."

In 1979, the California Legislature enacted the Judicial Arbitration Act. The act was in response to the increasing burden on the California courts and in view of the evident success of similar programs in other states, in particular Pennsylvania and New York. The act requires all civil cases in superior courts with ten or more judges and where the claim by any single party does not exceed $15,000 to be ordered to arbitration. In various counties, including Los Angeles County, the Legislature has required mandatory arbitration for any claim under $25,000.

Cases which fall within the jurisdictional limits of the act can be compelled into arbitration. However, parties who are dissatisfied with the outcome at arbitration are guaranteed their day in court. The Legislature expressly stated that "[a]ny party may elect to have a de novo trial, by court or jury, both as to law and facts." However, the Legislature's statutory language did not consider the question before this court: whether a party to an arbitration award is automatically required to retry his or her case if a co-party requests a trial de novo.

In circumstances where the statutory language is ambiguous or vague "[w]e have a statutory duty to construe each provision of the Code of Civil Procedure liberally and with a view to effect its objects and promote justice.... Wherever possible, potentially conflicting provisions should be reconciled in order to carry out the overriding legislative purpose as gleaned from a reading of the entire act. A construction which makes sense of an apparent inconsistency is to be preferred to one which renders statutory language useless or meaningless.' " "Finally, statutes must be construed in a reasonable and common sense manner consistent with their apparent purpose and the legislative intent underlying them--one practical, rather than technical, and one promoting a wise policy rather than mischief or absurdity." *Herbert Hawkins Realtors, Inc. v. Milheiser,* 140 Cal.App.3d 334, 338 (1983).

Undoubtedly, the Legislature's intent is to discourage trials de novo. "While there is no specific legislative language to that effect, it is apparent that the legislature desired alternative, not cumulative, dispute resolution . . ."

In the instant case, petitioner and his mother had independent claims. They happened to be against the same defendant and to have originated in the same automobile accident. The two plaintiffs in these two actions also happened to have been members of the same family. It is also true the two claims were consolidated in a single proceeding, a step which contributes to judicial economy. They remain different and distinct claims, nevertheless. The same judge, jury, or arbitrator--or different judges, juries, or arbitrators-- could have found petitioner's claim was valid but his mother's not, or vice versa. We believe to involuntarily require petitioner to retry his case, simply because a co-party requested a trial de novo, is inconsistent with the purpose of the arbitration act to "[p]rovide parties with a simplified and economical procedure for obtaining prompt and equitable resolution of their disputes." * * *

Let a pre-emptory writ of mandate issue compelling the respondent superior court to vacate its order of January 23, 1986, in Los Angeles Superior Court case no. C490665 denying petitioner's motion for an order entering judgment in his favor, and thereafter make a new and different order granting said motion.

QUESTIONS

1. If this case went to trial rather than to court-annexed arbitration, can you think of any reasons why the claims should be tried separately? Do those same reasons apply to court-annexed arbitration?

2. Why does Judge Johnson conclude that it is not necessary for all parties to multi-party court-annexed arbitration to retry their cases if only one party demands a trial de novo? What effect would a contrary decision have on party willingness to participate in court-annexed arbitration?

3. Is Leach in any way harmed by the decision in this case? Is Sarkis Demirgian in any way harmed by the decision? Would Sarkis Demirgian have been harmed if the opposite result had been reached? In what respect, if at all, is Judge Johnson concerned with the parties' interests in

arriving at a decision in this case? Would the result have been any different had Leach not breached the original settlement agreement and Sarkis Demirgian had not filed the supplemental cause of action?

Lyons v. Wickhorst

42 Cal.3d 911, 727 P.2d 1019, 321 Cal.Rptr. 738 (1986)

Bird, Chief Justice.

Does a trial court exceed its authority when it dismisses a plaintiff's action with prejudice because no evidence was presented at a court-ordered arbitration?

In June of 1980, appellant Edward Lyons filed a lawsuit against respondent Erwin Wickhorst seeking actual, compensatory, and punitive damages for unlawful arrest and false imprisonment. Since appellant did not seek damages in excess of $25,000, the trial court ordered mandatory arbitration.

The first arbitration hearing was set for November of 1982. Immediately prior to the arbitration, appellant informed the arbitrator and counsel for respondent that he did not intend to present any evidence in support of his case. In response, respondent made no attempt to refute appellant's claims. Thus, no evidence was introduced at the first hearing.

The superior court appointed a new arbitrator and set a new hearing for June of 1983. During this second attempt at arbitration, appellant once again declined to present evidence. Respondents did not attend the hearing after informing the arbitrator that attendance would be futile in light of appellant's refusal to proceed.

Although no evidence was presented during either of the two hearings, the arbitrator entered an award in favor of respondents. On the same day that the award was entered, appellant requested a trial de novo pursuant to section 1141.20. Upon motion by respondent, the court dismissed the action stating that appellant's refusal to offer any evidence at the court-ordered arbitration hearing "border[ed] on contempt," and was a "continuing and willful rejection of the whole arbitration program."

Appellant challenges the authority of the trial court to dismiss his action for failure to participate in the mandatory arbitration procedures.

In dismissing appellant's action, the trial court relied in part on section 581 and the "Rules of Court Ordered Arbitration." Section 581 authorizes dismissal by the court in any of the following situations: (1) neither party appears at the trial following 30 days notice of time and place; (2) a demurrer is sustained without leave to amend; (3) the plaintiff abandons the case prior to final submission, or (4) either party fails to appear and the other party requests dismissal. None of these scenarios occurred in the present case.

Similarly, neither the judicial arbitration statutes nor the rule of judicial arbitration permit [sic] the courts to dismiss an action because of a plaintiff's failure to present evidence at a judicially mandated arbitration proceeding. A separate provision authorizes a trial court to order a party to a judicial arbitration proceeding to pay "any reasonable expenses, including attorney's fees" which the opposing party incurs "as a result of bad-faith actions" or frivolous or delaying tactics in such a proceeding. Thus, the trial court's dismissal of appellant's action was not expressly authorized by statute.

In the absence of express statutory authority, a trial court may, under certain circumstances, invoke its limited, inherent discretionary power to dismiss claims with prejudice. However, this power has in the past been confined to two types of situations: (1) the plaintiff has failed to prosecute diligently or (2) the complaint has been shown to be "fictitious or a sham" such that the plaintiff has no valid cause of action.

The discretion to dismiss an action for lack of prosecution has recently been recodified in section 583.410. Section 583.410 permits the court to dismiss an action for lack of prosecution provided that one of several enumerated conditions has occurred. Generally, the court may not dismiss unless "(1) [s]ervice has not been made within two years after the action is commenced . . . (2) [t]he action is not brought to trial within ... [t]hree years after [it] is commenced . . . [or] (3) [a] new trial is granted and the action is not again brought to trial . . . within two years. . . ." (§ 583.420.)

In those situations in which a dismissal pursuant to the court's discretionary power has been upheld, affirmance has not been without reservation. See, e.g., *Karras v. Western Title Ins. Co.*, 270 Cal. App. 2d 753, 758 (1969). The courts have long recognized a policy favoring a trial on the merits. As the courts of this state have stressed, "[a]lthough a defendant is entitled to the weight of the policy underlying the dismissal statute, which seeks to prevent unreasonable delays in litigation, the policy is less powerful than that which seeks to dispose of litigation on the merits rather than on procedural grounds." *Denham v. Superior Court*, 2 Cal. 3d 557, 566 (1970). In sum, although the discretionary power to dismiss with prejudice has been upheld in this state, its use has been tightly circumscribed. * * *

[T]his court must examine the circumstances under which appellant's motion for a trial de novo was dismissed. The dismissal of appellant's complaint was both without notice and without an opportunity to be heard. At the time of appellant's motion, neither the judicial arbitration statutes, nor the rules of judicial arbitration provided standards to guide the exercise of the court's discretion in granting or denying the motion. * * *

An immediate and unconditional dismissal entered at the first suggestion of noncooperation is too drastic a remedy in light of the fact that arbitration was not intended to supplant traditional trial proceedings, but to expedite the resolution of small civil claims.

We, therefore, reverse the trial court's order dismissing appellant's action and remand for proceedings consistent with this opinion.

Mosk, Broussard and Grodin, J.J., concur.

Bird, Chief Justice, concurring.

In order to secure a majority for today's decision, I have omitted from my opinion any discussion of the implications of the trial court's actions on the constitutional jury trial guarantee. I write separately to express my concern regarding this issue.

Article I, section 16 of the California Constitution gives to all its citizens the inviolate right to

trial by jury. This right has been long protected and cherished in our jurisprudence.

The jury system is an essential part of our courts' ability to safeguard the rule of law in the face of constant challenges to the authority of that fundamental principle. In fact, our reliance on, and confidence in, the institution of the jury is primarily a function of the key role that the jury system plays in protecting our citizens against the unchecked powers of government, and concomitantly in providing a critical counter-balance to the power and persuasiveness of lawyers and judges.

The framers of our federal and state constitutions were "reluctan[t] to entrust plenary powers over the life and liberty of the citizen to one judge or to a group of judges." *Duncan v. Louisiana*, 391 U.S. 145, 156 (1968). The guarantee of a jury trial, therefore, reflects a profound judgment about the way in which law should be enforced and justice administered. On the most general level then, the function of the jury is to safeguard the citizen against the arbitrary exercise of official power. See *Williams v. Florida*, 399 U.S. 78, 87 (1970). * * *

Dismissal of an action for failure to comply with a court order does not always violate the right to a jury trial. The dismissal power is narrowly circumscribed because every litigant must be afforded the opportunity to present his claims before a jury of his peers. Cf. *Dorsey v. Barba*, 38 Cal. 2d 350, 355-356 (1952). The trial court denied appellant that opportunity here. Therefore, we must critically examine the purposes and policies underlying the involuntary dismissal power to determine whether the trial court's action violated appellant's right to a jury trial.

In a civil action, the plaintiff has a duty to comply with court orders and a duty to prosecute his case in a diligent manner. See *Oberkotter v. Spreckels*, 64 Cal. App. 470 (1923). A breach of either duty in most jurisdictions can result in the dismissal of the complaint. As the party seeking relief, the duty to prosecute with diligence and in accordance with court orders rests with the plaintiff. "[N]o affirmative duty to do more than meet the plaintiff step by step is case on the defendant.' " *Knight v. Pacific Gas & Elec. Co.*, 178 Cal. App. 2d 923, 929 (1960).

By seeking to resolve the dispute in a judicial forum, the plaintiff acknowledges the obligations that accompany his request. The plaintiff initiates the proceedings in order to vindicate his rights. In so doing, he or she accepts the responsibility of abiding by rules designed to facilitate the orderly and equitable resolution of the dispute.

The authority of a trial court to dismiss sua sponte for disobedience or lack of prosecution is founded on this conception of the judicial process. The dismissal sanction provides the courts with the power to "manage their own affairs so as to achieve the orderly and expeditious disposition of cases" *Link v. Wabash Railroad Co.,* 370 U.S. 626, 630-631 (1962), and in this way serves "the needs of the court[s] in ... preserving respect for the integrity of [their] internal procedures...." *Moore v. St. Louis Music Supply Co., Inc.* 539 F.2d 1191,1193 (9th Cir. 1976).

Although the practice varies from court to court at both the state and federal levels, involuntary dismissal is most frequently employed where the conduct of the plaintiff demonstrates an unwillingness to participate in the fact-gathering and disclosure process, thereby impeding the determination of the substantive rights of the parties.

In many of these cases, dismissals have been affirmed because the plaintiff exhibits a reluctance to assist in any disclosure of facts or issues or to proceed to the next stage of the litigation process. See, e.g., *Darms v. McCulloch Oil Corp.,* 720 F.2d 490, 495 (8th Cir. 1983) [dismissal affirmed where plaintiffs refused to put on any evidence although two years had elapsed since the denial of class certification].

The sanction of dismissal with prejudice is a quid pro quo for a plaintiff's intransigence. Having exercised his rights to utilize the forum, it is the plaintiff's own dilatory or disobedient conduct in prosecuting a lawsuit that forecloses his opportunity to have his rights determined upon the merits.
* * *

[In this case, however,] Appellant was not only denied the protections normally attendant upon an order of involuntary dismissal, but was precluded from moving the proceedings to the trial court altogether. Appellant's actions did not impede the litigation process. He stood ready to prove his allegations while concomitantly abiding by the rules pertaining to conduct of a jury trial. His action was dismissed with prejudice before he had a chance to present any evidence in court to support his claims. * * *

Moreover, the compulsory arbitration proceeding cannot operate as a substitute for the constitutional guarantee of a jury trial. The current scheme does not embody any of the features of the jury system deemed essential to the political viability of our legal system. Thus, the analogy implicitly accepted by the trial court here between a judicially mandated arbitration proceeding and a court proceeding does not support the drastic foreclosure of rights that an unconditional dismissal represents.

The judicial arbitration statute was enacted as an alternative to the traditional method of dispute resolution with the hope that it might help offset a seemingly ever increasing judicial workload. In responding to the demand for improving the efficient resolution of small civil claims, the Legislature made clear that the procedures employed should be simple, economical, and expedient. The arbitration scheme, however, was not intended entirely to supplant traditional trial proceedings.

As with other court-annexed arbitration systems, the scheme in this state provides for a hearing that is considerably less formal than a trial in a court of law. The arbitrator's powers are expressly limited to nine listed functions. The most important are: (1) to permit testimony to be offered by deposition; (2) to permit evidence to be offered and introduced as provided in the rules; (3) to rule on the admissibility and relevancy of evidence offered; (4) to decide the law and facts of the case and to make an award accordingly; and (5) to award costs, not to exceed the statutory cost of the suit. Cal. Rules of Court, rule 1614(a).

All disputes regarding procedural, evidentiary, or discovery matters beyond the scope of these powers must be brought to the attention of the supervising court. *Ibid.* In addition, the rules of evidence governing civil actions apply only partially to judicial arbitration. The Evidence Code is relaxed in several areas permitting the introduction of certain forms of written testimony and documentary evidence not admissible in court.

Under the present scheme, any person may serve as an arbitrator if selected by the parties. Legal training is not a prerequisite because arbitrators need not conform their decisions to judicial precedent. Furthermore, the arbitrator is not required to make findings of fact or conclusions of law, and no official record of the proceeding need be kept.

These characteristics of the compulsory arbitration scheme provide more than adequate proof that the system was not intended to be a substitute for a judicial determination on the merits in small civil cases. Arbitrators have limited powers and are free to disregard legal precedent. Procedural safeguards required in court proceedings are relaxed considerably in arbitration proceedings.

More significantly, the Legislature unconditionally provided for a trial de novo on demand following arbitration. The Legislature recognized the constitutional problems that could arise if the arbitration hearing were to be construed as a substitute for a judicially supervised trial.

The right to trial by an impartial jury is one of the oldest guarantees in the Constitution. It plays a fundamental role in maintaining our intricate system of governmental checks and balances by safeguarding our citizens against arbitrary or excessive governmental action, reinforcing personal commitment to society through concrete participation in an important governmental function, and permitting the infusion of the common sense judgment of laymen into an often rigid judicial process. Dedication to these concepts demands that the jury system remain a vital part of the American judicial system.

In searching for instant solutions to increasingly complex social and economic problems, various modifications of the legal process have been suggested. The court-annexed arbitration scheme is one of the results of efforts in recent years to streamline court procedures, relieve congestion of court calendars, and reduce expenditures.

Although complexity, congestion, delay, and expense are legitimate concerns, these factors have never justified the sacrifice of fundamental rights. Efforts to expedite and efficiently administer the legal process are commendable. However, our interest in economy and speed must be tempered by the recognition that certain fundamental institutions are so essential to our system of justice that we cannot change them drastically without dramatically altering the foundation of the rule of law and the basic shape of our governmental structure.

Despite its duty to "zealously" preserve the right to jury trial, *Byram v. Superior Court*, 74 Cal. App. 3d 648, 654 (1977), the trial court sacrificed this fundamental right in favor of its concerns with administrative efficiency. These concerns cannot support the drastic remedy of eliminating the long-standing practice of providing jury trials in all legal actions. See *People v. One 1941 Chevrolet Coupe*, 37 Cal. 2d 283, 299 (1951). This right is "so fundamental and sacred to the citizen . . . [that it] should be jealously guarded by the courts." *Jacob v. New York* 315 U.S. 752 (1942).

Penalizing a litigant by dismissing his action for failure to present evidence at a compulsory arbitration proceeding places too high a premium on achieving the goals of expediency and efficiency. An involuntary dismissal may clear the dockets of troublesome cases, but it demonstrates a strikingly indifferent attitude toward the fundamental constitutional right to a trial by jury.

The state's interest in providing a forum for the quick resolution of relatively small civil claims cannot overcome appellant's right to a jury trial. "Trifling economies . . . have not generally been thought sufficient reason for abandoning our great constitutional safeguards aimed at protecting freedom and other basic human rights of incalculable value." *Green v. U.S.*, 356 U.S. 165, 216 (1958) (dis. opn. of Black, J.).

I would therefore hold that the use of involuntary dismissals as a sanction to ensure full participation in judicially mandated arbitration proceedings creates an unconstitutional burden on a litigant's right to a jury trial.

Reynoso, Justice, concurring.

I agree with the majority that dismissal here was too drastic a penalty for appellant's refusal to present evidence at the arbitration proceedings, which took place (1) after *Hebert v. Harn*, 133 Cal.App.3d 165 (1982), had furnished a reasonable basis for assuming that such tactics would not impair appellant's right to a trial de novo and (2) before a contrary possibility had been indicated by the filing of *Genovia v. Cassidy*, 145 Cal. App.3d 452 (1983). Accordingly, I concur in reversing the judgment of dismissal.

On the other hand, since it is clear that the judicial arbitration program was intended by the Legislature to be mandatory, the trial courts should actively support it by taking appropriate measures to encourage or require good-faith participation by litigants. As the majority points out, Code of Civil Procedure section 128.5, empowering trial courts to require payment of reasonable expenses incurred as a result of bad-faith actions or tactics, is made expressly applicable to judicial arbitration proceedings. Section 128.5 provides a means of avoiding the danger that a party will refuse to participate in the judicial arbitration process as a strategic tactic, attempting to assure that the trial court judgment will be more favorable to it than the "default" arbitration award, thus permitting the party to avoid the award-of-costs penalty provided by section 1141.21. If a trial court concludes that a nonparticipating party has pursued such a tactic, it may appropriately award the costs that would have been recoverable under section 1141.21 as an element of the monetary sanctions authorized by section 128.5.

Moreover, subdivision (d) was added to section 1128.5 in 1985 to provide that "[t]he liability imposed by this section is in addition to any other liability imposed by law for acts or omissions within the purview of this section." In light of that subdivision, I agree with Justice Grodin that "in particular situations, additional statutorily-authorized [sic] sanctions may be properly invoked," such as dismissal under section 2034. I would leave open the question whether, in a particularly egregious case, a trial court would have inherent power to dismiss the action.

Lucas and Panneli, J.J., concur.

Grodin, Justice, concurring.

Unlike the Chief Justice, see conc. opn. of Bird, C.J., *ante*, I believe that the Legislature may constitutionally authorize a trial court to dismiss an action if a plaintiff intentionally refuses to participate in a legislatively-established, mandatory judicial arbitration process. Indeed, as a policy matter, it may well be that dismissal is the most appropriate sanction for such conduct.

I have joined the lead opinion, however, because as I read the relevant statutes, the Legislature has to date declined to authorize the denial of a trial de novo and the dismissal of the plaintiff's action as a sanction for such conduct. The provisions of the Judicial Arbitration Act explicitly embrace an alternative sanction, under which a party who requests a trial de novo is required to pay specified costs if the judgment after the trial de novo is not more favorable to such party than the arbitration award. * * *

If experience demonstrates that a dismissal sanction is necessary to make the judicial arbitration process effective, the Legislature, in my view, is free to adopt such a remedy.

QUESTIONS

1. Why does Chief Justice Bird write both a majority and concurring opinion in this case? What insight does this give into the process of judicial decision-making? What are the essential differences between her majority and concurring opinions?

2. Why do you think the trial court dismissed Lyons' case? What interests was the trial court seeking to protect by dismissal? Why did the Supreme Court disagree with the trial court's decisions? To whom is the trial court accountable according to the Supreme Court? Do you think trial courts deserve to have more discretion in these matters? Why or why not?

3. Which opinion do you find most persuasive in this case? Why? Which do you think the trial judge would find most persuasive? Why?

4. What could Lyons' attorney have done to avoid dismissal of his case by the trial court? What devices does a trial court have to respond to or deter sham arbitration proceedings?

Honeywell Protection Services

v.

Tandem Telecommunications, Inc.

131 Misc.2d 814, 495 N.Y.S.2d 130 (Supp. 1985)

Silbermann, Judge.

This is a motion by defendant seeking to vacate plaintiff's demand for a trial *de novo.*

Although counsel for plaintiff appeared at the arbitration hearing, no witnesses or evidence were presented in support of plaintiff's cause of action or in opposition to the defendant's counterclaim. As a result of plaintiff's failure to present evidence an award was made in favor of defendant dismissing plaintiff's cause of action and awarding defendant judgment on its counterclaim.

The Rules governing Compulsory Arbitration provide that a trial *de novo* may be demanded by any party not in default. The appearance by an attorney at the hearing does not excuse a default by a party in presenting evidence and proceeding with the hearing. An attorney cannot sit by, listen to his [adversary's] proof and demand a trial *de novo* as a result of the failure to affirmatively participate.

The plaintiff herein, in effect, defaulted in proceeding to trial even though it appeared at the hearing by an attorney. The Arbitrator noted an appearance of plaintiff's counsel but no appearance by the client.

Plaintiff's counsel contends that "there is no requirement that he must produce a witness at arbitration and a party may prove a claim or a defense by utilizing documents in its possession [sic] and using the other party's witnesses." Indeed this would be true if the court were to believe that plaintiff had no witnesses or evidence to produce and had in fact presented its entire case before the arbitration panel. In such a case a plaintiff would not be in default and could demand a trial *de novo.*

However, this court having been presented with two motions in separate cases on the same day wherein this same law firm proceeded in almost an identical manner before the arbitration panel has come to the conclusion that this is a ploy to circumvent mandatory arbitration.

Mandatory arbitration for cases in which the *ad damnum* clause is under $6,000 has been successful in alleviating calendar congestion of the Civil Court. If permitted to succeed such a ruse would create a loophole which would completely undermine compulsory arbitration and incidentally waste the time of the arbitrators and the adverse parties. To permit an attorney to appear at a hearing, not present any evidence and then be free to demand a trial *de novo,* would circumvent the statute providing for compulsory arbitration and render such law a nullity thereby defeating the intent of the arbitration procedure.

This practice should most probably be looked at by the legislature with a view towards closing this loophole. However this court is constrained to act. This loophole allows a party to use compulsory arbitration as a forum for free discovery and not for the purpose it was established to resolve disputes and relieve court congestion. [Sic.]

Accordingly, defendant's motion is denied on condition that plaintiff serve and file an affidavit with the court within five days after service of a copy of this order with notice of entry stating that it will present no evidence or witnesses at trial not already produced at the hearing. In the event plaintiff fails to file such an affidavit the motion is granted.

Plaintiff may if it so elects, move to vacate its default and have this case restored to the arbitration calendar.

QUESTIONS

1. What might have motivated counsel for plaintiff in this case to fail to present evidence at the arbitration hearing? Do you see a conflict between the court's interest in clearing dockets and counsel's duty of zealous advocacy?

2. Who is benefited by the decision in this case? Who, if anyone, is harmed? Why does the court give plaintiff's counsel another chance to avoid a default judgment when there is evidence that counsel's law firm had a practice of not participating in court-annexed arbitration?

3. Does this opinion resolve the issue of consequences for failure to participate in court-annexed arbitration in New York?

Valot v. Allcity Insurance Co.

131 Misc.2d 814, 501 N.Y.S.2d 597 (1986)

William Ritholtz, Judge:

Where a defendant at a compulsory arbitration hearing appears only by its attorney, does defendant's non-appearance constitute a default, thereby depriving it of the right to a trial de novo?

This is a motion to vacate defendant's demand for a trial de novo. Correspondingly, defendant cross-moves for said trial de novo. Plaintiff commenced this action to recover damages due to defendant's alleged breach of an insurance contract to pay for a loss by theft of plaintiff's automobile.

Pursuant to [civil court rules] any party not in default may, within thirty days after the award is filed, demand a trial de novo. A party's right to a trial de novo is, therefore, dependent upon what constitutes a default.

Plaintiff claims that defendant, in effect, defaulted at the arbitration hearing in that defense counsel merely sat by and listened to plaintiff's proof and introduced no evidence. No employee of defendant insurance company was present. In support, plaintiff cites the case of *Honeywell Protection Services v. Tandem Telecommunications, Inc.*, 130 Misc.2d 130 (1985). In Honeywell, the Court held that the appearance by an attorney at the hearing does not excuse a default by a party in presenting evidence and proceeding with the hearing. The Court reasoned that to permit an attorney to appear, not present any evidence and still reserve all rights to a trial de novo, would "circumvent the statute providing for compulsory arbitration and render such law a nullity thereby defeating the intent of the arbitration procedure." *Honeywell Protection Services v. Tandem Telecommunications, Inc.*, supra at 131.

Contrary to plaintiff's belief, however, the *Honeywell* case is not directly on point with the case at bar. *Honeywell* involved a plaintiff's attorney who failed to present any witnesses. A plaintiff bears the initial burden of proving and going forward with his claim. This duty applies to arbitration hearings as well as to trials. It necessarily follows, then, that a plaintiff who appears by his attorney only and neglects to present any evidence has clearly failed to meet the burden imposed upon him. To sanction the granting of a trial de novo to a plaintiff who makes no attempt to prove his prima facie case would render the arbitration process a sham. Under such circumstances, this Court agrees that "such a ruse would create a loophole which would completely undermine compulsory arbitration and incidentally waste the time of the arbitrators and the adverse parties." *Id.* Plaintiff's non-appearance, therefore, would be considered a default. A trial de novo would be available to him only after the case is restored to the arbitration calendar provided good cause is shown, and plaintiff then appears at the subsequent hearing.

In the instant case, it was the defendant's attorney who presented no witnesses. A defendant, on the other hand, is under no obligation to produce witnesses or any other evidence in defending claims against him. If there is no such obligation at trial, the right to which is a constitutional guarantee, then a more exacting standard may not be enforced at an arbitration proceeding. On the contrary, the arbitration rules, in particular the procedure governing trial de novo, should not be interpreted too narrowly since the compulsory arbitration program initially deprives the parties of their right to a jury trial. *Bayer v. Ras*, 71 Misc.2d 464, 465, 468 (1972). Evidence of the intent to liberally construe the procedure for trial de novo derives from the legislative history of the arbitration rules. Under the older rule, a demand for a trial *de novo* required an affidavit setting forth "substantial grounds" for such demand. The rule was then amended to require merely that the affidavit set forth "grounds" for the demand. *Id.* at 466. Under the current rule, filing a demand for the trial *de novo* is merely a procedural device for getting the case onto the calendar for a new trial. *Id.* It is not an issue subject to the discretion of the Court, but rather a procedure akin to filing a notice of trial, a means of assuring the right to trial. *Stanton v. Lumbermen's Mutual Casualty Co.*, 106 Misc.2d 442 (1980). The mechanism must be a simple one whereby a disappointed litigant may exercise his right to a jury trial. Without such recourse to a jury trial, the rules of the mandatory arbitration would be ineffective. *Bayer v. Ras, supra* at 467. "One reason the program has worked so well is that both litigants and lawyers are assured of a trial *de novo*, with or without a jury, if they are unhappy with the arbitration results." *Id.* at 466.

In this light, it would be incongruent in this case to narrowly interpret the arbitration rules to deny defendant its right to trial *de novo* based on a question of a technical default. Although it did not appear by an officer or other employee, defendant was represented by its attorney who appeared and actively participated in the hearing by cross-examining plaintiff's witness. This was not an instance, for example, where counsel's sole purpose in appearing was merely to request an adjournment without any semblance of participation in the hearing. *See First National Bank and Trust Co. of Ellenville v. Classic Collateral Corp.*, 44 A.D.2d 868 (1974). It is wholly defendant's prerogative to present its defense without calling its own witnesses. Such appearance does not constitute a default nor a willful subverting of the arbitration process as plaintiff alleges.

Therefore, plaintiff's motion to vacate defendant's demand for trial *de novo* is denied, and defendant's cross-motion for an order setting this matter down for a trial *de novo* is granted.

QUESTIONS

1. How does the court distinguish this case from *Honeywell*? If the purpose of court-annexed arbitration is to clear dockets, why should it make a difference whether it is plaintiff or defendant who fails to put on evidence at an arbitration hearing and then demands a trial *de novo*? Would the result have been different if defendant had cross-claimed against plaintiff? Why?

2. Does the decision in this case mean that defendants have more strategic opportunities in court-annexed arbitration than plaintiffs have? What opportunities, if any, does this decision create for the New York legislature?

New England Merchants National Bank v. Hughes

556 F. Supp. 712 (E.D. Pa.1983)

Raymond J. Broderick, District Judge.

In this diversity action, plaintiff New England Merchants National Bank (the "Bank") has brought suit against defendant Katy E. Hughes ("Hughes") averring that Hughes is liable to the Bank as guarantor of a Bank loan to Wheels for

the Handicapped, Inc. ("Wheels, Inc."), a company which she began and served as president. Pursuant to Local Rule 8 of this Court, the case was arbitrated before a panel of three arbitrators. It is undisputed that the defendant received notice of the arbitration hearing and that neither the defendant, nor her counsel, nor any witnesses on her behalf appeared at the arbitration hearing. Defendant has offered no excuse for her failure to appear. At a conference in chambers subsequent to the arbitration hearing, counsel for the defendant simply stated that the defendant had declined to participate in the arbitration hearing. Plaintiff did appear at the arbitration hearing and presented evidence and was awarded $31,963.16 by the arbitrators. After the entry of the arbitrators' award, defendant demanded a trial de novo within the 20-day period provided for by Local Rule of Civil Procedure 8. Plaintiff has now moved for summary judgment in its favor on the ground that defendant's wilful failure to attend the arbitration hearing precludes defendant's right to a trial de novo and also on the ground that the undisputed facts of this case imposed upon defendant Hughes the legal duty to pay the Bank the balance of the loan to Wheels, Inc., plus interest. For the reasons hereinafter set forth, the Court will grant plaintiff's motion and enter judgment against the defendant.

The material facts as to which there is no genuine issue are as follows. On March 5, 1981, defendant Hughes, on behalf of her corporation, Wheels, Inc., entered into a loan agreement with the Bank. The principal amount of the loan was $25,000; interest was to be paid at the rate of 19% per annum. Also on March 5, 1981, defendant Hughes, acting in her personal capacity, signed a Guaranty agreement with the Bank. The Guaranty expressly states that Hughes will indemnify the Bank for any losses incurred arising out of the Bank's loan to Wheels, Inc. Wheels, Inc., defaulted on the loan by failing to make timely payment of principal and interest to the Bank, as provided for in the loan agreement. Upon demand by the Bank, defendant Hughes failed to make the loan payments due and owing under the terms of the loan agreement and her Guaranty. Today, the outstanding principal balance of the loan is $23,050.00. As of September 2, 1982, $5,651.01 in interest had accrued on the loan. Unable to obtain payments from Hughes pursuant to the Guaranty, the Bank commenced this action on March 15, 1982. Jurisdiction is founded on diversity of citizenship pursuant to 28 U.S.C. § 1332, since the Bank is a Massachusetts citizen and Ms. Hughes is a Pennsylvania citizen. * * *

In this case, the defendant had notice of the arbitration hearing, its date, time, and location. Defendant never requested a continuance but simply declined to participate in the arbitration.

Under these circumstances, the defendant, by failing to follow this Court's Order of July 12, 1982 and the procedures of Local Rule 8, is precluded from demanding a trial de novo. Under these circumstances, the proper course of action by the plaintiff would have been to file a motion to strike defendant's demand for trial de novo. Instead, plaintiff addressed defendant's failure to participate in the arbitration hearing as one of two alternative grounds for summary judgment. As heretofore pointed out, the plaintiff's affidavit in support of its second ground for summary judgment, which has not been contradicted, establishes that there is no genuine issue of material fact and that plaintiff is entitled to judgment as a matter of law. It would therefore appear that defendant lacked a defense of this action. * * *

In its summary judgment motion, plaintiff notes that the deposition of the defendant sets forth the uncontradicted fact that she signed an unconditional guaranty which obligates her to indemnify the Bank should Wheels, Inc., fail to fulfill the terms of the loan agreement between Wheels, Inc., and the Bank. It is also undisputed that Wheels, Inc., ceased making payments and that the Bank made timely demand upon defendant Hughes to fulfill the express terms of the guaranty that she signed. Equally undisputed is the fact that defendant Hughes has not fulfilled her obligations to the Bank pursuant to the Guaranty.

In view of the fact that the record shows that there are no genuine issues of material fact, the plaintiff is entitled to summary judgment in the amount of the principal balance due on the obligation in the amount of $23,059.00 plus interest in the agreed amount of 19% per annum, which interest totals $7,732.74 plus a reasonable attorney's fee in the amount of $3,734.15, said amount being uncontested by the defendant.

Both Massachusetts law and Pennsylvania law, the only two bodies of law that could be applicable to this case, *see CBS, Inc. v. Film Corp. of America*, 545 F. Supp. 1382, 1385-87 (E.D.-Pa.1982), provide that a guaranty creates an enforceable contractual obligation against the guarantor (Hughes). The guaranteed party (the Bank) need not first sue the debtor (Wheels, Inc.) but may bring suit directly against the guarantor (Hughes). *See Downer v. United States Fidelity & Guaranty Co. of Maryland*, 46 F.2d 733 (3d Cir. 1931). Furthermore, the express terms of the Guaranty provide that "the rights and obligations of the parties hereto shall be governed, construed and interpreted according to the laws of the Commonwealth of Massachusetts" and that the liability of the guarantor (Hughes) "is direct and unconditional and may be enforced without requiring . . . resort to any other right, remedy, or security . . . ." An appropriate Order will be accordingly entered.

QUESTIONS

1. How do you account for the difference in result between this case and *Valot*? Under what set of facts might the result in the two cases have been the same? Why?

2. What is the relevance to this case, if any, of the fact that court-annexed arbitration in federal courts occurs by local court rule while court-annexed arbitration in state courts occurs as a result of legislative enactment?

5 NEGOTIATION

The term "negotiation" is derived from the Latin word for "carrying on business." As a dispute resolution method, negotiation is both the oldest and most commonly used technique. It can be defined narrowly as bargaining, conferring, or discussing the terms of a potential agreement between disputants or their representatives. It also is a communication process and a psychological confrontation. Negotiation is as varied as the individuals involved and as complex as human nature.

Negotiation conducted for the purpose of resolving a dispute must be distinguished from negotiation intended to put together a business deal. If parties negotiate to impasse over the price of a car, for example, no one will step in and force the buyer to buy or the seller to sell. If parties negotiate to impasse over a contract dispute, however, they may be forced to another forum, such as litigation or arbitration, where a third party can issue an order compelling an outcome. Dispute resolution negotiation, unlike other forms of negotiation, always is conducted in the shadow of adjudicatory processes that can be resorted to if negotiations fail.[1]

It also is important to distinguish negotiation from other major dispute resolution processes. Negotiation is informal, totally controlled by the parties or their representatives, unlike litigation and arbitration, which are governed by established rules. Negotiation follows no specified form. There are no required procedures or approaches. Negotiation occurs only if the parties agree to it; no party can compel another to participate. The parties control the outcome of negotiation. No neutral decision-maker hears evidence and renders a decision. Parties or their representatives must communicate directly or indirectly with one another. In addition to achieving an adequately satisfactory outcome, negotiators must persuade one another that a negotiated settlement over which they have total control is preferable to an uncertain outcome issued by a judge, jury or arbitrator.

The lack of participation by a neutral third party also distinguishes negotiation from mediation. Participants in negotiation must resolve all problems--substantive, communicative, stylistic--themselves. No one attempts to facilitate the process for them.

These differences between negotiation and other dispute resolution processes emphasize that negotiation is an interdependent process. Participants are decision-makers as well as advocates. Mutual persuasion is required to reach settlement. If a party refuses to participate or settle, negotiation ends and some other dispute resolution process must be invoked. Perhaps the interdependence of the parties in negotiation helps to explain why in negotiation so much attention is given to personal negotiating styles.[2]

A final characteristic of negotiation as a dispute resolution technique is that it is almost always attempted first in resolving a dispute and frequently occurs in tandem with other dispute resolution processes. An aggrieved party in a slander action, for example, may have failed at initial settlement negotiations and filed suit, yet will return to negotiations as the case progresses to trial. Negotiated settlements can occur at any point, even at the appellate stage of litigation. A defendant who prevailed at trial, for example, might be willing to settle with the plaintiff to avoid the possibility of an adverse judgment by appellate judges, or to avoid having to exhaust the appellate process before gaining any of the damages awarded at trial.

Background of Negotiation

The history of negotiation as a dispute resolution technique is as old as the history of humankind. People always have negotiated with one another to resolve disputes, be they personal or international in scope. Thucydides, for example, provided several examples of efforts of Sparta and Athens to negotiate settlements to the Peloponnesian Wars, 424-411 B.C.[3] Recent history is replete with successful and failed efforts to negotiate settlements in contexts including lawsuits, racial conflicts, employment discrimination claims and international border disputes.

The Judeo-Christian tradition and English common law consistently have supported settling civil disputes through negotiation. References in both the old and the new testaments of the Bible urge parties to attempt reconciliation with an adversary as a first, if not only, course of action.[4] Several early American religious communities carried this philosophy to the point of excluding members who insisted on litigating their differences rather than resolving them themselves.[5]

The common law has supported negotiated resolutions in several ways. First, the common law is bound by precedent. Precedent informs parties of the likely outcome if a case were decided by a court. By providing disputants with examples of what courts have regarded as appropriate outcomes in the past, it announces a norm for resolving present disagreements. Second, filing a case with a court compels parties to confront the dispute; the possibility of settlement increases once parties realize that if they do not settle their dispute, the court will. Third, under the common law's reliance on the adversary system parties retain the power to resolve disputes at any step in the litigation process. If parties settle, courts remove their cases from the dockets.

While negotiated settlements in civil cases enjoy a long history and widespread support, negotiation in the criminal law area has struggled to overcome opposition. Plea bargaining, as it generally is called, consists essentially of self-conviction by confession in return for leniency in punishment.[6] Initial opposition to plea bargaining focused on the confession.

English common law and early American decisions held that confessions resulting from plea bargains were not voluntary, and hence should not be accepted. The argument was that a promise of leniency extended by a person in authority as an inducement to plead guilty rendered confessions involuntary.[7]

After the Civil War, a change began to appear in American cases involving plea bargaining. Appellate courts began to draw distinctions between confessions given in court and those made out of court. Defendants fully advised of their rights were allowed to enter confessions in court. Assurance that defendants understood their rights was seen as adequate protection against the bargaining power of the state and its offer of leniency. By the 1920s, guilty pleas had become the dominant method of securing convictions in major American cities.[8]

The main argument supporting the use of plea bargaining in criminal cases is its efficiency: Why require the state to go to considerable expense, and frequently considerable emotional trauma for victims, when defendants are willing to admit to the commission of crimes? Likewise, why prevent the prosecution from ensuring a conviction for some offense when faced with facts that may not justify the original charge? The prosecutor remains responsible for advocating that the punishment be appropriate to the offense.[9]

Acceptance of plea bargaining has not been universal. Opponents of plea bargaining argue that it denies defendants the procedural fairness of forcing the state to prove cases. In situations where the state may have difficulty proving a case, attractive plea bargains may be offered to defendants, thus offering too lenient punishment to the guilty and too tempting punishments to the innocent who fear risking trial. Additionally, opponents argue, society has an interest in rational and appropriate sentences. Bargains may undermine that interest.[10]

How Negotiation Works

Dispute resolution negotiation is as varied as the parties who attempt it. Most negotiations, however, follow a common pattern: orientation, information exchange or argument, crisis, and settlement or breakdown.[11] This pattern and two of its major influences, the substantive and personal styles of the negotiators, provide an overview of how the process works.

Orientation is the first phase of negotiation. It includes all interactions, from personal contacts to letter or telephone exchanges, that occur prior to substantive discussions. Sometimes a lawsuit has been filed prior to initiating contact; frequently, however, negotiation preceeds filing. Orientation sets the initial tone of the subsequent interaction. Parties form impressions as to the other side's candor, style, intentions, and abilities, and prepare to negotiate consistent with those impressions.

Information exchange or argument is the body of the process. Whether the parties exchange information or argue with one another depends on the styles of the negotiators. This stage generally is delineated from the orientation stage by a shift in conversation from procedural matters and small talk to the substantive needs, desires, or positions of the parties. This stage can be completed in a single session or continue for months, depending on the parties and the issues.

The third stage of the process is more a point than a stage. Crisis, or turning point, is brought on most frequently by an approaching time deadline, such as the running of the statute of limitations, a trial date, or a date for an arbitration hearing. The intensity of negotiations tends to increase as deadlines approach. Crisis also may occur because one party concludes the other is not negotiating in good faith, or because a party grows frustrated with the failure to agree. Folklore holds that 90 percent of negotiations occur in the last 10 percent of available time.[12] So many lawsuits have settled on courthouse steps or in courthouse halls on the day of trial, that the term "courthouse settlement" has come into general use to describe last minute agreements. In one of the few studies on timing of settlements, data revealed that 32 percent of the criminal cases settled the day of trial, while another 36 percent of those cases settled from two to twenty days before trial. In the personal injury field, only 2.5 percent of cases settled the day of trial, but

42.5 percent settled between two and ten days of trial. A similar pattern was found to exist in commercial cases.[13]

A breakdown of negotiations or a settlement is the final phase of the process. Temporary breakdowns suspend direct bargaining between parties, but allow them to return to some earlier stage of the process. Final breakdown, a steadfast refusal to re-enter bargaining, returns each side to unilateral options for dealing with a conflict, including invoking other dispute resolution processes. If settlement is reached, this final phase allows negotiators to agree on details and to formalize their agreement.

The manner in which negotiations are conducted in the different phases is determined by the substantive and personal bargaining styles of the negotiators. Substantive bargaining styles may be distributive or collaborative, terms describing the approaches taken to issues at the heart of the dispute. Personal style, on the other hand, may be competitive or cooperative, terms describing the philosophies of the negotiators.[14]

Distributive bargaining may be characterized as issue oriented. It attempts to divide a fixed amount of resources between the parties to the negotiation. If the resource is money, for example, every dollar obtained by plaintiff in settlement is a dollar lost by defendant. Distributive bargaining offers no opportunity for mutual gain since the sum of one party's losses and the other party's gain will be zero. Distributive negotiations are characterized by a focus on what a party would be willing to give or take to settle a dispute. In a breach of contract case, for example, defendant might be willing to admit liability for the purpose of negotiating how much money should be paid to plaintiff to compensate for the breach. The parties would express their positions in monetary terms, with explanations designed to gain concessions from the other side.

Collaborative, or integrative, negotiation focuses on the motivations or interests behind positions taken in negotiations. The premise of collaborative negotiation is that parties bargain over issues as a means of satisfying underlying interests. While issues are specific, quantifiable expressions, interests are more abstract motivators.[15] In a personal injury action, for example, plaintiff might be seeking a specific amount of money damages from defendant. The issue would be how much money the parties would agree on to settle their dispute. Plaintiff's underlying interests, by contrast, might include fear of not being able to meet house payments and other monthly expenses because of the injury. A collaborative approach would attempt to determine why plaintiff sought the specific sum. Collaborative negotiation would seek other ways to satisfy plaintiff's interests. An annuity, for example, might allow defendant to pay fewer total dollars in settlement, yet allow plaintiff to meet the worrisome monthly expenses.

The personal approach adopted by negotiators--competitive or cooperative--affects the communication between the parties, their perceptions of each other and the process, and their stratgies and tactics. Neogotiators' styles will largely determine the type of relationship that develops between them and their ability to negotiate successfully with one another.

Communication is a good indication of personal bargaining style. Cooperative communication tends to be open, with relevant information shared freely. Competitive communication is guarded, with little information exchanged.

Cooperative and competitive negotiators typically perceive the negotiation process differently. Cooperative negotiators tend to have friendly, trusting attitudes and to view the process as necessary in order to solve a problem. They view the other side as an equal, also seeking a solution to a problem. Competitive negotiators tend to have hostile, threatening attitudes, and to view the process as an undesirable obstacle to a favorable settlement. They view the other side with suspicion and distrust.

The goals of cooperative and competitive negotiators also frequently are different. Cooperative negotiators seek to find a mutually satisfactory outcome, while competitive negotiators seek only the greatest gain possible for themselves or their clients.

Research shows that both cooperative and competitive neogtiators range from poor to excellent at achieving results.[16] Research also supports the theory that negotiators cannot adopt negotiating styles any more easily than they can take on new personalities. The best negotiators seek to perfect the style that is natural for them.

Burdens of Persuasion in Negotiation

Unlike litigation, negotiation does not assign a burden of persuasion. The burden of persuasion is met at the point where both parties are willing to forego the possibility of getting more, or giving less, for the certainty of what is offered. It is a question of individual satisfaction. Both parties must be adequately satisfied with the bargain or each will withhold voluntary acceptance. Consequently, each party establishes a subjective burden of persuasion.

Each individual's subjective needs are different. The emotional, psychological, and financial costs of carrying on a dispute influences a party's perception of settlement offers, as does the desirability of continuing the dispute. Parties may change their criteria for settlement at any moment.

The Role of the Lawyer in Negotiation

Lawyers generally play two roles in dispute resolution negotiation. First, as experts in the law, they advise clients. Clients look to them to evaluate the merits of a claim or defense, as well as to advise on how best to achieve the client's objectives. Second, they frequently are negotiators. They conduct the interactions with other parties (or their representatives), evaluate the information, and modify their recommendations to their client as appropriate.

As an expert on the law, the lawyer is charged with drawing important legal conclusions about a dispute. What law governs? What evidence would be admissible if the case were to go to arbitration or litigation? Based on the admissible evidence, what is the likelihood that specific elements of claims and defenses could be established to the required level of certainty? Answers to such questions contribute to the prognosis of what would likely occur if the dispute were submitted to a neutral third party for decision.

A lawyer's prediction of the outcome under an adjudicatory process also helps to establish the settlement value of a dispute. In personal injury litigation, for example, there usually are two questions at issue: liability (whether defendant was responsible), and damages (the amount due to plaintiff as a result of liability). Attorneys who specialize in personal injury cases use a variety of methods for predicting the probable result of a trial. One such formula recommends evaluating cases by assigning points to several factors. The factors and the number of points possible are: How easy it will be to prove liability (50 points); the severity of plaintiff's injuries (10 points); the likability and believability of plaintiff (10 points); the subjective impression made by defendant (10 points); plaintiff's out-of-pocket expenses for the injury (10 points); and age of plaintiff (10 points).[17] The attorney determines from previous similar cases in that jurisdiction the probable jury verdict if the case were won at trial. That probable verdict, divided by the total number of points assigned, becomes the suggested settlement value.

Recall, for example, the case of Sara Goings, discussed in the chapter on litigation. The primary problem in that case was Goings' inability to establish Dollar Department Store's liability under her state's law. In her favor were the facts that her injuries were severe, that she would make an excellent witness, and that she had expended a substantial amount of money on medical expenses and would have to spend more. Dollar Department Store was a cold, impersonal corporation. Goings' advanced age, however, would be likely to lower the amount of damages awarded her. Juries in her jurisdiction had awarded from $40,000 to $70,000 to plaintiffs who had suffered similar injuries. Using the settlement equation described above, her attorney might have awarded the following points and reached the following conclusion:

	Possible Points	Points Awarded
Liability	50	5
Severity	10	8
Likability of Plaintiff	10	10
Impression of Defendant	10	8
Expenses Paid	10	8
Age of Plaintiff	10	4
	100	43
Average Verdict	$55,000	
Points Awarded	X .43	
Settlement Value of Case	=$23,650	

The importance of these predictions of outcome is based on the concept that dispute resolution negotiation occurs with an alternative adjudicatory process available if resolution eludes the parties. Parties remain free to accept or reject proposed settlements, but the uncertainty of what will occur if the dispute is resolved by adjudication weighs heavily in their decision-making. Prior determinations by local courts and arbitrators in similar situations assume the status of fair market values as parties weigh their alternatives. Thus, a divorcing couple should know about the local courts' practices on permanent alimony in the dissolution of long term marriages. An accused criminal should compare the offer in a plea bargain against the type of sentence a defendant with a similar background convicted of a similar crime received in that jurisdiction. Clients look to attorneys for information and advice to make these comparisons.

Another responsibility of counsel during negotiations is to conduct the negotiations in such a manner as to protect the client. A major dilemma in negotiation is deciding what information to share with the other party. In a dispute alleging breach of contract, for example, assume that plaintiff seeks $15,000, and that defendant has responded with a settlement offer of $5,000. Plaintiff's minimum acceptable settlement is $9,000. Plaintiff's lawyer would have to convince defendant's lawyer that it is in defendant's best interest to settle this case for more than $5,000. To help make the argument, the lawyer could disclose the measure of plaintiff's damages, lost profits, and replacement costs suffered as a result of the alleged breach with no fear of giving up any tactical advantage. If plaintiff's lawyer shared information that could be used to prove breach, however, defendant's lawyer would have an opportunity to prepare to rebut that evidence. Plaintiff's lawyer faces the dilemma of persuading without risking compromise or making the ultimate case more difficult to prove.

An attorney's procedural recommendations also must include a determination of which dispute resolution process will best serve a client's interest should efforts at a negotiated settlement fail. Disputes involving a relationship that is likely to survive the resolution of the dispute, for example, should be processed through a resolution system that will respect the relationship. An attorney representing a party in a divorce action confronted by a breakdown in substantive negotiations, therefore, might attempt to negotiate the terms of a process for resolving the dispute that could keep it from proceeding to litigation.

Finally, the role of the lawyer in negotiation should be considered in light of the litigation system. Litigation forces attorneys into distributive, competitive postures. Pleading requirements, for example, compel attorneys to enumerate specific issues and to state the exact relief sought. Litigation also compels competitiveness as parties are charged with demonstrating why their contentions are correct and the other side's contentions are incorrect. The adversary nature inherent in litigation must be overcome or temporarily suspended if parties choose to deal cooperatively or collaboratively.

Example of Plea Negotiation

Erika Yamashita practices law in a community without a public defender's office. Attorneys are appointed to represent indigent people charged with crimes potentially punishable by a jail sentence. The state pays the attorney, then looks to the defendant later for reimbursement. Attorneys willing to accept these appointments have their names on a list, and are appointed on a rotating basis.

Yamashita was appointed to represent Michael Benson, charged with robbery in the second degree. The statutes in Yamashita's jurisdiction distinguish among three degrees of robbery. Robbery I is the intentional taking of property from a person with force or while armed with a deadly weapon. Robbery II is the same taking, but done by simulating that one is armed with a deadly weapon, or using a "fake" or unloaded weapon. Robbery III is the same taking accomplished by using threats of immediate use of physical force.

Yamashita conducted her first interview with Benson immediately after notification of her appointment. At that time her only knowledge of the crime came from the formal charging instrument that read, ". . . Michael Benson did on the 10th of June, 1986, commit Robbery in the Second Degree by taking money from the cash register at Arco Stop & Gas by simulating the use of a weapon to prevent resistance...."

She learned that Benson was a 25-year-old citizen of another state. He had been working as a tree planter for a local contractor. When he worked, he would be in the mountains for two or three weeks at a time. When he was in town, he stayed at one of two or three houses in the community where he could rent space on the floor for $5.00 a night.

Benson had been in the community for about eight months at the time of his arrest. He had been arrested twice before on shoplifting charges. The most recent was one month before the alleged robbery. He admitted he had taken a 12-pack of beer from a local grocery store and was caught outside. He had been released immediately after the incident and given a court date that had not yet arrived.

The other charge was for taking a pair of jeans from a local department store; that charge had a court date that had just passed. He did not show up for the court date. In Yamashita's jurisdiction that exposed Benson to another misdemeanor charge, Failure to Appear in the Second Degree, a charge that had not yet been filed against him.

Benson claimed to have no convictions. His record showed only the two arrests. He now was being held without bond in the local county jail because the local release authorities had a policy against releasing a person who had failed to appear on a previous charge unless a significant cash bond were posted.

Benson claimed that he had not robbed anyone. He said that he went to the Arco station the morning of June 10 and bought $3.00 worth of gas. Nothing unusual happened at the gas station; he left after paying.

Approximately 20 minutes later he was pulled over on the interstate highway by two squad cars and an officer in plain clothes in an unmarked car. He was ordered out, handcuffed, and ordered to lie on the pavement while the police searched his car. He claimed he was told he was a suspect in a robbery, but he denied any involvement with it.

Yamashita explained the likely sequence of legal events to Benson, and answered his questions about the criminal system. She advised him she would return to talk with him when she had learned more about the case.

Police reports told Yamashita a different story. The statement from the gas station attendant was that he had been working alone on the morning that Benson drove into the station. He waited on Benson, who purchased $3.00 worth of gasoline. Benson paid for the gasoline with a five dollar bill. The attendant walked to the attendant's booth between the gasoline pumps and opened the cash box. The cash box was visible from where Benson had parked. The cash box was not locked. The attendant made change, returned $2.00 to Benson, and watched as he pulled his car over to the side of the station and got out as though he were going to use the restroom. The attendant said he thought nothing of the stop, and walked back to his own car where he had been working on the radio when not waiting on customers. When he got into his car, he saw Benson at the side of the building, and still thought he was going to use the restroom. The attendant said that for about 60 seconds after that he was looking at his radio. When he looked up he saw Benson in the attendant's booth near the cash box. He said he ran to the booth yelling something like, "What are you doing in there?"

The attendant said that when he got to within about five feet of Benson, Benson jammed his hand into his pockets, and pointed a gun he had in one of them. Although the gun did not show in its entirety, the attendant saw its handle. The attendant stopped, and Benson fled. The attendant then called the police and gave a description of Benson and his car. He also counted the cash left in the cash bin, and determined that $260.00 had been taken.

The police report went on to explain that the description of Benson and his car was broadcast over the radio and heard by a plainclothes policeman on the interstate highway who realized that he was near the point where the car could enter the highway if Benson had fled in that direction. About 12 minutes later, the plainclothes officer spotted Benson's car and radioed for assistance. When joined by two squad cars, the officers pulled Benson over.

The police report included a statement given by Benson after he had received his *Miranda* warnings. In the statement he admitted taking money from the cash box. He said he got about $50.00. Because no weapon was found in the search, the officer asked him if he had taken the gun out of the car. He denied that he had a gun. When the officer asked him if he acted as if he had a gun, Benson replied "Yes." Benson indicated that he took the money from the cash register box because he needed to buy a "fix" of heroin. He indicated his heroin habit cost approximately $100 per day.

Additionally, the observations of the plainclothes officer prior to the two squads joining him was that Benson was driving erratically, and at one point rolled down his window and vomitted. The arresting officer who took the statement indicated that he concluded Benson was suffering from heroin withdrawal.

When confronted with these contradictions by Erika Yamashita, Benson offered no explanation. He continued to deny any involvement in the robbery, and could not explain where the officer might have gotten the statements that were attributed to him.

Yamashita discussed heroin addiction with Benson. She learned that he had been using heroin for two years, had never been to a drug treatment program, and wanted to kick the habit.

In Yamashita's first contact with the district attorney, plea negotiations were discussed. The district attorney indicated that in return for a plea of guilty to Robbery II, he would be willing to stand silent at the penalty phase, which meant that when the court asked the district attorney for a recommendation, he would indicate he had none. Yamashita would be allowed to make her argument for what she considered the appropriate sentence without an argument that the sentence should be more severe. Yamashita advised the district attorney that she would relay that offer to her client.

In her next conversation with Benson, Yamashita advised him of the offer from the district attorney. She also advised him that in all probability that it would mean a sentence to the state penitentiary. Additionally, because of Benson's clean record, and the state prison system's overcrowding problem, he could reasonably predict that he would be released within six months if sent to prison. Benson expressed no interest in the offer and maintained his claim of innocence.

Yamashita then raised a treatment option that might be discussed with the district attorney. She explained to Benson that the state hospital offered a drug program for first time offenders that involved medically supervised treatment for the addiction. The program required 30-60 days as an in-patient, then continued out-patient treatment. Benson was interested.

Yamashita advised the district attorney of her client's position and continued to prepare for trial. As part of that preparation, she advised the district attorney that she intended to file a motion to suppress the statement given to the police officer. She would argue that Benson's medical condition and severe heroin withdrawal prevented him from being able to knowingly waive his right to silence. She also pointed out that if the matter did go to trial, she thought there were two problems with the state's case. First, the attendant said that he saw a gun, yet no gun was recovered. Second, the defendant claimed that approximately $260 was taken from the cash box; only $61 was recovered from Benson.

By the time of Yamashita's conversation with the district attorney, one month had passed from the date of Benson's arrest. The district attorney, in response to Yamashita's notice of motion and discussion of the case, indicated that the district attorney's office would be willing to accept a plea of guilty to Robbery III, a lower class of felony, and would be willing to make a recommendation that Benson spend six months in jail, with credit for time already served. Yamashita responded that before she took that offer to her client, she wanted the district attorney to consider the drug treatment program. Another factor to consider, she argued, was that if Benson was accepted into the program, he would spend at least 30 days in the hospital.

The district attorney was willing to modify his position in response to that argument. Considering the one month that Benson already had served in jail, and the up to one month he probably would spend in the program, the district attorney modified his offer to a plea of guilty to Robbery III, and a district attorney recommendation of four months in jail from the date of sentencing.

In her next discussion with her client, Yamashita relayed the offer from the district attorney. Benson's position still was that he had committed no crime and that he should not be pleading guilty. He also indicated some suspicion of Yamashita's motives for bringing back another offer from the district attorney's office when he had steadfastly maintained his innocence. Yamashita pointed out that it was her obligation to relay all offers to him and it was his obligation to decide if and when he should accept one. She pointed out that to date her preparation for trial had indicated a high probability of conviction. If she was unsuccessful in having his statement suppressed, there would be a confession from him admitted into evidence, eyewitness testimony that he had taken the money, and testimony from the three officers who arrested him that his vehicle matched the description given by the attendant and testimony that he was stopped at a point that would have made it possible for him to have been at the station at the time the robbery was committed. In Yamashita's mind these things added up to a very good state's case, with a high probability of conviction.

The motion to suppress was heard during Benson's seventh week in custody. He testified to his heroin addiction, and to the fact that he was sick the day of the arrest. The arresting officers testified to their observation of his physical illness and to their conclusions about its cause. A physician testified to the effects of heroin withdrawal. The judge concluded that the severity of the illness, its ready manifestations, and its debilitating effects prevented Benson from making a knowing and intelligent waiver of his right. Consequently, the judge suppressed the statements given to the officer at the scene. Those statements would not be allowed into evidence if the case went to trial.

Armed with the order to suppress the confession, Yamashita again met with the district attorney. The district attorney was willing to be more cooperative in his negotiations at this point. He still maintained that even without the statements he had enough to convict Benson of robbery, but he was willing to accept a plea of Theft in the Second Degree, a Class A misdemeanor. Theft in the Second Degree was defined as the unauthorized taking of property with a value of less than $200. In return for such a plea, the state would recommend a period of incarceration of one additional month, which would mean a total of three months followed by release to the state hospital program. Additionally, the state would not file the charge of Failure to Appear in the Second Degree, and would drop one of the earlier shoplifting charges. The state would continue to require a plea to the other shoplifting charge.

Yamashita relayed this offer to Benson. At that point, Benson's trial was scheduled to begin one week later. They reviewed the possibility of conviction in light of the state's loss of the use of Benson's confession. Yamashita pointed out that even without the confession, the likelihood of conviction still was good. Benson admitted that the certainty of gaining his release four weeks after entering the plea had a great deal of attraction to him. Additionally, he was anxious to go to the hospital program. He also liked the fact that no matter what happened with the robbery trial, the other charges would be taken care of in this arrangement. He told Yamashita he would like to accept the district attorney's offer. As Yamashita was leaving, he also told her that he did indeed take some money from the cash box, but not $260.

The negotiations were relayed to the judge in open court. She accepted the change of plea and sentencing recommendations. Benson pled guilty to a Class A misdemeanor and was sentenced to a total of three months in jail. One month later, he was admitted to the state hospital.

QUESTIONS

1. Consider the range of negotiations that took place in this situation: Yamashita with the district attorney; Yamashita with Benson; Benson with himself. Were competing claims settled adequately? Which negotiations do you think were the most difficult?

2. A negotiated settlement was achieved in this situation. Do you think all parties were satisfied? Would all have been satisfied if the case had gone to trial?

3. Was it appropriate for Yamashita to advise Benson about the impact of prison overcrowding or his possible sentence?

4. Was society served by the settlement in this case? Who were the parties to the negotiation?

Trends in Negotiation

The lack of rules and structures in negotiation makes it difficult to graft innovations onto the process. Efforts have been made by legislatures to impose form and content requirements on certain classes of negotiation, however. Similarly, some attorneys have developed a technique called settlement brochures to aid in their negotiations. Finally, a technique called the minitrial has been devised to help parties to a dispute negotiate their own settlements.

An example of legislative imposition of form and content on negotiation is seen in the public sector labor-management field. Disputes between labor and management in the public sector are processed through statutory steps prescribed by legislatures.[18] Generally, parties are given a set period of time to conduct negotiations. If, at the expiration of that period, negotiations have not succeeded, parties must turn to mediation. If mediation also proves unsuccessful, the parties are required to submit the issues still in dispute to a third party fact-finder to conduct a hearing. Within a set period of days, the fact-finder issues a report with a recommendation either to be accepted or rejected by the parties. Another period of time must elapse before the dispute can be taken to another forum. The goal of these steps is to keep the parties talking. The requirement that a specific number of days elapses before another step can be taken is designed to allow the parties to "cool off" so they can return to negotiations. Mediation and fact-finding facilitate the process of negotiation and provide information that may be useful to the parties.

Rule 68 of the Federal Rules of Civil Procedure also provides incentives for parties to negotiate settlements to disputes rather than proceeding to trial. The rule allows one party to offer a settlement to the other side. The offer may involve money or property. If the offer is not accepted, and at trial the party rejecting the offer recovers less than the amount offered, that party must pay the costs incurred by the offeror from the date of the offer. Rule 68 is being used with increasing frequency by litigators seeking to avoid trial and by judges seeking to encourage settlements.[19]

A final example of legislative prescription of the form and content of negotiation is in the consumer area. Legislatures are enacting statutes that dictate the manner in which information will be shared in consumer fields, where it is believed that parties do not have equal bargaining power. Consumer credit is such a field. Credit companies can calculate and explain fees and interest rates in a variety of ways. Congress perceived consumers as unequal bargainers in credit negotiations. Hence the law dictates how interest and fee calculations will be made and requires clear disclosure before agreements are reached.[20] Congress's goal was to allow consumers to readily compare terms offered by various suppliers of credit.

Settlement brochures are being used with increasing frequency as a tool in negotiating personal injury cases.[21] A settlement brochure is a booklet prepared by plaintiff's counsel that lays out the case. It reveals the evidence plaintiff will rely on to establish liability, and documents the expenses associated with whatever injuries plaintiff may have suffered. It indicates the future losses associated with the injury, and makes an argument compelling settlement. The contents of the brochure are limited only by the attorney's imagination. Pictures frequently are used to demonstrate injuries, or to compare lifestyles before and after the injury. A separate section generally is included that covers the applicable law of the case and reaffirms the strength of plaintiff's position. The general criticism of settlement brochures is their potential to expose to defendant some theories or techniques that plaintiff's counsel may not wish to reveal.[22]

Minitrial

A minitrial is a technique to facilitate negotiated settlements by principals in some disputes. It derives its name from its reliance on trial-like procedures. It appears well suited to any case involving highly complex, technical issues where trained experts are in the best position to find a resolution. Lawyers play a different role in minitrials than they do in typical dispute resolution negotiations.[23]

If parties agree to the minitrial process, they hire a neutral advisor who, along with the disputants themselves, hears an abbreviated version of the case. Lawyers for each side present arguments on behalf of their clients within an agreed upon time limit. Sometimes the lawyers call witnesses; more often, they summarize depositions of witnesses taken during discovery.

Following their presentations, the lawyers depart, leaving the disputing parties and the neutral advisor to discuss whether a negotiated settlement is possible. Often the parties are willing to negotiate after they have heard the best arguments their lawyers can make, because they have a better understanding of the risks of going to trial. The neutral advisor can play whatever role the parties agree to. Sometimes the neutral advisor is asked to mediate negotiations between the parties. Other times the neutral advisor is asked to provide an opinion about how the dispute ought to be resolved. Occasionally the neutral advisor is asked to become an arbitrator, if the parties cannot resolve the dispute themselves.

No records are kept of minitrial proceedings. If the neutral advisor is asked to render an opinion, no record is made of the opinion. If the advisor is asked for advice, the advice remains confidential.

Although experimental, the minitrial already has demonstrated great promise. The United States Department of Defense and the Department of Justice have used the technique to resolve several defense contract disputes that otherwise would be tried before the United States Court of Claims.[24] The minitrial also has proved successful in several complex commercial cases. Even if a minitrial does not lead to a complete settlement of a case, often it can result in the resolution of some issues and narrow the questions to be presented at trial.

Example of Minitrial

Alpha Computer filed suit against Beta Computer for $23 million for patent infringement. Alpha engineers had designed a computer chip that allowed it to develop a line of mini-micro computer smaller than a portable typewriter. The "mini-micro" proved so successful that within six months Beta had a competitor machine on the market. Alpha claimed that Beta could not have developed its mini-micro without infringing on Alpha's computer chip patent. Beta responded that the idea behind Alpha's computer chip was not patented.

Many months of discovery and pretrial motions followed. Both companies hired engineers and computer experts to examine the chips. Alpha Computer spent over $500,000 in expert and legal fees during this time; Beta spent almost as much. The technical issues in the case were so complex that the team of lawyers on each side had to receive weeks of instruction in computer engineering and even then were not sure they fully grasped the arguments. Both sides dreaded taking the case to trial, fearing the facts would be unintelligible to most judges and juries.

Alpha Computer's attorneys finally decided to recommend a minitrial. Their clients agreed. Beta executives were receptive to the idea and persuaded their attorneys to try it. The two sides agreed to retain the services of a professional arbitrator, who also had an advanced degree in engineering, to be the neutral advisor. The neutral advisor's fee was $800 per day. The companies also agreed that each would have a financial vice-president with authority to settle the dispute and a senior engineer present at the minitrial.

The minitrial was held in a conference room at the airport of a city halfway between Alpha and Beta's corporate headquarters. The parties agreed to the following procedure:

Lawyers for each side would each have eight hours to present their arguments. Each could use exhibits and could call as many as three expert witnesses. Each side would have up to 30 minutes to cross-examine any expert witnesses called. Each side also would be allowed to quote from depositions taken during the prior discovery period. Neither side would be allowed to consult with the neutral advisor during recesses, meal or overnight breaks. In the discussions following the presentation of arguments the engineers from each side would meet with the neutral advisor to see if they could reach an agreement on technical issues. If agreement was reached, the vice-presidents would meet with the neutral advisor. The neutral advisor was asked to be a mediator only, but was encouraged to make non-binding suggestions if appropriate.

Following the two days of presentations the parties agreed to recess until noon the next day so the engineers and the neutral advisor could review the evidence. The three then met together. Within an hour Alpha engineers agreed with Beta engineers that they could not prove patent infringement and that the suit should be dropped. The vice-presidents then met and Alpha agreed to pay a percentage of Beta's attorney fees.

QUESTIONS

1. Why go through the formality and expense of a minitrial just to negotiate? Could the same benefits be achieved without the process?

2. Can you think of situations where the minitrial technique would not be appropriate? What criteria do you use to make the determination?

3. As a lawyer, would you have any reservations about participating in a minitrial?

Endnotes

[1] See e.g., Mnookin & Kornhauser, *Bargaining in the Shadow of the Law: The Case of Divorce*, 88 Yale L. J. 950 (1979).

[2] See generally the discussion of "hard/soft" negotiation in R. Fisher and W. Ury, Getting to Yes: Negotiating Without Giving In 13 (1981); "cooperative/competitive" negotiation in G. Williams, Legal Negotiation and Settlement 46 (1983); and the focus on twenty common techniques adopted by legal negotiators in C. Craver, Effective Legal Negotiation and Settlement 113 (1986).

[3] Thucydides, The History of the Pelopennesian War (R. Livingstone ed. 1943).

[4] "Mosiac law required that 'thou shalt in any wise rebuke thy neighbor' (Lev. 19:17), meaning that one should 'debate his cause' (Prov. 25:9) with his neighbor himself before threatening him." H. Clark, Clark's Biblical Law 292 (2d ed. 1944). In the New Testament, Jesus says, ". . . if any man will sue thee at law, and take away thy coat, let him have thy cloak also." (Matt. 5:40)

[5] J. Auerbach, Justice Without Law? 25 (1983).

[6] A. Alshuler, *Plea Bargaining and Its History*, 13 Law & Soc. 211, 213 (Winter 1979).

[7] *Id.* at 214.

[8] *Id.* at 223.

[9] See generally, In Defense of 'Bargain Justice,' " 13 Law & Soc. 509, 518 (1979); Santobello v. United States, 404 U.S. 257, 161 (1971).

[10] Alshuler, *supra* note 6.

[11] Williams, *supra* note 2, at 70.

[12] Address by T. Colosi, Vice-President, American Arbitration Association, *Washington State Education Association* (Ap. 20, 1985).

[13] Address by G. Williams, *Negotiation and Settlement* Continuing Legal Education Program, Annual Meeting (Oct. 8-11, 1980 (reprinted in *Negotiation and Settlement*, Oregon State Bar, 1980).

[14] Williams, *supra* note 2, at 47.

[15] See generally, A. Maslow, *A Theory of Human Motivation*, 40 Psych. Rev. 370 (1943).

[16] William *supra* note 2, at 41.

17 Sindell & Sindell, *Formulae to Evaluate Injury Cases,* in Settlement and Plea Bargaining (Am. Trial Law. Assn. ed. 1981).

18 *See, e.g.,* Or. Rev. Stat. §§ 243.650-243.782 (1987).

19 *E.g. Marek v. Chesny,* 473 U.S. 1 (1985) (Rule 68 may be applied to sanction civil rights plaintiffs who reject settlement offers on the way to obtaining a favorable trial verdict). *cf. Johnston v. Penrod Drilling Co.,* 803 F.2d 867 (5th Cir. 1986) (Rule 68 in applicable to rejected joint offers of settlement).

20 15 U.S.C. § 1601 et seq. (1982 and Supp. IV 1986) (Rules on calculation and disclosure of costs by providers of consumer credit).

21 Thomasch, *Objectives and Techniques in Negotiating a Settlement* in Settlement and Plea Bargaining, *supra* note 17.

22 Speiser, *The Psychology and Art of Settlement* in Settlement and Plea Bargaining, *supra* note 17, at 56.

23 Green, *Growth of the Mini-Trial,* 9 Lit. 12 (Fall 1982); Davis, *A New Approach to Resolving Costly Litigation,* 62 J. Pat. Arb. Soc. 482 (1979).

24 Dept. of the Army, U.S. Army Corp. of Engineers, Memorandum on Alternative Disputes Resolution Update (March 30, 1987) (reprinted in Sourcebook: Federal Agency Use of Alternative Means of Dispute Resolution 587-588 (1982)).

Sources

Am. Trial Law. Assn., ed., Settlement and Plea Bargaining (1981).

J. Auerbach, Justice Without Law? (1983).

Alshuler, *Plea Bargaining and Its History,* 13 Law & Soc. 211 (Winter 1979).

G. Bellow & B. Moulton, The Lawyering Process: Negotiation (1981).

L. Brown & E. Dauer, Planning by Lawyers: Materials on a Nonadversarial Legal Process (1978).

Church, *In Defense of 'Bargain Justice,' ",* 13 Law & Soc. 509 (1979).

H. Cohen, You Can Negotiate Anything (1980).

C. Craver, Effective Legal Negotiation and Settlement (1986).

Davis, *A New Approach to Resolving Costly Litigation* 62 J. Pat. Arb. Soc. 482 (1979).

H. Edwards & J. White, The Lawyer As A Negotiator (1977).

R. Fisher & W. Ury, Getting To Yes (1983).

Green, *Growth of the Mini-Trial,* 9 Lit. 12 (fall 1982).

J. Illich, The Art and Skill of Successful Negotiation (1973).

_____ & B. Jones, Successful Negotiating Skills for Women (1981).

D. Lewis, Power Negotiating Tactics & Techniques (1981).

Lowenthal, *A General Theory of Negotiation Process, Strategy and Behavior,* 31 U.Kan.L.Rev. 69 (1982).

Maslow, *A Theory of Human Motivation,* 40 Psychological Rev. (1943).

Mnookin & Kornhauser, *Bargaining in the Shadow of the Law: The Case of Divorce,* 88 Yale L.J. 950 (1979).

G. Nierenberg, The Art of Negotiation (1981).

H. Raiffa, The Art and Science of Negotiation (1982).

T. Warschaw, Winning By Negotiation (1979).

G. Williams, Legal Negotiation and Settlement (1983).

I. Zartman, The 50 Percent Solution: How to Bargain Successfully with Hijackers, Strikers, Bosses, Oil Managers, Arabs, Russians, and Other Worthy Opponents In This Modern World (1976).

_____ & M. Berman, The Practical Negotiator (1982).

Santobello v. New York

404 U.S. 257 (1971)

Mr. Chief Justice Burger delivered the opinion of the Court.

We granted certiorari in this case to determine whether the State's failure to keep a commitment concerning the sentence recommendation on a guilty plea required a new trial. The facts are not in dispute. The State of New York indicted petitioner in 1969 on two felony counts, Promoting Gambling in the First Degree, and Possession of Gambling Records in the First Degree. Petitioner first entered a plea of not guilty to both counts. After negotiations, the Assistant District Attorney in charge of the case agreed to permit petitioner to plead guilty to a lesser-included offense, Possession of Gambling Records in the Second Degree, conviction of which would carry a maximum prison sentence of one year. The prosecutor agreed to make no recommendation as to the sentence.

On June 16, 1969, petitioner accordingly withdrew his plea of not guilty and entered a plea of guilty to the lesser charge. Petitioner represented to the sentencing judge that the plea was voluntary and that the facts of the case, as described by the Assistant District Attorney, were true. The court accepted the plea and set a date for sentencing. A series of delays followed, owing primarily to the absence of a pre-sentence report, so that by September 23, 1969, petitioner had still not been sentenced. By that date petitioner acquired new defense counsel.

Petitioner's new counsel moved immediately to withdraw the guilty plea. In an accompanying affidavit, petitioner alleged that he did not know at the time of his plea that crucial evidence against him had been obtained as a result of an illegal search. The accuracy of this affidavit is subject to challenge since petitioner had filed and withdrawn a motion to suppress, before pleading guilty. In addition to his motion to withdraw his guilty plea, petitioner renewed the motion to suppress and filed a motion to inspect the grand jury minutes.

These three motions in turn caused further delay until November 26, 1969, when the court denied all three and set January 9, 1970, as the date for sentencing. On January 9, petitioner appeared before a different judge, the judge who had presided over the case to this juncture having retired.

Petitioner renewed his motions, and the court again rejected them. The court then turned to consideration of the sentence.

At this appearance, another prosecutor had replaced the prosecutor who had negotiated the plea. The new prosecutor recommended the maximum one-year sentence. In making this recommendation, he cited petitioner's criminal record and alleged links with organized crime. Defense counsel immediately objected on the ground that the State had promised petitioner before the plea was entered that there would be no sentence recommendation by the prosecution. He sought to adjourn the sentence hearing in order to have time to prepare proof of the first prosecutor's promise. The second prosecutor, apparently ignorant of his colleague's commitment, argued that there was nothing in the record to support petitioner's claim of a promise, but the State, in subsequent proceedings, has not contested that such a promise was made.

The sentencing judge ended discussion, with the following statement, quoting extensively from the pre-sentence report:

"Mr. Aronstein [Defense Counsel], I am not at all influenced by what the District Attorney says, so that there is no need to adjourn the sentence, and there is no need to have any testimony. It doesn't make a particle of difference what the District Attorney says he will do, or what he doesn't do.

"I have here, Mr. Aronstein, a probation report. I have here a history of a long, long serious criminal record. I have here a picture of the life history of this man . . .

" 'He is unamenable to supervision in the community. He is a professional criminal.' This is in quotes. 'And a recidivist. Institutionalization—; that means, in plain language, just putting him away, 'is the only means of halting his anti-social activities,' and protecting you, your family, me, my family, protecting society. 'Institutionalization.' Plain language, put him behind bars.

"Under the plea, I can only send him to the New York City Correctional Institution for men for one year, which I am hereby doing."

The judge then imposed the maximum sentence of one year.

Petitioner sought and obtained a certificate of reasonable doubt and was admitted to bail pending an appeal. The Supreme Court of the State of New York, Appellate Division, First Department, unanimously affirmed petitioner's conviction, 35 App. Div. 2d 1084 (1970), and petitioner was denied leave to appeal to the New York Court of Appeals. Petitioner then sought certiorari in this Court. Mr. Justice Harlan granted bail pending our disposition of the case.

This record represents another example of an unfortunate lapse in orderly prosecutorial procedures, in part, no doubt, because of the enormous increase in the workload of the often understaffed prosecutor's offices. The heavy workload may well explain these episodes, but it does not excuse them. The disposition of criminal charges by agreement between the prosecutor and the accused, sometimes loosely called "plea bargaining," is an essential component of the administration of justice. Properly administered, it is to be encouraged. If every criminal charge were subjected to a full-scale trial, the States and the Federal Government would need to multiply by many times the number of judges and court facilities.

Disposition of charges after plea discussions is not only an essential part of the process but a highly desirable part for many reasons. It leads to prompt and largely final disposition of most criminal cases; it avoids much of the corrosive impact of enforced idleness during pre-trial confinement for those who are denied release pending trial; it protects the public from those accused persons who are prone to continue criminal conduct even while on pre-trial release; and, by shortening the time between charge and disposition, it enhances whatever may be the rehabilitative prospects of the guilty when they are ultimately imprisoned.

However, all of these considerations presuppose fairness in securing agreement between an accused and a prosecutor. It is now clear, for example, that the accused pleading guilty must be counseled, absent a waiver. *Moore v. Michigan*, 355 U.S. 155 (1957). Fed. Rule Crim. Proc. 11, governing pleas in federal courts, now makes it clear that the sentencing judge must develop, *on the record*, the factual basis for the plea, as, for example, by having the accused describe the conduct that gave rise to the charge. The plea must, of course, be voluntary and knowing and if it was induced by promise, the essence of those promises must in some way be made known. There is, of course, no absolute right to have a guilty plea accepted.

This phase of the process of criminal justice, and the adjudicative element inherent in accepting a plea of guilty, must be attended by safeguards to insure the defendant what is reasonably due in the circumstances. Those circumstances will vary, but a constant factor is that when a plea rests in any significant degree on a promise or agreement of the prosecutor, so that it can be said to be part of the inducement or consideration, such promise must be fulfilled.

On this record, petitioner "bargained" and negotiated for a particular plea in order to secure dismissal of more serious charges, but also on condition that no sentence recommendation would be made by the prosecutor. It is now conceded that the promise to abstain from a recommendation was made, and at this stage the prosecution is not in a good position to argue that its inadvertent breach of agreement is immaterial. The staff lawyers in a prosecutor's office have the burden of "letting the left hand know what the right hand is doing" or has done. That the breach of agreement was inadvertent does not lessen its impact.

We need not reach the question whether the sentencing judge would or would not have been influenced had he known all the details of the negotiations for the plea. He stated that the prosecutor's recommendation did not influence him and we have no reason to doubt that. Nevertheless, we conclude that the interests of justice and appropriate recognition of the duties of the prosecution in relation to promises made in the negotiation of pleas of guilty will be best served by remanding the case to the state courts for further consideration. The ultimate relief to which petitioner is entitled we leave to the discretion of the state court, which is in a better position to decide whether the circumstances of this case require only that there be specific performance of the agreement on the plea, in which case petitioner should be re-sentenced by a different judge, or whether, in the view of the state court, the circumstances require granting the relief sought by petitioner, i.e., the opportunity to withdraw his plea of guilty. We emphasize that this is in no sense to question the fairness of the sentencing judge; the fault here rests on the prosecutor, not on the sentencing judge.

The judgment is vacated and the case is remanded for reconsideration not inconsistent with this opinion.

QUESTIONS

1. What was the bargain in this case? What were the benefits to each side as a result of the bargain? Should it be public policy to encourage such bargains?

2. Is granting Santobello specific performance of the bargain a realistic remedy in this case? What did Santobello seek?

3. What role, if any, should the United States Supreme Court play in the plea bargaining process? Is Santobello consistent with this role?

Rise v. Board of Parole

304 Or 385, 745 P.2d 1210 (1987)

Gillette, J.

This case involves the effect, if any, that a plea agreement between a criminal defendant and a district attorney can have on the Board of Parole's subsequent decisions regarding the defendant's parole date. The Board in the present case determined that it was not "bound" by the terms of such a plea agreement, and the Court of Appeals affirmed without opinion. *Rise v. Board of Parole*, 84 Or.App. 742, 735 P.2d 380 (1987). We hold that the Board was not bound by the terms of the plea agreement and that it did not err in refusing to enforce the agreement. Accordingly, we affirm.

Petitioner and his co-defendant, Troy Stewart, each were charged with two counts of aggravated murder, ORS 163.095, in connection with the death of Ralph Anderson. Elaborate pretrial negotiations between the district attorney and petitioner's attorney culminated in a plea agreement with the following pertinent provisions:

"The purpose of this agreement is to secure the cooperation of Mr. Rise in the prosecution and conviction of Troy Stewart. The State of Oregon is entering into this agreement because, although Mr. Rise is fully and completely guilty of the offenses he is charged with, his role in these offenses was secondary and subsidiary to the role of Troy Stewart.

"Mr. Rise agrees to meet with authorities from state law enforcement at such reasonable times and places as they may deem necessary to tell honestly, truthfully, and completely all he knows about the crimes set forth above and these persons involved in those crimes. He also agrees to appear at any grand jury, trial proceeding, or any other court proceeding in connection with these crimes and to testify fully and truthfully.

"In return for Mr. Rise's fulfilling each and every obligation of this agreement, the State of Oregon agrees to:

"1. Allow Mr. Rise to stipulate to the facts on a charge of Murder based on this incident. This stipulation will occur after trial or plea in *State v. Stewart,* supra.

"2. Not oppose Mr. Rise's truthful statement that he knew the victim, Mr. Anderson. *The purpose of this portion of this agreement is to assure that his crime is treated as a subcategory 2 Murder by the Oregon Board of Parole, thereby setting Mr. Rise's range at 10-13 years.*

"3. *To send a statement to the Oregon Board of Parole requesting that Mr. Rise serve 10 years. If Mr. Rise requests that the State provide the Parole Board with additional information or appear in person before the Parole Board, the State will do so.*

"4. To permit Mr. Rise to continue with the appeal of the remand proceedings which resulted in this case being sent to adult court.

These four obligations are the only obligations imposed on the State of Oregon by this agreement." (Emphasis applied.)

On July 17, 1985, petitioner entered a guilty plea to one count of murder, ORS 163.115, and was sentenced to life imprisonment. In accordance with the plea agreement, petitioner provided the district attorney with a detailed account of the crime. According to petitioner, that statement was included in a Parole Analysis Report, which was submitted to the Board of Parole. Petitioner's attorney requested that a new Parole Analysis Report be prepared without the inclusion of petitioner's statement because, under the terms of the plea agreement, the district attorney should not have submitted the statement to the Board. In response, the Board issued a Board Action Form that stated, in part:

"The Board is not bound by any agreement the D.A.'s office makes. If the material is relevant, the Board will make use of it. * * *"

Based on the facts set out in the Parole Analysis Report, the Board concluded that petitioner had engaged in "significant planning" in committing the murder. Therefore and in spite of the fact that petitioner knew the victim, the Board classified petitioner's crime as a "Subcategory 1" murder, and set his matrix range at 120-168 months (10-14 years).

Petitioner sought judicial review of the Parole Board decision, arguing, inter alia, that the Board erred in failing to honor the district attorney's promises that petitioner's crime would be treated as a "Subcategory 2" murder and that the district attorney would not submit any information to the Board unless petitioner requested additional information. The Court of Appeals affirmed without opinion. We allowed review to consider the effect of a district attorney's promises in a plea agreement on subsequent decisions by the Board of Parole. * * *

The Board itself took no part in the plea negotiations and was not a party to the plea agreement between the district attorney and petitioner. Therefore, it could be bound by the agreement only if the district attorney had the authority to bind the Board, requiring it to treat his crime as a Subcategory 2 murder. * * *

Petitioner argues that, under ORS 135.405(3), a district attorney has broad authority to make concessions in plea negotiations. Admittedly, the list of permissible concessions is not exclusive. However, the items on that list all are matters within the normal scope of a district attorney's duties. A district attorney has broad discretion to make charging decisions. As an advocate for the State, the district attorney has the authority to make, or to forego making, recommendations to the sentencing court. Parole decisions, however, are statutorily delegated to the Board of Parole. ORS 144.005 to 144.395. It is unlikely that, in creating the list of permissible promises, the legislature intended to authorize a district attorney to usurp the function of the Board of Parole. Neither the statutory language nor any legislative history of which we have been made aware supports such a construction of the authority of the district attorney. Accepting petitioner's reading of the plea agreement ot the effect that the district attorney promised petitioner that the Board would treat his offense as a Subcategory 2 murder, the Board was not bound by that unauthorized promise. * * *

Finally, petitioner argues that, even if the Board was not bound by the terms of the plea agreement, this court, nevertheless, should order the Board to enforce those terms. Petitioner's argument in favor of specific performance has force, because it is quite possible that rescission of the plea agreement would not be an adequate remedy in this case. In Santobello v. New York, 404 U.S. 257 (1971), the Supreme Court held that, when the prosecution breaches a plea agreement with the criminal defendant, the defendant is entitled either to specific enforcement of the agreement or vacation of the guilty plea. Here, petitioner agreed that he would enter his guilty plea after he had testified against his co-defendant. Presumably, then, petitioner already has performed his part of the bargain. If the state cannot be held to its promises, it is possible that petitioner would be left with no meaningful remedy for the state's breach of a plea agreement under which petitioner was induced to waive a battery of constitutional protections. The prospect of such a result is unsettling. * * *

Because of the posture of this case, however, we are not able to reach that issue. Our review of parole board decisions is limited to whether the Board erred in reaching its decision. We already have determined that the Board did not breach the plea agreement between petitioner and the district attorney, because the Board was not a party to the agreement and was not otherwise bound by the terms of the agreement. We further hold that the Board did not err in refusing to enforce the agreement. The Board of Parole is not in the business of construing plea agreements or of fashioning appropriate remedies for their breach. Those questions are matters for judicial determination. If the plea agreement was breached in this case, then petitioner's remedy lies elsewhere--perhaps in habeas corpus or post-conviction relief, where the court is authorized to fashion appropriate relief. * * *

The decisions of the Board of Parole and the Court of Appeals are affirmed.

QUESTIONS

1. Did the district attorney honor the commitments made to Rise? Did the district attorney agree to limit communication with the parole board in any way? What argument can be advanced that the district attorney has the power to bind the state?

2. Is the agreement in this case a traditional plea bargain involving "self conviction in return for leniency?" Do Rise's obligations under this bargain carry a greater potential cost to him or the state than the typical plea bargain? If so, should the court take that fact into consideration?

3. Who represented society in the plea bargain in this case? Were society's interests served?

Daniels

v.

Horace Mann Mut. Ins. Co.

422 F.2d 87 (4th Cir. 1970)

Albert V. Bryan, Circuit Judge:

For failing to settle a claim against them for an automobile personal injury, Ada L. Daniels and the committee for her incompetent husband, Nathan G. Daniels, sued the Horace Mann Mutual Insurance Company, their insurer, for the amount by which the judgment exceeded the limit of their liability policy. In a jury-waived trial, the District Court denied recovery and they appeal.

The contract, issued to Ada L. Daniels as the car owner, gave protection against responsibility due to negligence of that insured and her husband with a maximum coverage of $10,000 for injury to one person and $20,000 for all persons injured in a single accident. The company covenanted to defend, at its expense, any suits against the insured upon claims of this kind, but it reserved the right to settle them.

While driven by Nathan Daniels in West Virginia on October 14, 1966, the car struck 16-year-old Victoria Williams and broke her arm. An action in the State court against Nathan and Ada Daniels was appropriately brought to recover for her injuries and for her father's outlays in medical and hospital expenses on her behalf. Indemnity of $85,000 was asked.

The company undertook the defense of the Williams' action but upon investigation became persuaded that Nathan Daniels was grossly at fault. At a pretrial conference the trial judge entered a finding that Nathan's negligence was the cause of the accident. Hence the quantum of the damages was the only issue to be resolved. The jury awarded $25,000 to Victoria and $880 for her father's expenditures. Judgment was passed upon the verdict and was not altered on appeal. The insurance company paid $10,000 towards its satisfaction. When the plaintiffs demanded payment from the defendants of the unpaid balance, the present action followed.

In a controversy of this kind the insured can succeed only if the insurer's failure to settle within the indemnity provided is ascribable, as generally said, to its negligence or bad faith. West Virginia's highest court, by whose rulings we are bound in this diversity case, has not definitively declared whether both or which, if only one, of these factors must be shown. It was the District Court's belief that the State Supreme Court when called upon for a decision would join those jurisdictions--a majority at one time but now possibly the minority--adopting the good faith doctrine.

For this forecast the Court specially noted the espousal of this view by Virginia, as enunciated in *Aetna Casualty and Surety Co. v. Price*, 146 S.E.2d 220 (1966). Good faith and negligence, as detriments, "have tended to coalesce, and today there is more of a difference in verbiage than there is in result." In this case we find a choice unnecessary.

For exposition of the insurer's obligation, both the Virginia court and the opinion of the District Judge referred to *Radio Taxi Service, Inc. v. Lincoln Mut. Ins. Co.*, 157 A.2d 319, 322-323 (1960), where it is said:

"* * * [T]he obligation assumed by the insurer with respect to a settlement is to exercise good faith in dealing with offers of compromise, having both its own and the insured's interests in mind. And it may be said also that a reasonably diligent effort must be made to ascertain the facts upon which a good faith judgment as to settlement can be formulated. * * *"

"* * * A decision not to settle must be an honest one. It must result from a weighing of probabilities in a fair manner. * * * Where reasonable and probable cause appears for rejecting a settlement offer and for defending the damage action, the good faith of the insurer will be vindicated. * * *"

True, the Court there found for the insurer, but, nevertheless, it lucidly outlined the pertinent law.

In short, the demand of care and good faith arises from the dual and delicate position of the insurer. In its hands at one and the same time are its own and the interests of the insured. If not technically, certainly practically, a trusteeship is posed. Selfishness will not be tolerated, yet the insurer is not to be held for a sincere mistake of judgment.

The District Judge looked, too, at *American Casualty Co. of Reading Pa. v. Howard*, 187 F.2d 322, 329 (4 Cir. 1951). Although it involved the

law of South Carolina, Judge Dobie laid down a test which seems to be acceptable as a general proposition: that if the insurer acted "reasonably, in good faith and without negligence in refusing proffered settlements" it met its obligations to the insured. This pronouncement is our text for decision presently. It provides an understandable and a workable formula.

That the appellee insurer did not act "reasonably, in good faith and without negligence in refusing the proffered settlement" readily appears from the uncontested circumstances. They require the conclusion that the District Court's contrary ultimate finding--whether considered as one of fact or law--was clearly erroneous. Now recounted, the subsidiary facts found by the trial court disclose the absence of a full grasp, by the insurer throughout, of the gravity of the Williams' cause against the insured and culpable neglect in defense.

To start with, the investigation was, in certain respects, inadequate. The insurance company appears to have conducted the pretrial negotiations under the mistaken impression that the injury was no more than a slightly complicated arm fracture. Actually, it was a comminuted break, involving the median nerve followed by a limited paralysis of the right hand. One of her doctors testified to the uncertainty of a permanent cure. She was physically unable to continue in high school for the remaining seven or eight months of her senior year. Mental and bodily pain was experienced. Yet the insurance company never sought independent professional opinion in diagnosis or prognosis of her hurt. It was content to allow plaintiff's evidence of the extent of the injury to go uncontested at trial and introduced no evidence whatsoever of a mitigating nature.

Next, no serious negotiations toward settlement were pursued by the insurer, a firmly recognized responsibility of the insurer. The Williams' attorney initially tendered a compromise of $16,000. After learning of the $10,000 policy maximum, he advised his clients that $8,000 was a realistic figure. Prior to the trial the attorney clearly indicated to the insurer that he would settle within the policy limits, making a firm offer of $9,500. His omission to tell opposing counsel of the willingness to take less was, he explained, because the insurer had never inquired whether the Williams would consider a smaller figure. But the District Court found that he "allegedly mentioned to the company's claims representative that his clients would probably settle for $8,000."

Its adjuster reported to the company he thought it would have to pay in range of $7,500 to $8,000. The insurer first authorized its lawyer to settle for $3,000. This offer was refused as "insulting." The authority was then raised to $5,000, and finally to $7,500, but prior to trial the company's lawyer submitted nothing higher than $4,500. During trial he mentioned $5,500, in a manner characterized by the plaintiff's attorney as "perfunctory." He testified that he had recommended to the company that he be given the authority to go to $7,000, but the company never authorized him to offer more than $5,500.

The insured seems to have received little consideration from the company or its lawyer. Both the claims manager and lawyer testified that they had given no consideration to the possibility of a recovery greater than the policy limits. Although Ada Daniels and her husband's committee constantly pressed the insurer to compose the claim, she testified that she was not kept abreast of any negotiations to that end. On visits to the insurer's attorney, she was always assured that there would be a settlement within the policy limits. Admittedly, the usual "excess letter" informed her that, as the claim was more than the policy coverage, she might procure her own attorney but later she was told it was unnecessary.

Lastly, the probability of liability is, obviously, a foremost consideration in deciding whether to settle. Here liability has been confessed. In this circumstance the jeopardy of the insured demanded more than ordinary solicitude. The company thus knew it *had to pay.* The only question was how much. No commensurate exertion on the insured's behalf is manifest or demonstrated.

Nor after the Williams had won at trial was there any earnest attempt to appeal or settle. Even at that stage settlements are not uncommon. The party winning at nisi prius may prefer to take a sum below the verdict to avoid an appeal. It is a ripe time to discuss settlement.

Thus, the insurer from beginning to end did not act "reasonably, in good faith and without negligence". To summarize: (a) there was only a superficial investigation; (b) there was no serious attempt to settle; (c) the company did not accept the recommendations of its counsel and agents as to the amount it should offer in settlement of the case; (d) there was only scanty consideration given to the insured's predicament; and (e) there was neglect in appraising the danger of the outstanding determination of liability. * * *

Judgment must go for the appellants in the amount of the unpaid balance of the Williams' recovery.

Reversed with final judgment.

QUESTIONS

1. What is the relationship between Daniels and the insurance company? Why does Daniels have the burden of proving negligence or bad faith? How do "mistakes" or "errors of judgment" without bad faith or negligence fit into this type of case?

2. How would you characterize the bargaining styles of the attorneys in this case? Where does Judge Bryan find fault with defendant's negotiation? Do you agree?

3. Would your opinion of the outcome in this case change if the performance of Horace Mann's attorneys at trial had been different? Their performance in the post-trial phase? Judge Bryan suggests that the negotiation behavior of Horace Mann's attorneys can be inferred from their performance in litigation. Is this inference necessarily true?

Kothe v. Smith

771 F.2d 667 (2d Cir. 1985)

Van Graafeiland, Judge.

Dr. James Smith appeals from a judgment of the United States District Court for the Southern District of New York (Sweet, J.), which directed him to pay $1,000 to plaintiff-appellee's attorney, $1,000 to plaintiff-appellee's medical witness, and $480 to the Clerk of the Court. For the reasons hereinafter discussed, we direct that the judgment be vacated.

Patricia Kothe brought this suit for medical malpractice against four defendants, Dr. Smith, Dr. Andrew Kerr, Dr. Kerr's professional corporation, and Doctors Hospital seeking $2 million in damages. She discontinued her action against the hospital four months prior to trial. She discontinued against Dr. Kerr and his corporation on the opening day of trial. Three weeks prior thereto, Judge Sweet held a pretrial conference, during which he directed counsel for the parties to conduct settlement negotiations. Although it is not clear from the record, it appears that Judge Sweet recommended that the case be settled for between $20,000 and $30,000. He also warned the parties that, if they settled for a comparable figure after trial had begun, he would impose sanctions against the dilatory party. Smith, whose defense has been conducted throughout this litigation by his malpractice insurer, offered $5,000 on the day before trial, but it was rejected.

Although Kothe's attorney had indicated to Judge Sweet that this client would settle for $20,000, he had requested that the figure not be disclosed to Smith. Kothe's counsel conceded at oral argument that the lowest pretrial settlement demand communicated to Smith was $50,000. Nevertheless, when the case was settled for $20,000 after one day of trial, the district court proceeded to penalize Smith alone. In imposing the penalty, the court stated that it was "determined to get the attention of the carrier" and that "the carriers are going to have to wake up when a judge tells them that they want [sic] to settle a case and they don't want to settle it." Under the circumstances of this case, we believe that the district court's imposition of a penalty against Smith was an abuse of the sanction power given it by Fed.R.Civ.P. 16(f).

Although the law favors the voluntary settlement of civil suits, *ABKCO Music Inc. v. Harri-*songs Music, Ltd., 722 F.2d 988, 997 (2d Cir. 1983), it does not sanction efforts by trial judges to effect settlements through coercion. *Del Rio v. Northern Blower Co.*, 574 F.2d 23, 26 (1st Cir. 1978) (citing *Wolff v. Laverne, Inc.*, 17 A.2d 213, 233 N.Y.S.2d 555 (1962); see *MacLeod v. D.C. Transit System, Inc.*, 283 F.2d 194, 195 n. 1 (D.C.-.Cir. 1960)). In the *Wolff* case * * * the Court said:

> We view with disfavor all pressure tactics whether directly or obliquely, to coerce settlement by litigants and their counsel. Failure to concur in what the Justice presiding may consider an adequate settlement should not result in an imposition upon a litigant or his counsel, who reject it, of any retributive sanctions not specifically authorized by law. 17 A.2d at 215, 233 N.Y.S.2d 555.

In short, pressure tactics to coerce settlement simply are not permissible. *Schunk v. Schunk*, 84 A.2d 627, 299 N.Y.S.2d 896 (1969). "The judge must not compel agreement by arbitrary use of his power and the attorney must not meekly submit to a judge's suggestions, though it be strongly urged." *Brooks v. Great Atlantic & Pacific Tea Co.*, 92 F.2d 794, 796 (9th Cir. 1937).

Rule 16 of the Fed.R.Civ.P. was not designed as a means for clubbing the parties--or one of them--into an involuntary compromise. See *Padovani v. Bruchhausen*, 293 F.2d 546, 548 (2d Cir. 1961) * * *. Although subsection (c)(7) of Rule 16, added in the 1983 amendments of the Rule, was designed to encourage pretrial settlement discussions, it was not its purpose to "impose settlement negotiations on unwilling litigants." See Advisory Committee Note, 1983, 97 F.R.D. 205, 210.

We find the coercion in the instant case especially troublesome because the district court imposed sanctions on Smith alone. Offers to settle a claim are not made in a vacuum. They are part of a more complex process which includes "conferences, informal discussions, offers, counterdemands, more discussions, more haggling, and finally, in the great majority of cases, a compromise." J. & D. Sindell, Let's Talk Settlement 300 (1963). In other words, the process of settlement is a two-way street, and a defendant should not be expected to bid against himself. In the instant case, Smith never received a demand of less than $50,000. Having received no indication from

Kothe that an offer somewhere in the vicinity of $20,000 would at least be given careful consideration, Smith should not have been required to make an offer in this amount simply because the court wanted him to.

Smith's attorney should not be condemned for changing his evaluation of the case after listening to Kothe's testimony during the first day of trial. As every experienced trial lawyer knows, the personalities of the parties and their witnesses play an important role in litigation. It is one thing to have a valid claim; it is quite another to convince a jury

of this fact. It is not at all unusual, therefore, for a defendant to change his perception of a case based on the plaintiff's performance on the witness stand. We see nothing about that occurrence in the instant case that warranted the imposition of sanctions against the defendant alone.

Although we commend Judge Sweet for his efforts to encourage settlement negotiations, his excessive zeal leaves us no recourse but to remand the matter with instructions to vacate the judgment.

QUESTIONS

1. What standard of review does the court apply in this case? Why? Would the outcome have been different if the trial court had imposed sanctions on both parties?

2. Does the fact that Dr. Smith (or his insurer) raised his offer 400% after one day of trial indicate that prior negotiations were in bad faith? What factors could contribute to such a significant change in his offer?

3. Does the Court of Appeals in this circuit support efforts by trial courts to settle cases without trial? How does it communicate this support to the trial court?

[Reread in this context Lockhart v. Patel, Ch. 2.]

Quick v. Crane

111 Idaho 759, 727 P.2d 1187 (1986)

Donaldson, Chief Justice.

This case arises out of an accident that occurred on Interstate 86 near Pocatello, Idaho, in the early morning hours of January 3, 1981. Visibility was poor due to patches of fog. Defendant-appellant, Fred Arthur Turner, was driving a tractor-trailer rig leased by his employer, defendant-appellant, Sigman Meat Company, from defendant-appellant, Rollins Leasing Corporation. According to testimony at trial, Turner had either slowed to around 5 to 10 mph or had completely stopped in the right lane of traffic after he had entered a thick patch of fog. A van owned by respondent, James Crane, collided with the rear of

the tractor-trailer rig. A white Nova driven by Penny Caldwell then collided with the van, and a pickup driven by Roger Orme collided with the Nova. Several other vehicles were subsequently involved in this chain reaction of rear-end collisions, but are not involved in this litigation. All the occupants of the van--James Crane, Johnny King, and Rick Quick--were injured. Quick subsequently died.

Lori Quick, Rick Quick's widow, then filed a wrongful death action against many of the parties involved in the collision. Numerous cross-claims and counterclaims were asserted, but by the time the case came to trial on June 4, 1984, most of the claims between the parties had been settled. The trial, therefore, was based only on the claims of Crane and King (hereinafter plaintiffs) against Turner, Sigman Meat Company and Rollins Leasing Corporation (defendants). The trial lasted 7 days and resulted in a verdict in favor of Crane and King. A special verdict was returned which provided as follows:

Party	Percentage of Liability
Turner, Sigman Meat Co., and Rollins Leasing Corp.	87%
Johnny King	9%
James Crane	2%
Rick Quick	1%
Penny Caldwell	1%

The jury verdict awarded Crane $1,000,000 (one million dollars) in damages and King, $100,000 (one hundred thousand dollars) in damages. Each of these awards were subsequently reduced based on each plaintiff's proportion of negligence and settlements they entered into.

After most of the defendant's post-trial motions were denied they filed this appeal and have raised what we have categorized as six separate issues. Crane raises another issue in his cross-appeal. Because each issue is based on different facts, we will elaborate on any additional facts as we address each issue. * * *

In the original complaint filed in this action, Lori Quick, the widow of Rick Quick, filed suit against Turner, Sigman Meat Company and Rollins Leasing Corporation, as well as Johnny King and Jim Crane. King and Crane then joined Quick in filing claims for their injuries against Turner, Sigman and Rollins. Crane also filed a cross-claim against King, and King filed a cross-claim against Crane. Prior to trial on the claims by Crane and King against Turner, Sigman and Rollins (defendants), a settlement was reached between King and Crane whereby Crane released his claim against King in consideration for a $40,000 cash payment and payments of $450 per month for life with a 20-year guarantee. Crane's claim against King was then dismissed with prejudice by the Court, approximately six months before trial. Crane also settled with Lori Quick prior to trial.

Shortly before trial, defendants moved to instruct the jury of the existence of the settlement between King and Crane and/or to admit the re-

lease agreement itself into evidence along with any other agreements Crane had with other parties. Defendants argued that since King and Lori Quick were called as witnesses, their settlements with Crane should have been disclosed to insure the jury was aware of their interests in the outcome of the case. The trial court denied defendants' motion.

It should be noted at the outset that the release with which the defendants are particularly interested--the one between King and Crane--was fully disclosed to the defendants and the court well before trial. It was written to conform to the requirements of I.C. Sections 6-805 and - 806. Under I.C. Section 6-806, the general rule is that a tortfeasor who settles with an injured party is still liable to make contribution to other tortfeasors, *unless* the release (1) is given before the rights of the other tortfeasors to secure judgment for contribution has accrued, and (2) provides for a reduction, of the injured party's total damages equal to the pro-rata share attributable to the released tortfeasors." Since the release between King and Crane satisfied these two requirements, King is not liable to the defendants for contribution. The amount by which the release will reduce the injured party's damages is governed by I.C. Section 6-805.

Defendants urge this Court to adopt the rule, followed in some jurisdictions, which allows the admission of settlement agreements between a plaintiff and one of the co-defendants so that the other co-defendants will not be unduly prejudiced. *Firestone Tire & Rubber Company v. Little*, 639 S.W.2d 726, 728 (1982). This rule of admissability of settlements, however, governs only those types of settlement agreements known as "Mary Carter Agreements." The term "Mary Carter Agreements" arises from the agreement popularized by the case of *Booth v. Mary Carter Paint Company*, 202 So.3d 8 (Fla.Dist.App.1967), and is used generally to refer to any agreement between a plaintiff and one or some (but not all) of the defendants whereby the agreeing parties place limitations on the financial responsibility of the agreeing defendants, the amount of which is variable and usually is in some inverse ratio to the amount of recovery which the plaintiff is able to make against the non-agreeing defendants. *Soria, supra.*

The reason such agreements have been found to be admissible by some courts is because of the potential for misleading the judge or the jury as to the relationship between the plaintiff and one of the defendants when, in fact, they have an interest in common pursuant to a secret agreement; and interest that borders on collusion. *Ward v. Ochoa,* 284 So. 2d 385, 387 (Fla. 1973). It is this element of secrecy that is condemned, particularly because of the advantageous position the agreeing defendant can put himself in by painting a gruesome picture of his co-defendant's conduct and even by making admissions against himself. Also, because the non-agreeing co-defendants are ignorant of such secret agreements, they are not in a position to bargain with the plaintiff on the same basis as if they had known of the agreement. In fact, depending upon the terms of the agreement, it may actually behove the plaintiff not to settle with the non-agreeing defendants.

A review of the release agreement between Crane and King reveals that it comes neither within the definition of a "Mary Carter Agreement" nor within the policy justifications on which some courts have relied in admitting such settlements to the jury. By the time this case got to trial, all of the parties that remained had been defendants in Lori Quick's initial suit. At trial, however, it was clear that there were two plaintiffs— each with his own injuries arising out of the same accident--and three co-defendants. The defendants were fully aware that King would conduct his case as a plaintiff against them and not as a co-defendant defending himself with the defendants against Crane. Hence, a critical element of a "Mary Carter Agreement"—that the agreeing defendant remain as a defendant to defend himself against the plaintiff—is not present here.

Furthermore, no matter whether King is characterized as a plaintiff or a co-defendant in the eyes of the jury, the defendants in this case clearly always operated under the assumption that to succeed they would have to prove that King was the driver of the van and was comparatively more negligent than Turner. They knew this even before the release agreement was made and Crane's complaint against King was dismissed. The defendants were able to fully prepare their cases and reasonably anticipated the way Crane and King would present their cases. The secretive and collusive element that is inherent in "Mary Carter Agreements" is simply not present in the case at bar. In fact, the absence of collusiveness is apparent in the release itself which does not make the settlement amount variable depending upon the amount of recovery Crane is able to get from the defendants.

Rather than being like a "Mary Carter Agreement," the release between King and Crane is sim-ilar to the so-called *Pierringer*-type agreement, as all parties in this appeal concede. See *Pierringer v. Hoger,* 123 N.W.2d 106 (1963). *Pierringer* releases are general approved by the courts and are consistent with I.C. Sections 6-805 and -806. Basically, they entail an agreement whereby the plaintiff releases one co-defendant but reserves the right to proceed against the remaining defendants. The non-settling defendants' right to contribution can then be cut off by the plaintiff's agreement to indemnify the settling defendant against any claims of contribution. Under the terms of this type of release, the non-settling defendants will not be required to pay more than their fair share as determined by the jury's finding of comparative negligence. *Frey v. Snelgrove,* 269 N.W.2d 918, 921 (Minn.1978). Defendants in the present case point to *Frey* as the basis for admission of the *Pierringer*-type release between King and Crane.

The court in *Frey* noted that if the plaintiff has agreed to indemnify the settling defendant against all possible cross-claims of the non-settling defendants, the trial court should ordinarily dismiss the settling defendant from the case and, since he is deemed to have fixed his limits of financial liability, the settling defendant is deemed to have relinquished any cross-claims against the remaining defendants. *Id.* at 923. However, since the trial court will be submitting to the jury the issue of the fault of *all* parties, including that of the dismissed settling defendant, the *Frey* court concluded that the jury should usually be informed that "there has been a settlement if for no other reason than to explain the settling tortfeasor's conspicuous absence from the courtroom." *Id.*

The present case is clearly distinguishable from *Frey* since the release at issue did not relinquish King's cross-claims against the defendants and since King was not dismissed from the case. The release did not fix the limit of King's liability, and King remained, as did Crane, a plaintiff in this action. Each conducted their own separate case against the defendants and the jury evaluated the interests and biases of each as plaintiffs. The rationale the Frey court relied upon in allowing the trial court, in its discretion, to permit a Pierringer-type release to be disclosed to the jury is clearly distinguishable.

Ultimately, there are problems with the defendants' argument that settlements, even though they clearly do not involve "Mary Carter Agreements," must be disclosed simply because a settling party is called as a witness. To so hold would discourage almost all settlements in multi-party cases--including *Pierringer* releases which are agreed to in conformance with I.C. Section 66-806--since normally the best witnesses are parties or former parties. Cases would go to the jury with far more parties and issues than necessary, at great expense to both the litigants and judicial system. Ironically, if we were to accept defendants' argument that Crane's settlements with King and Rick Quick's estate must be disclosed because King and Lori Quick were called as witnesses, then logically any settlements that the defendants themselves entered into with Rick Quick's estate would also have to be disclosed to the jury.

This Court has always held to the strong public policy favoring amicable settlement of litigation. *See Lomas & Nettleton Company v. Tiger Enterprises, Inc.*, 585 P.2d 949 (1978). To allow the disclosure of settlement agreements to the jury cannot but have the effect of discouraging parties from settling. There is a strong probability that a settlement may be regarded by the jury as an admission of liability. This policy against disclosure may be overcome in the event the settlement involves an agreement such as a "Mary Carter Agreement" and the parties moving for disclosure can prove they will be prejudiced by non-disclosure. Additionally, rule 408 of the Idaho Rules of Evidence "does not require exclusion of evidence relating to compromises or offers to compromise if the evidence being introduced is used to show witness bias or prejudice. However, trial judges have broad discretion in determining the admissibility of such evidence and their decision "will not be overturned absent a clear showing of abuse." Here, the King-Crane release is clearly not a "Mary Carter Agreement" and we find that the trial court did not abuse its discretion by excluding the agreement. We therefore hold that the district court did not err in refusing to disclose the existence of the release agreement, or the release itself. * * *

[Case remanded for other reasons.]

QUESTIONS

1. Although titled *Quick v. Crane*, who are the real parties in this action? What "release" is at the center of this controversy? Why do defendants seek its admission?

2. What is the difference between a *Mary Carter* agreement and a *Pierringer* agreement? Why does Judge Donaldson suggest that the two should be treated differently? What rule regarding treatment of such agreements would serve the public interest? What interests need to be balanced?

Davidson v. Beco Corporation

112 Idaho 560, 733 P.2d 781 (1986)

Burnett, J.

May a statement contained in a settlement offer be used to impeach a party who gives contrary testimony at trial? That is the salient issue presented in this case. In addition, we were asked to decide whether personal liability should be imposed for a corporate debt and whether attorney fees should be awarded.

These issues arise from a debt collection suit filed by Howard Davidson against Doyle Beck, Elizabeth Beck, and two corporations controlled by the Becks. Davidson alleged that he had not been fully paid for trucking services. A jury agreed, returning a verdict against all defendants. Judgment was entered accordingly. For reasons explained below, we affirm the judgment against the corporations but reverse it as to the Becks individually.

The facts are these. Davidson provided services for Beco, Inc. (later renamed Beco Construction Company, Inc.), on two construction projects. Davidson submitted bills to Beco but they were not paid. Davidson went to Beco's office. There he met with Doyle Beck, Beco's president and controlling shareholder. Davidson requested payment of $20,712 as billed. When Beck disputed the amount, a compromise was struck at $9,740. Beck gave Davidson a corporate check for $1,000. Arrangements were made for paying the balance. However, those arrangements became shrouded in controversy.

According to Beck, he and Davidson reached an accord by which Davidson would receive a tractor in lieu of any further cash payment. The tractor would be appraised and if it was worth more than the balance owed, Davidson would pay the excess to the holder of a lien on the tractor. In contract, Davidson claims there was no such accord. He contends that he rejected the tractor proposal because he did not want to pay the tractor's excess value in order to collect a debt. According to Davidson, Beck agreed for Beco to pay the balance of the debt in cash at the rate of $1,000 per month, together with interest at fourteen percent. The upshot of the controversy is that Beco made no further cash payments and Davidson never took possession of the tractor. Davidson eventually sued Beck and Beco on the original billing.

While the suit was pending, Beco's attorney sent Davidson's attorney a letter. Among other things, the letter acknowledged that Davidson had performed services for Beco. The offer of a tractor in lieu of cash was reiterated. The letter also said that "a similar offer was made [to Davidson] some time ago, but it was refused." This statement, of course, was inconsistent with Beck's assertion that an accord had been reached.

Before trial, Beck and Beco filed a motion in limine, seeking to exclude the letter from evidence. They argued that the letter was inadmissible under I.R.E. 408 because it contained "statements made in compromise negotiations." The district judge ruled that the letter would not be admitted as an exhibit during Davidson's case-in-chief. However, the judge denied the motion insofar as cross-examination was concerned. At trial Beck testified about the accord. During cross-examination, Davidson's attorney read into the record several excerpts from the letter. They included the statement that a previous offer had

been "refused" and the statement acknowledging existence of a debt. The jury later returned a verdict for Davidson. This appeal followed. * * *

We now examine the limitations upon using settlement offers in evidence. These limitations long have existed in Idaho law. They are intended to promote settlements, a public policy recently reiterated by our Supreme Court. The limitations are defined by Rule 408, Idaho Rules of Evidence. The rule provides as follows:

Compromise and Offers to Compromise--*Evidence of* (1) furnishing, *offering,* or promising to furnish, or (2) accepting, offering, or promising to accept, *a valuable consideration in compromising or attempting to compromise a claim which was disputed as to either validity or amount, is not admissible to prove liability for, invalidity or, or amount of the claim* or any other claim. *Evidence of conduct or statements made in compromise negotiations is likewise not admissible.* This rule does not require the exclusion of any evidence otherwise discoverable merely because it is presented in the course of compromise negotiations. *This rule does not require exclusion if the evidence is offered for another purpose,* such as proving bias or prejudice of a witness, negativing a contention of undue delay, or proving an effort to obstruct a criminal investigation or prosecution. [Emphasis added.]

Rule 408, which is identical to its federal counterpart, flatly prohibits the use of settlement negotiations to prove "liability for, invalidity of, or amount of" a claim. Indeed, the federal rule's prohibition had been adopted by our Supreme Court even before Idaho Rule 408 was promulgated. However, the question posed by this case is * * * whether evidence of settlement negotiations may be used to impeach contrary statements at trial.

This question illustrates a tension between the truth-seeking function of a trial and the policy of encouraging settlements. Scholars are divided on how the tension should be resolved. Some commentators believe that allowing impeachment could defeat the policy of encouraging settlements. See K. Redden & S. Saltzburg, Federal Rules of Evidence Manual 285 (4th ed. 1985.) "[O]pening the door to impeachment evidence on a regular basis may well result in more restricted negotiations." Others have argued that encouragement of settlements must yield to the ascertainment of truth where misrepresentations allegedly have been made from the witness stand. See D. Louisell & C. Mueller, 1 Federal Evidence Section

172 (1985) ("Protecting the settlement process to the point of shielding apparently perjured testimony seems excessive"). The language of the rule itself--allowing evidence to be admitted for purposes other than proof of "liability for, invalidity of, or amount of" a claim--plainly suggests that the policy of encouraging settlements is restricted. Although impeachment is not among the purposes listed in the rule, the list is preceded by the phrase "such as." It is not exclusive. *See* Report of the Idaho State Bar Evidence Committee at p. C 408-1 (December 16, 1983).

We believe the policy of encouraging settlements stops short of being absolute. Rule 408 refrains from imposing an explicit ban against the use of statements made in settlement negotiations for the purpose of revealing the falsity of contrary statements made in the courtroom. We decline to infer such a prohibition.

Rather, we hold that prior inconsistent statements made during settlement negotiations may be used for the purpose of impeachment. Although very few courts in other jurisdictions have tackled this issue, their decisions are in accord with our holding today. *See County of Hennepin v. AFG Industries, Inc.,* 726 F.2d 149 (8th Cir. 1984).

Our holding is a narrow one. A trial court may admit evidence of settlement negotiations when contrary testimony has been given at trial, but the court is not *required* to do so. When evidence is offered for a purpose other than proving "liability for, invalidity of, or amount of" a claim, the decision to admit such evidence generally is committed to the discretion of the trial court. *See Soria v. Sierra Pacific Airlines, Inc.,* 726 P.2d 706 (1986) (discretionary standard applied where evidence of settlement is offered for purpose of showing bias). The trial judge must weigh the probative value of the evidence for the limited purpose of impeachment against the risk that unfair prejudice will result if the triers of fact improperly use the evidence to evaluate the merits of a claim or defense. Experienced judges and lawyers know that this risk is substantial, notwithstanding any cautionary instruction the court might give the jury. The risk may be minimized by excising any portions of the prior statement which are unnecessary to the impeachment process or which present a particular danger of impermissible use by the triers of fact. In any event, when exercising his discretion, the trial judge should be mindful that the competing values of truth-seeking and encouraging settlements are at stake. Consequently, a prior inconsistent statement made during settlement negotiations should be admitted only if it strongly suggests that a witness is perjuring himself at trial or if any unfair prejudice is likely to be insubstantial.

We now apply these guidelines to the case at hand. Our analysis is in two steps. First we address the contention that the trial judge erred in allowing Davidson's counsel to use portions of the settlement letter beyond the stipulated first paragraph. Second, we consider whether such error was harmless.

The letter was used on cross-examination for impeachment and to establish liability. As noted above, Davidson's counsel read into the record not only the language concerning the tractor offer but also a passage acknowledging the existence of a debt. In that passage, counsel for Beck and Beco stated, "My client does recognize that your client provided necessary services and is entitled to payment." Plainly, this language served no permissible purpose under Rule 408.

The tractor offer presents a closer question. The language in question is as follows:

> Beco, Inc., currently possesses a 301 John Deere Tractor Loader valued at approximately $14,000.00. Beco, Inc., has no currently (sic) use for this tractor and has attempted to sell it previously but has been unable to do so. [The lienholder] has agreed to release this tractor . . . provided [the lienholder] is paid the difference between the principal owed to your client and its current value. If such an agreement is acceptable to you we will obtain a current appraisal for purposes of exchange. * * * By way of information, a similar offer was made to your client some time ago but it was refused.

The record before us contains no indication that the trial court weighed the probative value of this evidence for impeachment against the risk of unfair prejudice. Accordingly, we must examine the issue independently.

The letter's statement that "a similar offer" had been "refused" was probative for the purpose of impeachment. It conflicted with Beck's assertion at trial that Davidson had accepted an earlier offer but then had failed to honor the accord. However, the conflict was not blatant. The distinction between an offer that had been "refused" and an offer that had been accepted but repudiated is one that could elude a lay witness. Moreover, * * * the word "refused" had been employed not by Beck but by his lawyer. Thus, although the letter cast some doubt on the veracity of Beck's testimony, it did not rise to the level of strongly suggesting perjury.

On the other hand, the risk of unfair prejudice was substantial and manifest. Any offer of compromise would invite an inference that the offeror believed his claim or defense to be weak. Here, the problem was compounded by the fact that the settlement offer was accompanied by a statement bearing directly on the offeror's affirmative defense of an accord. When this excerpt from the letter is coupled with the excerpt acknowledging a debt, we believe the risk of unfair prejudice outweighed the probative value of the evidence. The trial court should not have allowed these excerpts from the letter to be used on cross-examination.

* * *

[The court went on to hold the admission of the letter as harmless error and affirmed the case in part and reversed in part on other grounds.]

QUESTIONS

1. Why does Davidson seek to have the letter from Beco's attorney admitted? On what grounds do Beck and Beco argue against its admission? Would negotiations have been as forthright if the parties had known that what was said would be used in court? Is confidentiality necessary to facilitate negotiations?

2. Under Idaho Rule of Evidence 408, under what circumstances is a statement made in negotiation not admissible? Why? Did the court rule that prior inconsistent statements made in negotiation are admissible? How will such statements be handled? Why would a party seek to introduce a prior inconsistent statement if not to prove the contents of that statement?

3. How does the court's ruling affect the future conduct of negotiation in Idaho? Is the effect good or bad?

4. In an unissued opinion, 1987 WL 2568, the Idaho Supreme Court affirmed Judge Burnett's decision for the Court of Appeals, but criticized the court for being too restrictive about the uses to which negotiation statements could be put. The Supreme Court suggested that impeachment was only one use that a court might make of such statements. What impact could this decision have on negotiations in Idaho?

6 MEDIATION

Mediation is defined most simply as facilitated negotiation. An impartial third party (the mediator) facilitates negotiations between disputants or the disputants' representatives in their search for a resolution of their dispute. The disputants remain responsible for negotiating a settlement; the mediator's role is to assist the process in ways acceptable to the disputants. Sometimes this means merely providing a forum for negotiations or convening the negotiations. More often it means helping the disputants find areas of common ground for resolution, offering alternatives, supervising the bargaining, then drafting the final settlement. Mediation can occur between two disputants seeking to resolve one issue, or among many disputants seeking to resolve several issues. The disputants can participate in mediation themselves or they can have representatives negotiate for them. Mediation most often is a voluntary process, but in some jurisdictions also can be mandated by statute or by court order.

Mediation has several characteristics. First, it is private. Even when ordered by a court (as it frequently is in the case of divorce), or mandated by legislation (as it frequently is in the case of labor disputes), mediation takes place out of the public eye. What goes on in mediation is known only to the disputants and their mediator.

Second, mediation is confidential. There are two dimensions to this confidentiality. One is that the disputants must have good rapport with their mediator and be willing to make disclosures they might not be willing to make publicly or to someone they did not trust. The second aspect of confidentiality is that following mediation, neither the disputants nor the mediator divulges what went on during the process. A central goal of mediation is to encourage disputants to put forth whatever information may be needed to resolve the dispute. If disputants feared that information shared during mediation would be used subsequently as evidence at trial, for example, they would be unlikely to disclose the information.

A third characteristic of mediation is that the process typically is created and controlled by the disputants and their mediator. If mediation is voluntary, they must decide where and when mediation is to occur, who should be involved in the negotiations, how the costs of mediation will be paid, and all the details of the mediation process itself. Before mediated negotiations occur, disputants and their mediator generally agree on rules to govern the process. These rules can cover such matters as whether the disputants will negotiate directly with one another or will make offers through the mediator, whether the mediator will be permitted to meet individually with the disputants, and what form a settlement will take. Even when mediation is mandated by statute, such as in situations where bargaining has reached impasse, or where it is ordered by a court as a precondition to trial, disputants and their mediator control many of the details of the process that is to govern their mediation.

Finally, like negotiation, mediation is a "forward looking" process. The adjudicatory processes, litigation and arbitration, require findings of fact about events that occurred in the past. Based on the findings of fact, rights and responsibilities are established and assigned according to the applicable law, contract provision, or public policy. The focus of mediation, by contrast, is on the future conduct of the parties required to resolve their dispute. Determining what occurred in the past is not the central focus of mediation. In fact, attempts to fix blame for past behavior can create obstacles to otherwise acceptable solutions.

Background of Mediation

The roots of mediation are deep in western and non-western cultures. The Bible, for example, refers to Christ as a mediator between human beings and God. Mediation was recognized as an integral part of the legal system of early Medieval Europe.[1] In Japan, Africa and China, mediation always has been valued because of its emphasis on consensus, moral persuasion, and maintaining harmony in human relationships.[2]

Mediation may have come to the United States formally via religious colonies, whose charters prescribed mediation of disputes that arose among members of the colony. A trusted member of the congregation would help members resolve their disputes in a manner consistent with the colony's religious beliefs.[3] Mediation always has been popular in the commercial world, where the desire to maintain business relationships and to achieve rapid, private resolution of disputes has led to mediation rather than to litigation.

While mediation is an ancient dispute resolution process and has been used informally since colonial times, the most institutional support for it in the United States has come in the 20th Century. In 1926, the American Arbitration Association (AAA), a private sector dispute resolution organization, began offering mediation and arbitration services to disputants who preferred private, voluntary resolution over public litigation. It now has dispute settlement centers throughout the United States.[4] Congress expressed its interest in the peaceful resolution of labor disputes in the transportation industry in the Railway Labor Act of 1926.[5] In 1934, Congress created the National Mediation Board to mediate railway disputes, then expanded the Board's jurisdiction to include mediation of airline disputes as well.[6] In 1947, Congress created the Federal Mediation and Conciliation Service (FMCS).[7] The FMCS provides mediation services during the collective bargaining process to assist parties in coming to agreement over the terms of a contract. On rare occasions the FMCS will provide mediation services at the grievance stage as well, if labor and management have agreed by contract to submit to mediation a dispute that has arisen concerning the contract. In addition, state legislatures have been active in enacting statutes that require mediation of labor-management disputes and in providing mediation services for the disputants. The goal of such legislation and service is to create mechanisms that encourage self-government in the labor-management context and to promote an opportunity to avoid strikes or lockouts.

In the latter years of the 20th Century, mediation also has been recommended or required by court order. Courts increasingly require couples seeking a dissolution of their marriage to mediate issues such as child custody, visitation rights, and child and spousal support. If the couple reaches agreement on these issues in mediation, their agreement is submitted to the court as a recommendation for its final order. Some courts allow mediation in criminal misdemeanor cases, if the victim consents to the process. Some judges also are experimenting with a form of mediation through settlement conferences. The judge meets with counsel and sometimes with parties prior to the commencement of trial to explore areas of possible agreement.

Voluntary Mediation

In voluntary mediation it is the responsibility of the parties to initiate the process, select a mediator, create rules to govern the negotiations, and negotiate an agreement. Voluntary mediation tends to be popular in situations where the disputants have an ongoing relationship, want or need to preserve that relationship, and wish to resolve their dispute privately. Business disputes, where parties have an ongoing relationship by contract or custom, are one example.

Voluntary mediation also is used frequently in marriage dissolution situations where the parties want to retain control over the resolution of such issues as child custody, visitation rights, and support. Despite that desire, or perhaps because of it, couples on the edge of divorce often are unable to interact at all, let alone negotiate effectively with one another. A neutral party frequently can make negotiation possible. Among the services a mediator can perform are focusing the discussion, chanelling emotions, and packaging proposals in such a way that parties can react to the proposals instead of to one another. In addition to helping couples resolve immediate issues surrounding dissolution, mediation may be able to help them develop an ability to work together in the future to solve problems that might arise surrounding the rearing of their children.

Mediation often is the only dispute resolution technique available for the resolution of international disputes. Sometimes the disputants agree to submit their dispute to mediation; other times the United States or some other country will send a mediator or team of mediators to a troubled area in order to convince the disputants to participate in a negotiated settlement.

There are several other areas in which voluntary mediation is increasingly popular. One is consumer disputes. Manufacturers of products ranging from automobiles to computers are offering to submit disputes with consumers to mediation. Many chambers of commerce throughout the country also offer mediation services to deal with consumer complaints.

Mediation is being used with increasing frequency to resolve environmental disputes. Environmental mediation can be controversial, since the mediation process puts pressures on disputants to agree to compromises in order to solve problems. The criticism wanes, however, when environmental standards have already been set and the dispute focuses on methods of implementation.

Voluntary mediation also is proving useful for the resolution of disputes that arise in schools, churches, the work place, and within or among government agencies. It is employed frequently to resolve prison disputes, a context in which mistrust among the disputants frequently runs high.

Finally, some criminal disputes are being resolved through voluntary mediation, if the court and the victim consent to the process. Typically criminal mediation occurs only when the victim and the accused have an ongoing relationship and the alleged criminal behavior has been classified as a misdemeanor. A mediated settlement, such as the accused agreeing to seek drug or alcohol treatment, can result in criminal charges being dropped.

How Voluntary Mediation Works

The decision to mediate a dispute typically occurs when disputants have tried to resolve their dispute through unassisted negotiations, but have failed to reach a settlement. Once they have agreed to mediate, they must select their mediator. There are a variety of ways to locate mediators. Some advertise their services in the telephone directory. Others rely on referrals from lawyers, counselors, or the clergy. Since mediators often are drawn from the ranks of academia, local colleges and universities frequently will maintain lists of mediators. Similarly, state, municipal, or county social service agencies sometimes maintain files of mediators. State mediation and conciliation services sometimes can refer disputants to individuals who provide mediation services. Finally, the American Arbitration Association maintains lists of mediators, although most of the AAA's work tends to be in the commercial or labor fields.

Success in mediation requires that disputants select a mediator who is trusted and respected by both sides. Some mediators are very directive and participate actively in the negotiations, making suggestions, offering alternatives, and going to great lengths to get the parties to agree to a resolution of their dispute. Others see their role more as conciliators, whose duty is to provide a forum in which the parties can work out their differences. Sometimes parties to mediation must interview several prospective mediators before selecting one to help them resolve their dispute.

Unlike litigation, mediation has no prescribed form or set of rules the disputants must follow. No two mediations are identical; each responds to the needs and expectations of the disputants and the style of the mediator. Most mediations have three steps, however: introduction to the process and establishment of ground rules, development of issues and options, and negotiation of an agreement. Each step can be very complicated, though with experienced parties it is possible for the process to move relatively quickly.

1. *Introduction to the Process and Establishment of Ground Rules*

Disputants in mediation remain responsible for settling their dispute. They cannot turn it over to the mediator for resolution. One of the most important aspects of the introductory phase, therefore, is for the mediator to educate the parties about their responsibilities in mediation and to clarify the role of the mediator. The amount of time required for the introduction to mediation depends on the background and sophistication of the parties.

Even if the parties come to mediation with a good understanding of the process, they may bring to it hostilities or unequal bargaining skills that will hinder successful negotiation. Most mediators pay close attention to the attitudes and skills of the parties in the early phases of mediation. They confront hostilities directly and attempt to orient the parties to the task of resolving the problem or problems that brought them to mediation and away from the usually futile exercise of attaching blame. Some mediators also feel it is their responsibility to help the parties develop effective and more equal bargaining skills. If the imbalances are significant, some mediators will recommend suspending mediation, while the party with inferior bargaining skills receives outside assistance in developing these skills.

The most important procedure in the first step of mediation is the establishment of ground rules. The ground rules are the equivalent of rules of procedure in litigation. They govern how mediation will work, binding both the parties and the mediator. Ground rules vary to meet the needs of particular mediations. Frequently, however, they include answers to the following questions:

1. When will mediation sessions occur? How long will each session last? Where will the sessions take place? Will there be a limit on how many sessions the parties will have before they pursue some other dispute resolution alternative?
2. What kind of behavior is acceptable or unacceptable during mediation? What commitments is each party willing to make in order to help the mediation process succeed? Should the parties seek legal counsel prior to mediation? If one of the parties is unable to attend a session, what kind of notice is to be given to the other party and the mediator?
3. What kind of settlement do the parties seek to achieve? Will they formalize their agreement in writing? Will the agreement be filed as a contract or submitted to a court as a proposed settlement? What role, if any, will the mediator play in drafting the agreement?
4. What rules should the mediator follow? May the mediator meet individually with the parties? If so, should information conveyed in such meetings be shared with the other party or be kept confidential? Should the mediator be invited to make suggestions for resolving the dispute or merely facilitate negotiation?
5. If the parties reach an agreement in mediation but subsequently discover that they need to renegotiate certain issues, what procedures will they follow to reopen negotiations or mediation?
6. How will the costs of mediation be paid?

Ground rules include whatever other rules are important to the parties. The ground rules literally provide the framework for the mediation process and emphasize to the parties that they are in control of the resolution of their dispute.

Establishing ground rules is the first opportunity the parties have to practice coming to agreement. Agreement at this preliminary stage can help pave the way for agreement on substantive issues later.

Some mediators draft the ground rules in the form of a contract for the parties and the mediator to sign before actual negotiations begin. The contract then binds all the participants and is a symbol of their rights and duties during the negotiations.

Parties have other important decisions to make during the first step of mediation. One is whether they are committed to mediation as a method for resolving their dispute. By the end of the first step, parties who did not realize it initially are fully aware that in mediation they retain control over the process for resolving their dispute and for the content of the resolution. At no point do they turn their dispute over to a neutral party for resolution. Another important decision is whether they have selected the appropriate mediator. If either party decides that the mediator or process is unacceptable, they have the power and responsibility to find a mediator who is acceptable or to seek another method for resolving their dispute.

2. *Development of Issues and Options*

After ground rules have been set, and it appears that the parties understand the mediation process, most mediators begin to help the parties identify the facts and issues in their dispute. If there are multiple parties and interests involved, as is common in environmental, prison, and many commercial mediations, this step can be very complex. Sometimes the parties disagree about the relevant facts or issues; sometimes they are even reluctant to talk to one another.

At least three levels of issues usually need to be explored in the process of developing issues and options: immediate, concrete problems, underlying interests and needs, and principles or values.

Immediate, concrete problems are those that brought the parties to mediation. In a contract dispute, for example, they might involve the fact that the supplier of computer chips has been substituting foreign made chips when the contract called for chips made in the United States. In a divorce mediation, concrete issues might involve the question of which spouse will have custody of the children or which will continue to reside in the family home.

Underlying interests and needs are the motivations behind the positions parties take on concrete issues. In the contract dispute just mentioned, the supplier's underlying interest might be establishing or maintaining an ongoing relationship with the overseas manufacturer of computer chips. Fearing that American chips will become too expensive, the supplier may be attempting to establish a position in the overseas market. In the divorce situation, one parent may fear that losing custody of the children will destroy that parent's relationship with them. The parent's underlying interest in maintaining the relationship would have to be explored before the custody issue could be resolved.

Parties also bring principles and values to a dispute. Sometimes those principles and values can make resolution of a dispute impossible; sometimes they must be preserved if a mediated settlement is to last. The buyer of the computer chips in the contract case, for example, might have ideological rather than financial reasons for preferring American made computer chips. Successful mediation of the dispute with the supplier would require a frank discussion of this ideological commitment. Similarly, the parents in the divorce mediation might have strong differences about the importance of religious training for their children. Resolution of the immediate, concrete issue of child custody would be unlikely without exploring the principles and values of each spouse regarding religious education.

Exploration of all three levels in a dispute can be very emotional and expose deep psychological differences between or among the parties. In most other dispute resolution forums, the parties and decision-makers strive to overlook emotional issues and to focus only on the "facts." Mediation tends to regard facts as ancillary to the relationship between the parties that has given rise to the dispute. This broader view of the dispute has the potential to result in resolution of more than the issues that triggered mediation.

Another important task in the second step of mediation is to identify who is and will be affected by the dispute and its resolution. Is the dispute limited to the parties in mediation or are there other persons and interests that should be taken into account while seeking resolution? In divorce mediation it is obvious that the interests of people other than the spouses are affected--children, parents, relatives, and even friends. The ethical code of divorce mediators requires them to protect children's interests in mediation.[8] Business disputes also can involve interests beyond those of the immediate parties. If partners in an accounting firm, for example, have a dispute over their partnership agreement, they need to take into account the interests of their employees and clients when they negotiate a new agreement.

Parties in mediation can begin to explore options for resolution only after they have a clear understanding of the breadth and depth of the issues in their dispute. Many mediators include a brainstorming session at this juncture. It is not uncommon for parties to be defensive about suggestions for resolution offered by the other side. In order to get a variety of options on the table, some mediators conduct a session designed to solicit ideas without evaluation. Parties, and in some cases the mediator, offer any solution imaginable, with the goal that each suggestion inspire others, and that in the later cool light of evaluation, some will prove workable.

Legal rules do have a role to play in mediated agreements. Divorcing spouses, for example, could not agree, or expect a court to endorse, an agreement under which the custodial parent would remove minor children from school without an approved plan of home instruction. Such an agreement would violate school attendance laws.

Parties to voluntary mediation nonetheless have considerable discretion over the role the law plays in their negotiations. The partnership agreement for partners in a restaurant business, for example, required each to work approximately fifty hours per week in the restaurant. One partner claimed the other was working only thirty-five hours per week. In the eyes of the law, the complaining partner would be entitled to file an action to have the partnership dissolved. Dissolution was not in neither party's interest, however, since the restaurant was doing well financially and both partners brought unique skills to the business. Mediation does not compel parties to exercise their legal rights.

The process of developing issues and options can be very complicated and time consuming, as well as emotionally draining on the parties and the mediator. The nature of the dispute and the parties' attitudes and skills will determine how many sessions are required to complete this step of the process. Many mediators conclude this step by helping the parties rephrase the issues in dispute and the options for resolution in concise, neutral language, giving the parties a clear understanding of the problem or problems they need to address before moving to the next step.

3. Negotiation of An Agreement

The goal of this step in mediation is for the parties to agree on a resolution of their dispute in a form provided for in their ground rules. Typically this means a written agreement. No matter how much progress the parties may appear to have made during earlier phases of the process, it is easy for negotiations to bog down at the point of actually agreeing on the language that will symbolize an agreement.

A technique frequently used by mediators to help parties come to agreement is to refer to the priorities they established during the introductory phase of mediation. If they agreed on basic principles, reference to those principles can provide a framework for resolving other controversies. Union and management representatives, for example, may have agreed early in mediation that free speech should be protected in the work place. Agreement on the principle of free speech might be a useful point of reference, if the parties cannot agree on what materials can be placed on the employee bulletin board.

Mediators frequently are assigned the task of drafting an agreement or plan once parties have agreed to a resolution of their dispute. Most mediators strive to produce a document that can be understood by both or all the parties, and which is clear and unambiguous. An agreement that provides for "reasonable behavior" on the part of a student in a dispute with a school district over disciplinary rules, for example, invites disputes in the future over what constitutes "reasonable behavior." If parties cannot agree on specific language for their agreement, many mediators believe that agreement has not been reached and that more negotiations are needed.

Once parties have agreed on a settlement, some mediators advise them to seek independent legal or financial review of the document. The Family Law Section of the American Bar Association has adopted standards that require mediators to strongly recommend independent legal review of mediated divorce settlements.[9] Some state bar associations in their codes of professional responsibility have adopted or are adopting rules that require lawyers who serve as mediators to advise parties to seek independent legal review of mediated agreements. Some mediators applaud this trend, claiming that outside legal or financial review gives the parties confidence in their agreement and creates an additional incentive to abide by its terms. Other mediators feel strongly that independent review could destroy the mediation process, fearing that it would be costly and that at least some lawyers might urge their clients to not agree to a mediated settlement in the hope of gaining more through litigation or arbitration.

Sometimes parties discover that the agreement they wrote at the end of mediation does not prove satisfactory. The agreement may not have been drafted with sufficient precision, or a subsequent problem may have arisen that the parties did not foresee in their original agreement. Many mediators, therefore, recommend that the agreement contain a provision for reentering mediation. If the parties know they can return to mediation to resolve differences, they may be able to avoid taking more adversary positions toward one another if a subsequent dispute arises. Renegotiation often can be completed more quickly than the original mediation, because the parties are accustomed to working together and can follow the ground rules established initially.

Burdens of Persuasion in Voluntary Mediation

The law imposes no burdens of persuasion or proof on parties in voluntary mediation because it occurs outside of the formal legal system and the parties have no decision-maker to persuade. The mediation process does have requirements for the parties, however.

One requirement is that the parties want to resolve their dispute. Ironic though it may seem, sometimes parties say they want their dispute resolved when in fact one or both has a stake in perpetuating it. Couples seeking a divorce, for example, may allow a disagreement over a property settlement to go unresolved indefinitely, because the disagreement gives them an excuse to stay in contact with one another even though that contact is not pleasant or productive. They will be unable to agree on a property settlement as long as one or both has a psychological interest in maintaining the conflict. A similar phenomenon sometimes is encountered in the international arena. Nations that have been disputing for years may claim to want resolution, yet seem to have more interest in maintaining the conflict than in finding ways to resolve it.

The second requirement of mediation is that the parties accept responsibility for resolving their dispute, even if doing so means that one or both must change their attitudes or behaviors. Each side has the responsibility to persuade the other that it is better to resolve the dispute themselves than to turn it over to a court or arbitrator and have a decision imposed on them.

Some believe that a third requirement of mediation is that the parties approach the process with an attitude of problem solving. The focus of mediation, they claim, should be on problem solving rather than on attaching blame. Parties should emerge from mediation feeling that they have been able to discuss issues openly and freely, and feeling satisfied with the agreement.[10]

Mandatory Mediation

As noted earlier, mandatory mediation occurs either by statute or by court order. Statutes provide for mediation in disputes where, according to state legislatures or the United States Congress, parties should at least try to resolve disagreements themselves before they have the right to take more drastic actions such as strikes or lockouts. If bilateral negotiations break down between labor and management, for example, mediation is required by statute. Mediation and conciliation services exist with staffs of professional mediators to work with the parties in an effort to avoid industrial strife and to create an environment in which positive negotiations can occur. News reports frequently contain statements that a dispute involving telephone employees, teachers, factory, or transportation workers and their employers has gone to mediation to help the parties agree on the terms of a contract or to resolve a dispute that has occurred under an existing contract.

Mediation also can be ordered by a court. Domestic relations disputes frequently are referred to mediation by courts in jurisdictions that do not require mediation of such disputes by statute. When a divorce petition is filed with the court, it is reviewed by the judge or court staff to determine whether it should be referred to mediation. If the jurisdiction provides mediation services and it appears the parties should attempt to mediate issues of property division, spousal support, or child custody, the case can be referred to mediation. The couple meets with family counselors who have been trained in mediation and who help the couple resolve many or all of the unsettled issues in the proposed dissolution. If mediation succeeds, the agreement is submitted to the court for approval and can be entered as the judge's order. If mediation fails, the case resumes its adversary posture and a judge decides the contested issues for the parties. Failure to reach agreement on all issues does not mean that mediation has been futile. Sometimes couples are able to resolve some of the issues through mediation. Such partial resolution reduces burdens on the court and lets the couple retain control over part of their dispute.

A growing number of state and federal judges believe they should play an active role in the settlement of cases before trial, both because settlements help reduce the number of cases on the trial docket and because settlement is seen as better for the parties than dragging a dispute through a trial. Some judges therefore assume the role of mediator in settlement conferences in civil cases.[11] Power to hold settlement conferences is provided by state or federal rules of civil procedure. Rule 16 of the Federal Rules of Civil Procedure, for example, authorizes the court to direct the parties to appear "for a conference to consider. . .such other matters as may aid in the disposition of the action."

The conduct of settlement conferences depends primarily on the judges who call them. Some judges meet with lawyers and discuss the merits of the case from the judge's perspective, then leave it to the lawyers to try to negotiate a settlement. Other judges participate actively in the negotiations between lawyers, and insist that the parties be present so there will be no delay while the lawyers consult with their clients on proposed settlements. The personality and experience of the individual judge is a dominant factor in whether and how a settlement conference is conducted, how many such conferences are called to discuss a particular case, at what stage in the litigation process it occurs, how long it lasts, and how much pressure to settle is put on lawyers and their clients by the judge.[12] Since settlement conferences can be ordered by judges, parties have no choice about participating, little control over the process, and must engage in negotiations with the assistance of the judge or magistrate assigned to the case.

In these respects, settlement conferences are a variation on mediation. The parties retain control over the content of any agreements reached as a result of settlement conferences, however, even though some attorneys and parties feel particular pressure to settle when negotiations are being supervised by a judge.

How Mandatory Mediation Works

Mandatory mediation works much like voluntary mediation: the process is introduced and ground rules are established, issues and options are developed, then final agreement is reached or breakdown occurs. Mandating mediation by court order or statute, however, changes its complexion considerably. Disputants no longer are voluntary participants in search of a solution. For the unsophisticated, a court order may equate with pressure to settle. For the sophisticated, mandatory mediation may be viewed simply as a hurdle to overcome before reaching the dispute resolution process of choice.

Procedurally, parties have far less control over the process in mandatory mediation than in voluntary mediation. The mediator may be assigned, for example, rather than selected. Mediation sessions may follow a pre-ordained schedule, and the issues to be dealt with in mediation may be delineated by someone other than the parties. Finally, in situations such as labor-management disputes, the parties in mandatory mediation are professional negotiators who have been through the process many times. Their high level of sophistication allows procedures to be streamlined.

Burdens of Persuasion in Mandatory Mediation

As is the case in voluntary mediation, the law imposes no burden of proof on parties in mandatory mediation. The parties remain responsible for any settlement they reach. The burden, as in negotiation, remains one of convincing the other party that the certainty offered through settlement is better than the uncertainty of alternatives.

The Role of The Lawyer in Mediation

Lawyers play four primary roles in mediation. They practice as mediators, they represent parties in the mediation process, they prepare clients to represent themselves in the process, and they review agreements prepared in mediation.

A growing number of lawyers are devoting some portion of their practices to mediation. The most common area is in marriage dissolution cases where the lawyer is asked to help couples resolve issues arising from the dissolution. Lawyers who provide mediation services claim that their legal training is excellent background for mediation and that mediation often is more satisfying than litigation or arbitration because of the possibility of mutual party satisfaction with the agreement.[13]

Lawyers also participate in mediation as representatives when their clients are groups such as companies, unions, interest groups or governmental units. The perception of lawyers as skilled in negotiation and knowledgeable about legal rights and duties commends them to this role. Lawyers seldom play the representative role when their clients are individuals and the disputes involve potential ongoing relationships. Lawyer participation as a representative in settlement conferences depends upon the processes established by the judges conducting the conferences.

A third role lawyers play in mediation is to help their clients prepare for mediation by providing legal advice, skill training, or both. There are situations, for example, where an attorney's client needs legal advice before entering mediation. This is common in the business world. The owner of a business may feel comfortable participating in mediation and know all the business ramifications of various options that might be proposed, but be uncertain about some of the legal ramifications. Lawyers also may work with clients to help them develop the negotiating skills they need to be effective in mediation. This is very common in divorce situations. A person about to enter mediation may meet with a lawyer to learn ways to participate more effectively in the process.

Finally, lawyers frequently are asked to review mediation agreements. Parties to mediation need to know that their settlement is legal and that they have negotiated a settlement that is not contrary to their own interests. Independent review of the agreement can give them greater confidence in the integrity of their settlement. Sometimes legal review will lead to renegotiation in mediation because the parties have neglected something the reviewing lawyers believe important. Based on the legal advice, parties can return to mediation to resolve problems identified by the lawyers.

Examples of Mediation

Divorce Mediation

Karen and Eric Jolson have been married for twelve years. She is thirty-one; he is thirty-three. They have two children, Vicki, 11, and Erin, 8. Karen and Eric were married when she graduated from high school. Eric has been in construction work since he graduated from high school. For the last two years he has been a foreman for a commercial construction company. Karen and Eric wanted a family and had their daughter, Vicki, the year after they married. At the time of Vicki's birth, Karen was committed to staying at home with her family. Eric encouraged her to do so. He wanted a marriage in which he would be responsible for providing the income and his wife would be responsible for the home.

Within a year of Erin's birth, however, Karen was feeling dissatisfied with being a "mere housewife." With Eric's approval she enrolled in the local community college and earned an associate's degree in nursing. It took her three years to complete the two-year program because she went only part-time so as to cause minimal interruption at home. Karen found great satisfaction in her education and was anxious to find at least a part-time job as a nurse.

When Erin started kindergarten Karen felt free to find a job. Eric was not pleased with her decision. He continued to feel that Karen was primarily responsible for the home and rearing the children. He thought working mothers were unfair to their children. Eric loved Vicki and Erin but felt that his most important role was to make sure the family had an adequate income. He did not particularly enjoy young children and resisted Karen's suggestions that he spend more time with them at night and on weekends.

Karen found a part-time job as an emergency room nurse at the hospital. She loved the job and the freedom it gave her. For twenty hours a week she was involved in an exciting, active environment where her nursing skills were needed and appreciated. She liked being around other professionals and being involved in the life-and-death decisions that were made daily. She felt guilty about "abandoning" her family, however, a term Eric had used on a night when she got home late, Eric was sick and dinner was later than usual.

Karen's job required her to work a rotating schedule. During her weeks on night and swing-shifts things became very tense at home. She would rarely see Eric since he worked days and left the house by 7:00 each morning. She arranged day care for Vicki and Erin after school until Eric could pick them up. Eric resented Karen's disruption of their family life, while Karen resented Eric's refusal to help make things work out for her. Karen tried to find a part-time job that would require her to work only daytime hours, but was unable to do so. Meanwhile, her relationship with Eric deteriorated. She felt that he was threatened by her independence and her competence. He felt that his dreams about marriage and family were being destroyed and that somehow he must be inadequate if Karen needed mental stimulation from other people. He continued to feel that Vicki and Erin were the real victims of their mother's career.

Approximately two years after Karen started working, Eric told her that she would have to choose between her job and her family. He was simply unable to live with the unpredictable situation at home. After several months of discussion, they agreed that their marriage could not continue.

The decision to end their marriage was hard on Karen and Eric. Both felt guilty about their inability to adapt or to change. Finally Eric moved into his own apartment, approximately a mile from the family home. Vicki and Erin continued to live with Karen but spent at least half their time with Eric. When the children were with him, Eric slept on the couch in the living room so that each child could have a bedroom.

After several months of separation Karen filed for divorce. She met with her attorney and explained that she and Eric would like to make the dissolution process as painless as possible. Her attorney explained what needed to be done and asked if Karen and Eric could work out a property settlement, support and child custody agreement. She said they would try.

Karen and Eric were able to agree on a property settlement and support plan, and also agreed that they would have joint custody of the children. They were unable to agree on where the children would live and how much time each of them would have with the children.

One of Eric's friends at work recommended that they try mediation. He gave Eric the name of Lee Erixson, the mediator who had worked with him and his former wife when he was divorced. Eric mentioned the idea to Karen. Karen was not sure she could trust a mediator selected by Eric but agreed to meet with Erixson.

Eric called Erixson, who told him he would like to meet with Karen and Eric together. They scheduled an appointment for the following week. When they arrived at Erixson's office Karen was obviously upset. She listened to Erixson explain what mediation involved and that he would help them with their immediate dispute as well as help them learn a process for resolving the conflicts they undoubtedly would have as the children got older. Erixson also explained his training in psychology and mediation. Finally Karen admitted that she felt she was being teamed up on by two men and feared that her interests would not be properly protected. Erixson suggested that they consider having two mediators and told them about a female colleague, Adrian Finley. Erixson explained that he and Finley frequently worked together in divorce mediation but emphasized that both of them were neutrals in the process and refused to become advocates for either party. Eric agreed with Karen that the team approach might be a good idea. They set up an appointment to meet Finley. Following that meeting both Karen and Eric felt comfortable enough to proceed.

At their first meeting Erixson and Finley gave Karen and Eric a list of ground rules that they thought important to follow in mediation. They asked them to read the ground rules and discuss adding others. The ground rules were as follows:

1. The parties agree to stay focused on the issues they have chosen to submit to mediation.
2. The parties agree to give the other a chance to talk, and to listen without interrupting.
3. The parties agree that all information shared in mediation is confidential and that it will not be used by them should this matter go to court.
4. The parties agree that the mediator(s) may call in experts to help if necessary; e.g., school counselor, family physician, accountant.
5. The parties agree that the mediator(s) may meet with the parties individually but that if such meetings occur, the other party will be informed of the meeting and have an equal opportunity to meet.
6. The parties agree to give each other advance notice if an emergency arises that prevents them from attending a mediation session.
7. The parties agree that mediation sessions will last no longer than 90 minutes.
8. The parties agree to have independent legal review of any agreement they reach in mediation.
9. The parties agree that the mediator(s) may make suggestions but that the parties themselves are responsible for any settlement.
10. The parties agree that the primary bread winner will pay the cost of mediation, each 90-minute session being $95.00.
11. The parties agree that if they encounter problems carrying out any agreement they make in mediation they will return to mediation, though not necessarily with these mediators, to attempt to work out their differences.

Karen and Eric added to the ground rules that the mediators could meet with Vicki and Erin if they thought it appropriate. They amended the pay ground rule to provide that they would each pay half the cost of mediation. Finally, they added a provision that if after the fourth mediation session it appeared no progress was being made, they would each consult a lawyer about how to resolve the time sharing issue. They signed the ground rules, an act Erixson and Finley explained was an important symbol of their commitment to the mediation process.

During the first session Erixson and Finley sought to get a better understanding of how Karen and Eric had made decisions during their marriage, who was more involved with the rearing of the children, whether one personality was more dominant in the relationship, and how the current time sharing arrangement was working out. As they explored these issues with Karen and Eric they discovered that neither appeared ready to discuss the issue of time sharing that had brought them to mediation. Karen was very nervous. She admitted to feeling guilty about her marriage ending, but said she knew she would be unable to go back to the way things were before she earned her nursing degree. Eric admitted he was only marginally involved with the children when they were younger, but he was ready now to make a greater commitment to them. He refused to allow them to be cut out of his life. Further, he expressed sadness and anger about the divorce. He admitted to a highly romantic view of marriage and said he really thought Karen had shared that vision with him when they were married. Now he felt he could not trust Karen and wondered if he would be able to trust any woman in the future.

Near the end of the first session Erixson and Finley suggested to Karen and Eric that both of them still had many emotional issues weighing them down and that they each needed a safe environment in which to deal with them. They suggested the names of several counselors who they thought might be able to help them deal with some of the hurt, guilt and fear involved in their divorce. They stressed the normalcy of people in Karen and Eric's position seeking counseling. They strongly recommended that mediation not continue until the emotional issues had been dealt with. Karen and Eric were relieved by the suggestion and were able to admit to each other that they were more upset by the divorce than they had been able to admit before.

Following the first mediation session Karen and Eric each sought counseling. The second mediation session did not occur for approximately six weeks. At the second session Erixson and Finley had Karen and Eric talk to one another about what they had learned in counseling. Each seemed more reconciled to the divorce and ready to move to the next phase. The mediators explained that even though they might be going separate ways they must remain partners on one point, the rearing of their children. They said the couple must learn to interact with one another as business partners, their products being Vicki and Erin.

The second session focused on the time sharing issue. Karen said she did not trust Eric's ability to take care of the children, although she readily acknowledged his love for them. The couple then discussed the differences in their ways of living. Karen was highly organized, thought it important for the house to be neat and for the children to have meals on a regular basis. She admitted that it was not always possible for meals to be on time given her work schedule, but she always insured they were fed properly. She took responsibility for doing the laundry and ironing. Eric, on the other hand, characterized himself as more "laid back." He said he had so much pressure at work that he liked to relax at home. A sink full of dirty dishes and clutter in the apartment did not bother him when he was tired or thought something else in life more important. One Saturday, for example, he thought it was more important to take the children to the zoo than to clean the apartment. When Karen picked up the children that night she was furious because the apartment was a mess. Eric wondered if Karen's values weren't too rigid. He did acknowledge Karen's love of the children and her desire to do what was best for them.

Erixson and Finley got the couple to focus on each parent's strengths with the children. After approximately forty-five minutes Karen and Eric agreed that their differences in lifestyle were not that significant. During this time Erixson and Finley worked with Karen and Eric on listening skills. Occasionally they would interrupt the discussion to get Karen or Eric to paraphrase what the other had said. They would also interrupt for clarification when they thought either spouse was sending a confused message.

The second session ended with brainstorming on the time sharing question. Karen and Eric left with a list of possible options, which they were to think about before the third session. Although some of the options on the list were clearly unacceptable, each was to return ready to discuss options on the list they thought might have merit. Erixson and Finley asked Karen and Eric to meet for an hour in a neutral place between sessions to discuss options.

The third session focused exclusively on options for time sharing. Karen and Eric reported that their meeting at a conference room at the local library had gone quite well. They were able to laugh together as they explained to the mediators why they had chosen that location, and said after about half-an-hour of discussion were able to move to a restaurant where they continued to talk about options over coffee and pastry. Their meeting lasted a little over an hour and they left feeling more confident that they would be able to talk effectively with each other again.

Before the end of the third session Karen and Eric had agreed to a plan they were willing to try for time sharing. They had the mediators write down the following:

1. Karen and Eric Jolson agree to joint custody of their children, Vicki and Erin, following their divorce.
2. Karen and Eric Jolson agree that the children's primary home will be with their mother, Karen.
3. Karen and Eric Jolson agree that Eric will live in a house or apartment in the same school attendance boundary as Karen's home.
4. Karen and Eric Jolson agree that the Vicki and Erin will alternate homes on a two-week rotation. In order to facilitate this rotation Karen and Eric further agree that:
   a. Should either parent's work schedule make this arrangement infeasible, they will consult with the other to see if the other parent is available as a backup.
   b. They will employ the same day care center and babysitters so that if they cannot serve as backup for one another, the children will have consistent care.
   c. Should either parent be unable to be backup for the other, neither will complain nor hold a grudge because both understand and accept their primary responsibilities.
5. Karen and Eric Jolson agree that this time sharing arrangement automatically will be re-evaluated when Vicki enters high school.
6. Karen and Eric Jolson agree to return to mediation if the arrangement they have worked out is not satisfactory.

Karen and Eric reviewed what had been written and agreed that it stated accurately what they had agreed to for time sharing. They further agreed that they would give a copy of the agreement to their lawyers for the lawyers to include as the proposed settlement to be submitted to the court for approval.

QUESTIONS

1. Do you think it was appropriate for the mediator to recommend outside counselling to Karen and Eric in this situation? Why or why not? How do you think the process would have proceeded if they had not received counselling?

2. Assume that Karen and Eric had not entered mediation voluntarily. Is this the kind of situation in which a court should have ordered mediation? Why or why not?

3. What do you perceive to be the strengths and weaknesses of team mediation?

4. Who represented the children in this mediation?

Criminal Mediation

Late one Friday night several residents of a neighborhood populated mostly by elderly and low income persons were awakened by the sound of screeching car tires, and a loud "thud," followed by the sound of a car speeding away. Cecelia Gustufson, a retired teacher, went to her front window to find that the car had driven over the curb onto her lawn, tearing up the grass, and knocking down a magnolia tree she had planted about six feet from the curb the year before. Her neighbor, Homer Winslow, had been watching television in his living room, looked out the window, and took down the license plate number of the car.

Gustufson called the police, who arrested Jeffery Sargent approximately thirty minutes later. Sargent admitted to having had a "few beers" before getting into his car. Sargent, twenty-two years of age, lived about a block south of Gustufson and told police he had been fired from his job as an automobile mechanic that afternoon. He was depressed and angry when he decided to go for a drive. Sargent was charged with criminal trespass and criminal damage to property. It was his first arrest. The damage to Gustufson's yard was approximately $75. The magnolia tree, which she had planted right after her husband's death, had cost $60 and had great emotional signifi-cance for her because it was her late husband's favorite kind of tree.

The officer investigating the incident discovered that Sargent had done yard work for Gustuf-son and her husband when he was a student at the local high school, but that she had not had contact with him since he graduated four years ago. Attorneys assigned to the case agreed with the presiding judge that this might be an appropriate case for mediation. Gustufson agreed to meet with Sargent and a mediator to discuss the situation.

During mediation Gustufson learned that Sargent had not intended to damage her property, an insight she found helpful because she was increasingly worried about living alone in the neighborhood. She found through talking with Sargent that she still liked him, just as she had when he used to do odd jobs for her. Sargent admitted to having trouble with alcohol, particu-larly when he was angry or frustrated. He also said that he did not have the $135 it would take to restore Gustufson's lawn and tree. After approximately a two hour mediation session Gustufson agreed that she would not press charges against Sargent if he would agree to get help with his drinking problem. Sargent agreed to do the physical work of replanting Gustufson's grass and to pay her $10 per week to cover the cost of materials and a new tree as soon as he found work. The mediator asked Sargent to get information on alcohol programs that week and to return with a specific proposal within a week. With the details of a program worked out, the prosecuting attorney agreed to drop the charges against Sargent. A few days later Gustufson called Sargent to ask if he would be interested in painting her house while he looked for other work. He agreed, and suggested that she deduct from his pay what he owed her for the materials and cost of a new magnolia tree.

QUESTIONS

1. Do you think mediation was appropriate in this situation? Why or why not? How much choice did Gustufson have about participating in the process? If she had preferred that Sargent be prosecuted, should her wish have been followed? Why or why not?

2. Identify situations in which mediation in criminal misdemeanor cases might be inappro-priate. What are your criteria for making the determination?

3. Can you envision any situations in which mediation might be appropriate in felony cases? Why should mediation be limited to misdemeanor cases?

Trends in Mediation

At least two trends in mediation deserve emphasis. One is the growth of community dispute resolution programs, which rely on mediation as their primary dispute resolution technique. The other is a process called med-arb, a hybrid of mediation and arbitration.

Community Dispute Resolution

Community dispute resolution is an umbrella term describing a wide variety of programs. Some programs are traditional parts of particular subcultures or religions, such as Jewish conciliation boards. Other programs began in the 1970s in response to dissatisfaction with the formal justice system and commitment to informal community structures to maintain social harmony and norms within neighborhoods and communities. Most community dispute resolution programs are voluntary, deriving their legitimacy from community consensus or religious norms rather than from the exercise of state power.[14] They provide forums where members of a community can get help resolving their family, consumer and neighborhood disputes without giving up decision-making power to the formal, adversary, sometimes alien judicial system.

Some community dispute resolution programs have close ties with local courts or law enforcement agencies. Selected misdemeanor offenses or disputes involving neighbors can be referred to community dispute resolution programs. If no satisfactory resolution occurs, the case is placed on the regular court docket or returned to the district attorney's office for criminal processing. Cases referred to community dispute resolution programs typically involve alcohol abuse in the family or neighborhood, or petty misdemeanors for which restitution is seen as more appropriate than punishment.

Mediation and fact-finding are the methods most commonly used in community dispute resolution programs that serve geographic areas rather than cultural groups.[15] The programs usually are staffed by volunteer mediators who have received some formal training in mediation. Sometimes a combination of mediation and arbitration is used. Volunteer mediators help the disputants find their own solutions to problems, but if they are unable to do so, the mediator will recommend a solution that the parties agree will be binding.

Community dispute resolution programs frequently act as a source of referrals to other agencies. Disputes arising out of drug abuse, for example, sometimes are most appropriately handled through referral to a drug treatment program. Finally, community dispute resolution centers serve as a place people can call to discuss their disputes. Often just talking with a volunteer leads to a solution of a problem. Although community dispute resolution programs differ in their details, the basic idea is that the people involved in the dispute are encouraged to explore their problem, accept responsibility for it, and find a solution with the aid of volunteers.

Community dispute resolution programs have been hailed as a grassroots response to an alien judicial system, and as a positive way to reinforce community values in an increasingly autonomous society.[16] But the programs also have been criticized as informal judicial systems lacking the procedural safeguards of the formal judicial system and as another means by which the dominant culture imposes its values on nonconformists.[17]

Example of Community Dispute Resolution

Jack Renfro and Peter Giordano have been neighbors for two years. They did not become close friends, but their relationship was never strained until Giordano decided to put up a fence to separate his backyard from Renfro's backyard. Giordano bought the fencing material and rented a post hole digger. He paid an engineer $50 to read the property description on the survey Giordano had done of the property and to identify where the post holes should be dug. When Giordano began to set the posts, Renfro came running out of his house and told him to get off his property. Renfro claimed that Giordano was setting the posts at least two feet beyond Giordano's boundary. The two became involved in a screaming match. A neighbor, fearing that the confrontation would become physical, called the police.

The police officer called to the scene listened to both sides of the argument. The officer concluded that it was pointless to give a citation to either Giordano or Renfro, but told them they would have to quit yelling at each other if they wanted to avoid arrest. The officer gave both men a brochure explaining the community dispute resolution program, and later called Betty Altschuler, an outreach counsellor in the dispute resolution program, to suggest that the disputing neighbors be contacted. Giordano recalled reading about the program in his neighborhood newsletter.

Altschuler contacted Giordano and Renfro the following Monday. She suggested that they meet with a trained mediator the next evening to discuss the dispute. She recommended that they each bring their property surveys and any other information they had about their property boundaries. Giordano and Renfro agreed, and at 7:00 on Tuesday evening met at a room in the community center with Norma Jason, a volunteer mediator. Jason explained mediation to Renfro and Giordano, emphasizing that it was her role to help them facilitate their own resolution of their dispute. She explained that any agreement they reached would be voluntary and nonbinding, and that everything that went on in mediation would be strictly confidential.

During mediation Giordano and Renfro discovered that their property surveys showed that each of them owned the disputed parcel of property. Hence, each had objective evidence to support his side of the dispute. With Jason's help, they agreed to approach city officials for help in obtaining an accurate survey. Jason wrote down what she understood to be their agreement and read it to them. Renfro and Giordano confirmed the accuracy of her memorandum. Jason put the statement in a file at the community dispute resolution office.

One month later Altschuler called Renfro and Giordano to find out what had happened with their dispute. They reported that with the help of a city surveyor they were able to establish their property lines and that Giordano had put up the fence. Neither indicated a need to return to mediation nor to take legal action.

QUESTIONS

1. What function did the mediation serve in this dispute? Could the same function have been served by another dispute resolution process?

2. Should neighborhood dispute resolution centers be funded publicly? Why or why not? Should courts have the discretion to assign certain cases to neighborhood dispute resolution centers? Why or why not?

Med-Arb

As its name implies, med-arb is a hybrid of mediation and arbitration. Parties to a dispute first meet with a neutral person who attempts to help them resolve their dispute through mediation. If mediation fails, the mediator either becomes an arbitrator and issues an award, or an arbitrator is called in to hear the dispute and issue an award.[18]

Med-arb enjoys growing popularity in commercial and business disputes, where the parties are committed to resolving their disputes outside of court. Med-arb also is being used in some jurisdictions that require mediation in domestic relations cases. If mediation is unsuccessful, the mediator is authorized to offer a solution, which either party can appeal to a trial *de novo*.

In some med-arb situations different persons serve as mediators and arbitrators. It is not uncommon, however, for the same person to serve in both capacities. Med-arb requires unusual skills on the part of the person who plays both roles. Mediators, after all, are retained to facilitate discussion and to help parties agree on their own solutions to problems. Arbitrators are retained to take evidence and to render a judgment following the parties' presentation of evidence. The dynamics of the two processes are substantially different: mediation strives to minimize the adversary nature of disputes, while arbitration works well within an adversary model. Because of its hybrid nature, med-arb seems most appropriate as a voluntary, private dispute resolution method with the parties having control over the choice of forum and the person or persons who serve as mediator-arbitrators.

Example of Med-Arb

John Cotesworth, Evan Handy and Cynthia Paul attended veterinary school together in the mid-1960s. During school they were best friends and decided to go into partnership together in a small town in the mid-west when they graduated. Because they were such close friends they decided to run their practice on a very informal basis. They each contributed money to buy equipment and supplies, rent a clinic, and advertise their services. Handy's father had been a veterinarian and gave them a lot of good advice, some equipment, and his patient list when he retired. Cotesworth, Handy and Paul agreed to share profits equally.

For almost fifteen years the practice went quite smoothly. The clinic developed an excellent reputation in the community and each of the veterinarians was highly respected and well known. Paul served three terms as mayor, Cotesworth was active in United Way, and Handy was named Citizen of the Year in 1984 for his work with senior citizens.

In May 1986, the three started to have problems. Cotesworth and his wife were divorced after several months of a child custody battle. Cotesworth's ex-wife remained Cynthia Paul's best friend. Paul found it increasingly hard to work with Cotesworth given what his former wife told her about him. Handy, who had always been a social drinker, occasionally showed up for work intoxicated or hung over and sometimes was unable to perform even routine surgeries. Cotesworth had no patience with Handy's drinking and would refuse to speak to Handy for several days after Handy had come to work intoxicated. Soon the personal problems started having professional ramifications. Cotesworth felt that because he was single Paul and Handy expected him to do most of the weekend emergency work but were unwilling to compensate him for it.

Paul felt that both Cotesworth and Handy assigned the temperamental cases to her because of her diplomacy with people and her ability to calm nervous animals. By mid-year the three veterinarians could barely speak to one another and realized that they should stop trying to work together.

Every time Cotesworth, Handy and Paul tried to discuss the best way to end their partnership they got into serious arguments. None was content with a three-way split. Paul and Cotesworth felt they had contributed much more than their share of time to the practice, while Handy contended they should not be allowed to benefit from all the help they had received from his father when they were starting their practice. Neither Cotesworth nor Paul wanted to stop practicing veterinary medicine, although Handy readily admitted that he was ready for a career change. Both Cotesworth and Paul wanted the equipment and the clinic; Handy said he would rather sell his share to anybody else than Cotesworth and Paul.

Cotesworth finally consulted his lawyer about the best way to dissolve the partnership. His attorney asked to see a copy of the original partnership agreement in order to study the provisions for dissolution. Cotesworth explained that when the three had started out they were best friends and that they had operated all these years without a partnership agreement.

Cotesworth's lawyer listened to her client's explanation of the problem confronting the veterinarians and explained med-arb. The three could try to negotiate a settlement to their dispute with the aid of a neutral mediator. Lacking agreement, the mediator either could offer an opinion or could turn the dispute over to an arbitrator. Cotesworth's lawyer gave him a list of three people in the community who practiced mediation.

Cotesworth, Handy and Paul interviewed the three mediators and agreed that one would be acceptable. They agreed that they did not want everyone in the town to know about their problems and concluded that the mediator should be authorized to arbitrate the dispute if they were unable to resolve their dispute.

The mediator spent several hours with the three explaining mediation and establishing ground rules. Achieving agreement on a process was a big step. In addition to agreeing on a process, they agreed to meet twice a week for two hours until they either came to agreement or reached stalemate.

The three veterinarians stayed in mediation for almost five weeks. Sometimes they met together; sometimes the mediator met with them individually or in pairs. The mediator was able to get them to talk about what had happened to their friendship as well as the best way to dissolve the partnership. Cotesworth finally understood that Paul had been angry with him because of his divorce and comments from his ex-wife. He thought she disapproved of the way he had handled a case several months ago and was holding a grudge. Cotesworth and Paul both came to a better understanding of Handy's drinking problem, apparently precipitated by the fact that he no longer liked veterinary medicine but thought he was too old to make a career change. Cotesworth and Handy listened to Paul's resentment about being given the most difficult patients. All were able to acknowledge how important their friendship had been over the years.

Through mediation Cotesworth and Paul were able to agree that they both wanted to continue to practice veterinary medicine in the same town and that they did not want to be in competition with one another. They knew, however, that they would never be close friends as they once had been. They agreed to retain a lawyer to draw up a formal partnership agreement.

Despite their progress in mediation, the three were not able to agree how much Handy should be paid for his share of the partnership. That issue eventually was turned over to the mediator, now arbitrator, for a decision. Cotesworth and Paul then agreed on what percentage of the award each of them should pay Handy. Handy used his share of the settlement to relocate in another community to work with a group of cattle breeders.

QUESTIONS

1. Would any other dispute resolution forum have been appropriate for this dispute? Why or why not?

2. In what situations might it be inappropriate for a mediator to "change hats" and serve as an arbitrator?

3. The case law of the jurisdiction probably contained a rough formula for partnership divisions. Should the parties have followed it? Should they have been aware of it? What role do you think legal rules should have played in this mediation? Why?

Endnotes

[1] W. Davies & P. Fouracre, The Settlement of Disputes in Early Medieval Europe 236-237 (1987).

[2] J. Folberg & A. Taylor, Mediation--A Comprehensive Guide to Resolving Conflicts Without Litigation 1-7 (1984).

[3] See J. Auerbach, Justice Without Law? 35-36 (1983).

[4] R. Coulson, Business Arbitration--What You Need to Know 8 (1986).

[5] Ch. 347, 44 Stat. 577 (1926) (codified as amended at 15 U.S.C. §§ 21, 45; 18 U.S.C. § 373; 28 U.S.C. §§ 1291-1294; 45 U.S.C. AA 151-163, 181-88 (1982)).

[6] 45 U.S.C. §§ 154, 183 (1982).

[7] 29 U.S.C. § 172 (1982).

[8] Task Force on Mediation, *Divorce and Family Mediation Standards of Practice*, 1986 A.B.A. Sec. Fam. Law 24 (Standard IIID).

[9] *Id*. at 32-33 (Standard VIA).

[10] Pirie, *The Lawyer as Mediator: Professional Responsibility Problems or Profession Problems?*, 63 Canadian B. Rev. 378, 383 (1985).

[11] W. Brazil, Settling Civil Suits (1985).

[12] Will, Merhige & Rubin, *The Role of the Judge in the Settlement Process*, 75 F.R.D. 203 (1978); see Schiller & Wall, *Judicial Settlement Techniques*, 5 Am. J. Tr. Ad. 39, 41-44 (1981).

[13] Friedman & Anderson, *Divorce Mediation's Strength*, 3 Cal. Law. 36 (7) (1983).

[14] R. Shonholtz, Neighborhood Justice Forums: An Expression of Neighborhood Covergence (1983).

[15] See J. Beer, Peacemaking in Your Neighborhood (1986).

[16] Ford Foundation, New Approaches to Conflict Resolution (1978).

[17] See Fiss, *Against Settlement*, 93 Yale L. J. 1073 (1984).

[18] See Goldberg, *The Mediation of Grievances Under a Collective Bargaining Contract*, 77 Nw. U. L. Rev. 170, 281-293 (1982).

Sources

The American Bar Association, Model Code of Professional Responsibility (1980).

_____, Divorce and Family Mediation Standards of Practice (1986).

J. Auerbach, Justice Without Law? (1983).

J. Beer, Peacemaking in Your Neighborhood (1986).

_____, Standards of Practice for Lawyer-Mediators in Family Disputes, Dispute Resolution Forum 5 (1984).

W. Brazil, Settling Civil Suits (1986).

Bureau of National Affairs, Public Sector Mediation (1983).

R. Coulson, Business Arbitration--What You Need to Know (1986).

W. Davies & P. Fouracre, The Settlement of Disputes in Early Medieval Europe (1987).

Disputes Processing Research Program, The Emergence of the Judge as a Mediator in Civil Cases, Working Paper, University of Wisconsin (1984).

Fiss, *Against Settlement,* 93 Yale L. J. 1073 (1984).

J. Folberg & A. Taylor, Mediation--A Comprehensive Guide to Resolving Conflicts Without LItigation (1984).

Ford Foundation, New Approaches to Conflict Resolution (1978).

Friedman, *Mediation: Reducing Dependence on Lawyers and Courts to Achieve Justice,* 1980 People's Law Review 42 (1980).

Friedman & Anderson, *Divorce Mediation's Strengths,* 3 Cal. Law. 36 (7) (1983).

Fuller, *Mediation: Its Forms and Functions,* 44 S. Cal. L. Rev. 305 (1971).

Goldberg, *The Mediation of Grievances Under a Collective Bargaining Contract,* 77 Nw. U. L. Rev. 270 (1982).

Lerman, *Mediation of Wife Abuse Cases: The Adverse Impact of Informal Dispute Resolution on Women,* 7 Harv. Women's L. J. 57 (1984).

C. Moore, The Mediation Process (1986).

Phillips & Piazza, *The Role of Mediation in Public Interest Disputes,* 34 Hastings L. J. 1231 (1983).

Pirie, *The Lawyer As Mediator: Professional Responsibility Problems or Profession Problems?,"* 63 Canadian B. Rev. 378 (1985).

Riskin, *Mediation and Lawyers,"* 43 Ohio St. L. J. 29 (1982).

Schiller & Wall, *Judicial Settlement Techniques,* 5 Am. J. Tr. Ad. 39 (1981).

R. Shonholtz, Neighborhood Justice Forums: An Expression of Neighborhood Convergence (1983).

W. Simkin & N. Fidandis, Mediation and the Dynamics of Collective Bargaining (1986).

Will, Merhige, & Rubin, *The Role of the Judge in the Settlement Process,* 75 F.R.D. 203 (1978).

Anderson v. Anderson

494 So.2d 237 (Fla.Dist.Ct. App.1986)

Glickstein, Judge.

This case is a perfect example of why the legislature in the closing hours of its session in June 1986 adopted enlightened legislation by the creation of section 61.183, Florida Statutes (1986), which provides:

61.183 Mediation of certain contested issues.

(1) In any proceeding in which the issues of custody, primary residence, or visitation of a child are contested, the court may refer the parties to mediation. Mediation services may be provided by the court or by any court-approved mediator.

(2) If an agreement is reached by the parties on the contested issues, a consent order incorporating the agreement shall be prepared by the mediator and submitted to the parties and their

attorneys for review. Upon approval by the parties, the consent order shall be reviewed by the court and, if approved, entered. Thereafter, the consent order may be enforced in the same manner as any other court order.

(3) Any information from the files, reports, case summaries, mediator's notes, or other communications or materials, oral or written, relating to a mediation proceeding pursuant to this section, obtained by any person performing mediation duties, is privileged and confidential and may not be disclosed without the written consent of all parties to the proceeding. Any research or evaluation effort directed at assessing program activities or performance must protect the confidentiality of such information. Each party to a mediation proceeding has a privilege during and after the proceeding to refuse to disclose and to prevent another from disclosing communications made during the proceeding, whether or not the contested issues are successfully resolved. This subsection shall not be construed to prevent or inhibit the discovery or admissibility of any information that is otherwise subject to discovery or that is admissible under applicable law or rules of court, except that any conduct or statements made during a mediation proceeding or in negotiations concerning the proceeding are inadmissible in any judicial proceeding.

Hopefully, now every circuit will put in place what Dade County has already been doing by providing for the mediation of matters which involve children. There, twenty-five of the thirty-one judges in that court's General Jurisdiction (Civil) Division, by administrative memorandum, require mediation in all dissolution actions where the issue of primary residential parental contact of the non-residential parent is to be resolved. Statistical data from that court shows [sic] that for the period of January to April, 1986, of the 1,276 mandated referrals to the Family Mediation Unit, 1,116 reached agreement by the unit or through the parties' counsel and submitted to the unit, which translates to an eighty-six percent settlement rate at an early stage in the proceeding.

Here, two nice people have gone through the wrenching adversarial process over the primary physical residence of their two small children, now five and eight. The wife has lost, because the husband proved that he was more emotionally stable than the wife, whose difficulties have been exacerbated by the fight over the children in the system. Hopefully, the above statute will be considered as an alternative to an adversary resolution of these parties' post-dissolution controversies. There is, however, competent evidence upon which to place these children with the husband. Thus the wife must leave the marital home and the children, as we affirm the trial court's decision with the hope that the children will be sheltered, as much as possible, by both parties from the breakup and the adversarial decision as to the parent with whom they are presently to reside. * * *

This case points out the wisdom of first determining the issues involving children, hopefully by mediation, and if not, then by the adversary process. Following that decision, the parties can best proceed to achieve an informed decision as to their individual economic welfare.

QUESTIONS

1. Why does Judge Glickstein think the Florida mediation statute is "enlightened"? Are his reasons consistent? Why might the judge have chosen this case to praise mediation?

2. Is divorce mediation more or less justified when children are involved? Why? How does the judge envision domestic relations cases being processed in the future?

Sonenstahl v. E.L.S., Inc.

372 N.W.2d 1 (Minn.Ct.App. 1985)

Foley, Judge.

The appellants, who are detectives in the Hennepin County Sheriff's Department, appeal from a judgment and an order denying their motion for a new trial. The trial court determined that the respondent union (L.E.L.S.) did not breach its duty to fairly represent the detectives when it negotiated the 1982 and 1983 collective bargaining agreements between the Sheriff's Department and the County. The court also held that the detectives did not have the right to a jury trial and that they could not properly subpoena the mediator from the Bureau of Mediation Services who had assisted with the negotiation process. We affirm.

The appellants are detectives in the Hennepin County Sheriff's Department. The respondent union L.E.L.S. and its local have represented the sheriff's department in the negotiation of labor contracts with the county since 1978.

In the spring of 1981 the union became aware that the county might be willing to reopen the 1981 wage rate for all sheriff's department personnel in order to negotiate a cost-of-living increase which had been given to other county personnel for 1981. The county also expressed a willingness to offer the detectives in the sheriff's department an additional 2 1/2% pay increase to bring them up to the increased salary which had been approved for non-union County Investigators. This similar wage level between the departments is referred to as "parity." The chief negotiator for the union, Roland Miles, determined that since the negotiations for the 1982 contract would begin in the summer of 1981, the cost-of-living and parity issues should be deferred until then.

Negotiations for the 1982 contract then began in the summer of 1981. The parity issue was submitted to the county, along with a package of other issues. The county initially accepted the detectives' parity request, but reserved the other issues for negotiation. However, sometime in mid-fall of 1981, Roland Miles indicated that the parity issue could possibly be used as a trade-off for other benefits.

A meeting of the general union membership was held in December 1981. Approximately 20 to 50 members were present. A 10% overall increase in salary was being requested and, in addition to the detectives' parity request, a group of junior deputies in the sheriff's department was also requesting a further salary increase.

At the December meeting, the members voiced their strong feelings that the detectives should not receive the parity increase. They expressed hostility towards the detectives, and the mood was tense. A motion was offered and passed that the detectives' parity should be traded for other benefits, if possible, although nothing specific was indicated.

In January 1982 the detectives formally requested withdrawal from union representation. They also refused to vote for the 10% across-the-board increase submitted to the general members, which included the request for the junior deputies but which did not include the detectives' parity request. The 10% proposal was not ratified by the general members.

In March 1982 another general meeting was held, at which Roland Miles presented an overall across-the-board package of a 9% increase, plus concessions for the junior deputies. That contract was ratified by the general members.

Although the negotiating committee had apparently been aware that the county would accept the parity increase, and that the union could not obtain additional benefits for other members by giving up the detectives' parity, the committee nonetheless had voted to exclude the parity issue from the final package submitted to the general members. The reason given for this decision was that inclusion of the parity proposal would jeopardize the entire package, due to the general members' demonstrated negative attitude towards the detectives at the December meeting. The county had indicated that the parity issue should not be included if it would cause ratification problems.

After the 1982 contract was ratified, the detectives went to the union and requested release from union representation. The union indicated that it was not interested in releasing the detectives, but would request the local to pursue the parity issue in the negotiations for the 1983 contract.

In 1983, no equity (i.e. parity) adjustments were allowed by the county, due to the state and county's financial situation. However, because the investigators would only be receiving a 5 to 6%

increase in salary, Roland Miles asked for an across-the-board increase of 9% for the sheriff's department, which would have brought the detectives' salary above parity. He did not ask for a greater amount for the detectives than the others fearing that the others would get less. The matter went to arbitration, since the county would not agree to the 9% increase. The parity argument was submitted to the arbitrator, but he eventually ordered only a 6% across-the-board increase.
* * *

The final issue raised by the appellant detectives is whether the trial court erred when it quashed the subpoena of the mediator who had participated in the negotiations between the union and the county. The detectives contend the mediator would have testified that Roland Miles "flagrantly misrepresented" the detectives' interests and "continuously rejected" offers from the county regarding the parity issue. The detectives also allege, and testimony indicates, that the mediator himself expressed a willingness to testify to this alleged breach of the union's duty in court.

The detectives correctly note that a provision of P.E.L.R.A. [Public Employment Labor Relations Act] states that all mediation sessions between public employers and employees or their representatives are public meetings unless otherwise provided by the Director of Mediation Services. Minn. Stat. 179A.14, subd. 3 (1984). In the present situation there is no indication that the negotiation proceedings were intended to be private. The trial court, however, found that "the proffered reasons for [the mediator's] testimony are insufficient to overcome the compelling need for a mediator to maintain the confidences of the parties and the appearance of impartiality". Thus, the court clearly believed that the policy of promoting successful mediation of public employ-

ment disputes outweighed the need for disclosing what the mediator believed was happening in this instance. As the respondent union and amicus Bureau of Mediation Services note, P.E.L.R.A. itself provides that successful mediation furthers the public interest:

[Unresolved] disputes between the public employer and its employee are injurious to the public as well as to the parties. Adequate means must be established for minimizing them and providing for their resolution * * *. (Minn. Stat. § 179A.01 (1984).

This language supports the trial court's decision to disallow the mediator's testimony, based upon policy reasons.

The legislature has recently recognized the need to maintain confidential certain communications made during the mediation process. In 1984 by amendment to the statute regarding privileges the legislature stated:

A person cannot be examined as to any communication or document, including worknotes, made or used in the course of or because of mediation pursuant to an agreement to mediate. This does not apply to the parties in the dispute in an application to a court by a party to have a mediated settlement agreement set aside or reformed. A communication or document otherwise not privileged does not become privileged because of this paragraph. This paragraph is not intended to limit the privilege accorded to communication during mediation by the common law. Minn. Stat. § 595.02, subd. 1(k) (1984).

In view of this statutory mandate, we believe the reasoning of the trial court was correct, and its decision to quash the subpoena is therefore affirmed.

QUESTIONS

1. Why do the detectives seek the mediator's testimony in this case? Were the detectives represented at the session the mediator conducted? Whose interest is served by the court's refusal to subpoena the mediator's testimony? Is it an appropriate interest for courts to consider when deciding whether to subpoena mediator testimony?

2. What "policy reasons" are behind the 1984 amendment to the Minnesota mediation statute? How, if at all, is that policy abrogated by giving a disaffected party access to evidence that will help resolve an ongoing dispute? Does it matter that the actions complained of in this case occurred before the amendment?

State v. Castellano

460 So.2d. 480 (Fla.Dist.Ct.App.1984)

Grimes, Acting Chief Judge.

The state seeks to appeal an order denying its motion to quash respondent's deposition subpoena of Roger Mallory. Since this is a nonappealable order, we treat the matter as a petition for writ of certiorari.

The respondent was charged with attempted first degree murder. In responding to a demand for discovery, the state listed Mallory as a person having information about the case. The respondent subpoenaed Mallory for the taking of his deposition. Mallory is a mediator in the Citizen's Dispute Settlement Program (CDSP) in the Tenth Judicial Circuit. The respondent asserts that Mallory will be able to testify that during the course of mediation the person who became the victim of the alleged attempted murder made life-threatening statements to the respondent. He maintains such testimony will support his contention of self-defense. The state filed a motion to quash the deposition subpoena urging that statements made to CDSP mediators were privileged. The court denied the motion to quash.

At the outset, we note that section 90.501, Florida Statutes (1983) provides:

> 90.501 *Privileges recognized only as provided.*—Except as otherwise provided by this chapter, any other statute, or the Constitution of the United States or of the State of Florida, no person in a legal proceeding has a privilege to:
>
> (1) Refuse to be a witness.
> (2) Refuse to disclose any matter.
> (3) Refuse to produce any object or writing.
> (4) Prevent another from being a witness, from disclosing any matter, or from producing any object or writing.

Thus, privileges in Florida are no longer creatures of judicial decision. *Marshall v. Anderson,* 459 So.2d 384 (1984).

In this case, the state argues for privilege on two grounds. First, the state contends that communications made by parties in the CDSP are privileged as being in the nature of offers of compromise. However, the rule protecting offers of compromise appears to be one more of admissibility than privilege. The admissibility of offers to compromise is addressed in section 90.408, Florida Statutes (1983):

> 90.408 *Compromise and offers to compromise.*—Evidence of an offer to compromise a claim which was disputed as to validity or amount, as well as any relevant conduct or statements made in negotiations concerning a compromise, is inadmissible to prove liability or absence of liability for the claim or its value.

The plain language of the provision only excludes evidence of an offer of compromise presented to prove liability or the absence of liability for a claim or its value. Therefore, even if the admissibility of such evidence could be equated with the privilege not to disclose the evidence, there is nothing in the statute remotely applicable to the testimony sought herein. This section is simply not relevant to the situation where a mediator testifies in a criminal proceeding regarding an alleged threat made by one party to another in a prior CDSP setting.

Alternatively, the state asserts that since the CDSP is an investigatory arm of the state attorney, the privilege accorded to statements made to a prosecuting attorney should be extended to those made to a CDSP mediator. *See Widener v. Croft,* 184 So. 2d 444 (1966). We know of no rationale to make such an extension. The parties to a CDSP program are simply attempting to resolve a dispute so that a criminal prosecution will be unnecessary. All statements are made voluntarily by persons under no legal compulsion to attend. The record reflects no authority for the mediator's statement that the parties' communications were confidential. The fact that he may have so advised the parties that their communications would be held confidential does not now excuse him from being compelled by respondent to testify concerning what was said.

There is no legal basis for a privilege which would prevent the respondent from obtaining Mallory's testimony. If confidentiality is essential to the success of the CDSP program, the legislature is the proper branch of government from which to obtain the necessary protection.

Certiorari denied.

QUESTIONS

1. Why does Castellano want the mediator's testimony in this case? What is the result if the testimony is unavailable? Is the court's reasoning in this case consistent with the reasoning in *Sonenstahl*? Do you think it relevant that *Sonenstahl* was a civil case and this is a criminal case? Would your answer be the same if the state were seeking the evidence to establish that Castellano knew the victim?

2. With this case as precedent, what advice, if any, should lawyers give clients about whether to participate in a dispute settlement program? Do you think this decision will have a negative effect on the Community Dispute Settlement Program?

3. Judge Grimes indicates that the legislature, not the judiciary or the parties, is responsible for deciding whether mediation should be confidential. Do you agree?

People v. Snyder

492 Misc.2d 137, 492 N.Y.S.2d 890 (1985)

John J. Connell, Acting Justice.

The above named defendant was indicted by the Erie County Grand Jury on charges of Murder in the Second Degree and Criminal Possession of a Weapon in the Second Degree involving an alleged incident on August 16, 1983 in which William Fugate was shot to death by the defendant.

In the case at bar, the defense, both in the voir dire and opening statement to the jury, had raised the defense of justification claiming that the defendant shot and killed William Fugate in self defense. Mention was also made by defense counsel in his opening statement of the victim and defendant's participation with the Community Dispute Resolution Center prior to the fatal shooting. Because of these statements, the District Attorney subpoenaed any and all records pertaining to such mediation between the defendant and the victim and involving a third person, Deborah Nelson.

Attorneys for the Better Business Bureau Foundation which administers the Community Dispute Resolution Center program in Erie County served an Order to Show Cause on the District Attorney's Office signed June 7, 1985 and made returnable on June 10, 1985 seeking that the said subpoena be quashed pursuant to CPLR 2304. On the return date arguments were heard from the attorney for the Better Business Bureau Foundation, the District Attorney's Office and defense counsel for George Snyder. Subsequent to the oral argument, and after review of the paper submitted in support of and in opposition to the motion, and upon review of the applicable statutory law, the motion to quash the subpoena was granted. There appears to be no reported case construing Section 849-b(6) of the Judiciary Law.

The Community Dispute Resolution Center's Program was established in 1981 by the New York State Legislature to enable the creation of community dispute centers to resolve neighborhood and interpersonal disputes. The goal of the Legislature in creating these centers was to provide a "quick, inexpensive and voluntary resolution of disagreements, while at the same time serving the overall public interests by permitting the criminal justice community to concentrate its resources on more serious criminal matters." It was the feeling of the Legislature that in order for such programs to be successful, the parties availing themselves of the services of these forums must feel that they can air their disputes "in an informal atmosphere without restraint and intimidation."

In order to assure confidentiality to the parties involved, and thereby encourage their full, frank, and open participation, Section 849-b(6) of the Judiciary Law was enacted as follows:

"Except as otherwise expressly provided in this Article, all memoranda, work products, or case files of the mediator are confidential and not subject to disclosure in any judicial or administrative proceeding. Any communication relating to the subject matter of the resolution made during the resolution process by any participant, mediator, or any other person present at the dispute resolution shall be a confidential communication."

In spite of the first sentence in this statute, there appears no where [sic] else in the article an exception to the restrictive language of the statute.

I find that even if the defendant can be found to have waived the confidentiality of the records pertaining to the mediation sessions in which he was involved, the statute, as drafted, permits no such waiver. The items sought by the District Attorney are by definition, "confidential communications."

Confidential communications are, by their very nature, guided by rules of exclusion. Most commonly, rules of exclusion are drafted to prevent evidence being presented to a jury that is of no probative value or of a kind that may unfairly prejudice one of the parties or misdirect the jury's attention from the primary issue at hand. The confidentiality of certain communications, however, is meant to nurture very specific interpersonal or professional relationships that the Courts, society and the legislature deem desirable. * * *

To grant the District Attorney's request to review the records of the Community Dispute Resolution Center would subvert the legislature's clear intention to guarantee the confidentiality of all such records and communications.

Accordingly, the subpoena is hereby quashed.

QUESTIONS

1. What evidence is being sought in this case? By whom? How do you account for the differences in result between this case and Castellano? Could Judge Connell have construed the New York statute to come to the opposite conclusion?

2. Who objected to the district attorney's subpoena? What position did Snyder take? Is it fair that Snyder can refer to participating in the Community Dispute Resolution Program without fearing contradiction on the nature of that participation?

3. What criteria should legislatures or courts use in deciding whether information disclosed in mediation remain confidential?

In re Marriage of Moran

136 Ill. App.3d 331, 483 N.E.2d 580 (1985)

Buckley, Justice.

On July 26, 1983, the trial court entered a judgment dissolving the marriage of petitioner Marianne Moran (Marianne) and respondent John McElroy Moran (John). Incorporated into the judgment was the parties' marital settlement agreement. On August 24, 1983, within 30 days of the entry of the judgment, Marianne filed a motion to vacate the judgment, alleging that the settlement agreement was obtained by fraud, duress and coercion and was unconscionable. Following an evidentiary hearing, the trial court denied Marianne's motion to vacate, and this appeal followed. For the following reasons, we reverse and remand. * * *

On July 20, 1983, Marianne attended the first pretrial conference with [her attorney, Edward] Rosenberg accompanied by her friend, Barbara Purdy. [The purpose of the conference was to discuss settlement offers by Marianne and John.] She testified that she wanted Purdy, a housewife, to accompany her and act as her "spokesman" because she felt "very, very dense and dull and not very articulate and very sick." Marianne stated that at the pretrial conference, the judge advised her that ERA had really changed things for women and that she could do no better at trial, but much worse.

The second pretrial conference was held on July 25, 1983. The trial court did not permit Purdy to attend this conference. Marianne stated that the judge told her about the *Asch* case [*In re Marriage of Asch* (1981), 100 Ill.App.3d 293, 55 Ill.Dec. 741, 426 N.E.2d 1066], and that under that decision she could very well end up with only five years of maintenance. The judge again told her the settlement agreement was the best she could do and that her attorney would lose if she went to trial. * * *

The undisputed evidence * * * discloses that the trial court misled Marianne and coerced her into signing the settlement agreement. The court advised Marianne that under [the *Asch*] case she would not be entitled to more than five years of maintenance. The court, however, mischaracterized the holding in *Asch*. Marianne was never told that while the wife in *Asch* was awarded only three years of maintenance, the trial court in that case retained jurisdiction to review the award at the end of three years. Although this review concept has become quite common (see *In re Marriage of Carney (1984)*, 122 Ill.App.3d 705, 716-17, 78 Ill.Dec. 477, 462 N.E.2d 596), it was never explained to Marianne. Under the property settlement in this case, Marianne's maintenance is substantially reduced after five years and terminates after seven years with no review. We must also point out that John's salary is approximately five times the annual salary of the husband in *Asch*.

The trial court also coerced Marianne into signing the agreement by repeatedly warning her that the agreement was the best she could do and that her attorney would lose if the case went to trial. We initally observe that the court made these warnings without even having evidence as to the actual values of most of the parties' assets. * * *

After 27 years of marriage and raising the parties' four children, Marianne should be entitled to more than five years of maintenance at 40,000

taxable dollars and two years of maintenance at 20,000 taxable dollars considering that John has an annual gross income of nearly $200,000 and was awarded virtually all of the remaining assets. * * * These assets are substantial. * * * Given the lengthy duration of the parties' marriage and John's superior opportunity for the future acquisition of assets and income, Marianne certainly was entitled to receive more property pursuant to the [Marriage and Dissolution of Marriage] Act [Ill.-Rev.Stat. 1983, ch. 40]. The trial court clearly misled her by warning her she could do no better at trial.

We further note that it is undisputed that the trial court told Marianne that if she was untrained, then how could she possibly have contributed to her husband's career. This statement was also misleading. Under the Act, Marianne's contribution as a homemaker and parent during the 27-year marriage are to be considered in dividing marital property; it is held that the marital relationship is to be viewed as a shared enterprise or partnership. (*In re Marriage of Komnick* (1981), 84 Ill.2d 89, 49 Ill.Dec.291, 417 N.E.2d 1305). Additionally, Marianne testified her father gave them substantial monthly payments during the first five years of their marriage when they were struggling to make ends meet, and that she had contributed considerable funds and furnishings that she had inherited. Marianne obviously needed no special training to make these contributions.

Other examples of the subtle coercion by the trial court are illustrated in the colloquy during pretrial on June 25, 1983, wherein Marianne complained that the value of the household furniture being given her was closer to $5,000 than to John's evaluation of $75,000 and the trial court responded, "Your house must look like a dump," and when Marianne complained that no consideration was being given to the fact that John, in dissipation of the family's assets, had lavished gifts on his paramour in excess of $10,000 to which the trial court replied, "That was peanuts." Little wonder that on July 26, 1983, the day of trial, Marianne surrendered and agreed to an unconscionable settlement.

The facts in the instant case are strikingly similar to *James v. James* (1958), 14 Ill.2d 295, 305, 152 N.E.2d 582, where our supreme court set aside a property settlement, reasoning that "its accomplishment does not clearly appear to have been entirely free from coercion and misrepresentation." In *James*, as in this case, the wife alleged that the trial court made certain misleading statements concerning the law in order to exert pressure on her to settle. * * * In *James,* the wife was also told by her attorneys that she had to settle the case because the matter had been set for hearing. Similarly, in the instant case, Marianne asked Rosenberg if the case could be continued so that more changes could be made to the settlement agreement and Rosenberg responded that John "will freeze you out."

The extreme coercion and duress by the court and [Marianne's] counsel mandate that the portion of the judgment of dissolution approving and incorporating the marital settlement agreement be and is reversed and the cause is remanded for a new trial as to the property and maintenance provisions.

Reversed and remanded.

QUESTIONS

1. In what sense is a pretrial conference equivalent to mediation? Is it accurate to characterize a pretrial conference as mandatory mediation?

2. How would you characterize the trial judge's interest in the pretrial conference? How does it compare with the interest of a mediator in mediation?

3. What impact did the judge's discussion of *Asch* have on Mrs. Moran? Why does the court reverse the trial judge? Should not parties be charged with relying on their attorneys to analyze the law?

INDEX